Principles of Economic Growth

Principles of Economic Growth

Thorvaldur Gylfason
Research Professor of Economics,
University of Iceland

OXFORD
UNIVERSITY PRESS

OXFORD
UNIVERSITY PRESS

Great Clarendon Street, Oxford OX2 6DP
Oxford University Press is a department of the University of Oxford.
It furthers the University's objective of excellence in research, scholarship,
and education by publishing worldwide in

Oxford New York

Athens Auckland Bangkok Bogotá Buenos Aires Calcutta
Cape Town Chennai Dar es Salaam Delhi Florence Hong Kong Istanbul
Karachi Kuala Lampur Madrid Melbourne Mexico City Mumbai
Nairobi Paris São Paulo Singapore Taipei Tokyo Toronto Warsaw

with associated companies in Berlin Ibadan

Oxford is a registered trade mark of Oxford University Press
in the UK and in certain other countries

Published in the United States
by Oxford University Press Inc., New York

British Library Cataloguing in Publication Data

Data available

Library of Congress Cataloging in Publication Data

Thorvaldur Gylfason, 1951–
    Principles of economic growth / Thorvaldur Gylfason.
        p.   cm.
    Includes bibliographical references.
    1. Economic development.   2. Economic history.   I. Title.
    HD75.T48   1999   338.9–dc21   98–56187

ISBN 0–19–877614–4 (pbk.)
ISBN 0–19–877613–6

10 9 8 7 6 5 4 3 2 1

Typeset in Swift and Frutiger
by J&L Composition Ltd, Filey, North Yorkshire
Printed by Bath Press Ltd, Bath, Somerset

To Anna and my parents

Average annual growth of GNP per capita 1990–96 (%)
Source: World Bank Atlas 1998

Preface

This book is an attempt to explain, in plain prose and pictures, the theory and empirical evidence of economic growth around the world. It is essentially a non-technical book. All equations are confined to appendices at the end of the book (with one exception: $E = mc^2$). Having taught economic growth for some time to undergraduate and postgraduate students at the University of Iceland, I felt that there might be a need for such a book, because much of the new theory and evidence of economic growth has not yet found its way into books other than those intended mostly for doctoral students. Hence this attempt to provide an accessible account of economic growth. The book is intended primarily for students of economics and business administration as well as for business managers, economists, journalists, politicians, public officials, and others who are interested in understanding economic growth.

Richard Feynman was once asked by a younger colleague: 'Dick, explain to me, so that I can understand it, why spin one-half particles obey Fermi–Dirac statistics.' Feynman answered: 'I'll prepare a freshman lecture on it.' Feynman came back a few days later and said: 'I couldn't do it. I couldn't reduce it to the freshman level. That means we don't really understand it.'[1] This book is written in a similar spirit. It deliberately bypasses some technical aspects of recent growth theory in an attempt to reduce the risk that the reader does not see the forest for the trees.

Moreover, the book has a message, and it is this: To grow or not to grow is in large measure a matter of choice. It is also a matter of justice, for those who usually pay the highest price for the economic growth that did not take place are the poor. The book discusses old and new research that shows that many of the most important determinants of economic growth are clearly within the purview of economic policy. Liberalization, stabilization, privatization, and education are good for growth. The government has an important role to play—and, indeed, responsibility—in all of these areas. It takes a government to privatize, for one thing.

The book was originally commissioned by SNS—the Swedish Center for Business and Policy Studies—and was published in a preliminary version under the title *Understanding Economic Growth* in connection with the XII International Conference of Private Business Associations in Stockholm, 11–12 June 1998, on the occasion of the 50th anniversary of SNS. The theme of the conference was Creating an Environment for Growth. I am especially grateful to Professor Hans Tson Söderström, president of SNS, and to Torgny Wadensjö, director of SNS Förlag, for their encouragement and support.

I have received advice and help from many people. Torben M. Andersen, Gylfi Th. Gíslason, Arne Jon Isachsen, Agnar Sandmo, Gylfi Zoega, and an anonymous referee read an earlier version of the manuscript and made many useful comments and suggestions. Marian Radetzki, Stefan Sandström, Johann Schulz, Birgitta Swedenborg, and Hans Tson Söderström commented on individual chapters in draft, and so did Tryggvi Thor Herbertsson, who also helped prepare the empirical figures in Chapter 4. Guðmundur Ólafsson assisted with the cast of characters at the end of the book. Dagfinnur Sveinbjörnsson helped prepare the indexes. I thank them all, but they should not in any way be held responsible for the book's content.

THORVALDUR GYLFASON

Reykjavik
August 1998

---

1. This story is told in David L. Goodstein and Judith R. Goodstein, *Feynman's Lost Lecture: The Motion of the Planets Around the Sun*, Vintage, California Institute of Technology, 1997. For further information on Feynman and other *dramatis personae*, see the cast of characters at the end of the book.

Contents

1

Growing Apart

Great nations are never impoverished by private, though they sometimes are by publick prodigality and misconduct.[1]

ADAM SMITH

It is obviously true that there are many countries, not essentially different either in the degree of security which they afford to property, or in the moral and religious instruction received by the people, which yet, with nearly equal natural capabilities, make a very different progress in wealth.[2]

THOMAS MALTHUS

There was a time, not long ago, when most economists regarded economic growth in the long run as being essentially immune to all but technological progress. Those were the days when technology had captured people's hearts and minds perhaps to a greater extent than ever before or since. The Soviets had launched the first manned sputnik into space. Around the world, Yury Gagarin was a household name and no one had yet heard of Neil Armstrong. Nikita Khrushchev was thus apparently not in much doubt when, in the late 1950s, he declared: 'We will bury you.' Privately, however, Khrushchev was slightly more circumspect; in 1961, he told an American visitor that 'we are perfectly willing to leave it to history as to which system is the better for mankind and which will survive'.[3] Meanwhile, in America, the most influential introductory economics textbook featured a diagram extrapolating Soviet and American economic growth into the future, showing how real gross national product (GNP) in the Soviet Union seemed quite capable of overtaking that of the United States by the year 2005, and perhaps even before 1990.[4] Ragnar Frisch, the Nobel-prize winning Norwegian economist, went even further, in 1961: 'The vast majority of Western economists lives and theorizes with blinders on ... The blinders will fall off towards the end of the 1960s (perhaps earlier). At that time industrial production in the Soviet Union will exceed that of the United States. *However, the day of reckoning will then come too late.'*[5] Throughout the 1970s and 1980s, the writings of many other good and influential economists reflected a similar mood.

Not only did many good economists not fully understand the destructive force of communism until the writing was on the wall in the 1990s,[6] but most also tended to overlook the effects of gross economic mismanagement in many parts of the third world on the growth potential of poor countries by failing to build their experience into mainstream models of economic growth. The adverse effects of political disturbances, like those of natural calamities, were acknowledged, but the effects of bad management were not. After all, the main focus of macroeconomic policy in those years was stabilization and redistribution, and neither inflation nor inequality in the distribution of income and wealth were considered harmful to growth. By the same token, the effects of *good* management on long-run growth were also, for the most part, underrated or overlooked. Worse than that, economic development and economic growth were generally viewed and taught as two separate subjects at universities, development typically as a soft-core, quasi-historical subject confined to poor countries, and growth as a hard-core, high-tech branch of macroeconomics reserved for rich countries. Growth theorists, including Robert Solow, felt that development economics showed some signs of 'being ripe for textbook treatment',[7] meaning that it needed to be mathematized.

In retrospect, this separation between economic development and growth seems odd. After all, 200 years earlier Adam Smith had explained, in his *Wealth of Nations* (1776), how good governance coupled with free trade, private enterprise, and private property was a source of wealth and, thereby, also of economic growth. In Smith's own words:

> Nations tolerably well advanced as to skill, dexterity, and judgment, in the application of labour, have followed very different plans in the general conduct or direction of it; and those plans have not all been equally favourable to the greatness of its produce.[8]

Smith was a growth theorist, more so than he has commonly been given credit for until quite recently. His main message in *The Wealth of Nations* was, in short, that division of labour enhances efficiency (that is, the amount of output that is produced by given inputs), but is limited by the extent of the market.[9] It follows immediately that, for example, international trade, by enlarging the market, increases efficiency and hence also wealth and, thereby, increases economic growth at least as long as it takes for the efficiency gains so induced to be reaped in full. Presumably, Smith would not have had much difficulty in sizing up the long-run growth effects of the inward-looking economic policies pursued by, say, Kwame Nkrumah in Ghana after independence in 1958 or, to take an extreme example, by Enver Hoxha in Albania, where foreign trade and foreign investment were virtually forbidden by the constitution, or of similar tendencies in smaller doses elsewhere, for that matter. After all, it was Adam Smith who first traced the economic stagnation and subsequent decline of China to its policy of virtual isolation and self-sufficiency after 1433, a policy that was not abandoned until 1978. In his words:

> China seems long to have been stationary, and had probably long ago acquired that full complement of riches which is consistent with the nature of its laws and institutions. But this complement may be much inferior to what, with other laws and institutions, the nature of its soil, climate, and situation might admit of. A country which neglects or despises foreign commerce, and which admits the vessels of foreign nations into one or two of its ports only, cannot transact the same quantity of business which it might do with different laws and institutions.[10]

But now is another age. Now that communism has been relegated to the scrap-heap of history, leaving the mixed market economy as the only game in town, it suddenly seems almost obvious that economic systems, policies, and institutions must have played an important role all along in determining the long-run economic performance of countries—that is, in explaining why growth rates differ. How else could we explain the vastly different experience of Finland and Estonia, West and East Germany, Austria and Czechoslovakia, South and North Korea, and Taiwan and China?—adjacent countries that started out in roughly comparable economic circumstances and had much else in common, e.g. similar natural resources and culture and even shared languages, but adopted diametrically different economic systems and developed so very differently over the past half-century. How else?

The contrast between each of the above-mentioned pairs of countries was not clear to all for a long time, as was mentioned before. In the 1960s, for example, South and North Korea registered comparable economic growth. In both places, national economic output increased rapidly, not least through investment. The difference was that, unlike the profit-oriented investments undertaken in the South, the ideologically motivated investment plans in North Korea did not result in the build-up of productive capital. So, even if large investment expenditures stimulated output for a time from the demand side, the accumulation of unproductive capital was bound ultimately to drag the economy down from the supply side. And now the contrast is clear: for the reason just mentioned and many others, monolithic, all-encompassing communism based on central planning and public ownership of almost all productive resources turned out to be a colossal failure wherever it was put into practice, no less so in Asia than in Europe. In 1995, for example, Russia's GNP per capita was one-twelfth of that of the United States.[11] There is no need now to dwell on such comparisons, not any more. There is no exception to this pattern; specifically, China and Vietnam are not, for their rapid growth since 1978 and 1987 can be traced in large measure to their deliberate, albeit selective, departures from planning.[12]

There are, however, other pairs of countries whose economic development strategies over the past generation or so are, perhaps, more interesting for comparison, because the border lines between their economic systems as such are not as clearly drawn. If the economic systems adopted by two countries are not completely different, is it nonetheless possible to trace the differences in their economic performance to their different economic policies? Or does technology dictate growth differentials in such cases? Or perhaps geography? Or history? Or all of the above?

Let us now, to set the stage for our examination of economic growth in theory and practice in subsequent chapters, consider the growth performance of four such pairs or clusters of countries over the past quarter century or so. We do this in order to demonstrate that not only economic systems, but also economic policies, arrangements, and institutions seem relevant for economic growth. Economic laws, like the laws of nature, are essentially the same everywhere: demand is inversely related to price almost as surely as rivers flow downstream by the force of gravity. So, even if our brief examples are taken mostly from low- and middle-income countries in different parts of the world, most of the points to emerge from what follows apply also to high-income countries, *pari passu*.

All four pairs or clusters of countries have one main thing in common: their economies have developed quite differently over the past 30–40 years despite roughly comparable initial conditions. We begin our journey in Asia by comparing the economic development of Thailand and Burma (renamed Myanmar by the governing military junta some years ago). We then continue to Africa and provide a brief comparative sketch of Botswana, Nigeria, and Ghana. Thereafter we move on to South America and discuss the economic record of Uruguay and Argentina and compare it with that of their erstwhile colonial ruler, Spain. At last we compare and contrast Madagascar and Mauritius.

Burma and Thailand

Earlier in this century Burma was the rice basket of South-East Asia, and was considered well ahead of Thailand in economic affairs. Since 1962, however, when General Ne Win came to power in a *coup d'état*, 14 years after the country gained independence from Britain in 1948, Burma has continued its 'victorious march towards socialism'—this is approximately how it was put in those days, and still is in Burma. The hallmark of the Burmese way has been self-reliance, without, however, going so far as isolating the country completely and deliberately from the rest of the world. Thus, Burma has been an active client of international organizations such as the International Monetary Fund (IMF) and the World Bank, unlike, for example, the former Soviet Union and several of its satellites in Central and Eastern Europe in the communist period. Moreover, unlike their colleagues in communist countries, many Burmese officials had been trained at some of the best universities in Britain.

In the 1970s, many outside observers still thought that Burma was doing all right, for those were the years when many good economists still thought that, in the long run, central planning was capable of producing more rapid growth than a market economy, not least in developing countries, even if most had by then admitted that human rights were grossly neglected under socialism. The available national income statistics seemed to confirm this impression by indicating adequate economic growth in Burma, roughly on par with Thailand (Figure 1.1).[13] Investment in Burma proceeded apace, rising from less than 10 per cent of gross domestic product (GDP) in 1962 to almost 20 per cent in 1980, a respectable ratio by world standards. The poor quality of much of this centrally planned investment, however, was not yet a matter of general concern. Not much either was made of the fact that exports were stagnant: they amounted to only about 8 per cent of GDP in 1980, down from 18 per cent in 1962. Meanwhile, in Thailand next door, the export ratio had risen from 17 to 24 per cent over the same period. Economics, as we know it, was not taught at the University of Rangoon; to be on the safe side, the economists at the university lectured on stochastic processes and such instead. Little by little, Burma began to show more and clearer signs of decay. The difference between Burma and Thailand began to feel more and more like the border between the Soviet Union and Finland: to many travellers from far away places, returning to Bangkok from Rangoon was like coming home.

And thus, from the 1980s onwards, it began to sink in that something had gone seriously wrong in Burma. While Thailand surged forward, Burma remained stagnant.

Fig 1.1
**Burma and Thailand:
GNP per capita,
1960–1994
(constant 1987 US$,
1960 = 100)**

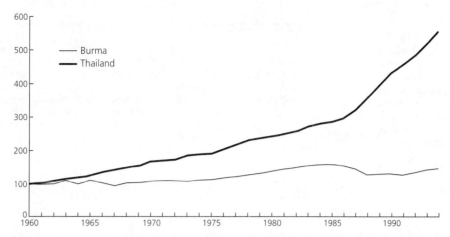

Yet, intermittent spurts of rapid growth, as, for example, in the early 1990s, blurred the picture and blinded some observers to the underlying weakness of the Burmese economy. Depressed investments of low quality (i.e. without adequate regard to commercial profit), plummeting exports, and deteriorating education, including the virtual evaporation of up-to-date economic expertise from public service and from the universities, jointly produced this outcome, which was compounded by an excessive reliance on political control of economic affairs. In 1990, Burma's military junta refused to abide by the general election victory of the opposition, led by Aung San Suu Kyi, who remained under house arrest in Rangoon until 1995. In 1996, the universities were shut down.

Thailand made few of these mistakes, even if the military has played an active, intermittent role in the country's politics over the years. Thailand's saving and investment performance has been strong, with investment around 40 per cent of GDP in 1994 (and 43 per cent in 1995), compared with 12 per cent in Burma (Table 1.1). Even so, the quality of some of this investment has proved questionable, partly because Thailand's banking system has been strongly influenced by politicians preferring votes to profits. Thai exports have surged: in 1994, they amounted to 39 per cent of GDP (and 42 per cent in 1995), compared with only 2 per cent in Burma—the latter, the lowest export ratio on record anywhere (Table 1.1). In education, the Thai record is also quite strong: for example, secondary and tertiary school enrolment rates increased by a third to a half from 1980 to 1993, even if they are still far below the enrolment rates typical of high-income countries.[14] Thus, if investment, exports, and education are important sources of growth, then there is little wonder why Thailand has surged past Burma.

From 1960 to 1994, GNP per capita increased by more than 5 per cent per year on average in Thailand compared with 1 per cent in Burma (Figure 1.1, Table 1.1). So, if GNP per capita was the same in 1960, as the figure shows, Thailand had become almost four times as rich as Burma in 1994. This is what happens with a growth differential of 4 percentage points over 34 years. Moreover, with considerable scope for (a) improved quality of investments (through better banking, as advised, e.g. by the IMF in 1997), (b) further expansion of exports, and (c) further progress in education, among other things, it would seem that Thailand's growth prospects continue to look bright. Even if it has proved more serious than many observers anticipated at first, the crash in stock-market and currency values in 1997–8 does not look likely to

	Annual average growth of GNP per capita 1970–95 (%)[a]	GNP per capita 1995 (US$), adjusted for purchasing power	Investment as percentage of GNP 1995	Exports of goods and services as percentage of GNP 1995	Enrolment in secondary education as percentage of relevant age group 1993	Annual average inflation 1970–95 (%)
Burma	1.2	—	12[b]	2[b]	—	13[c]
Thailand	5.2	7,540	43	42	37	6
Botswana	7.3	5,580	25	49	52[d]	11
Nigeria	−0.9	1,220	9[b]	24[b]	29	19
Ghana	−1.2	1,990	19	25	36	36
Uruguay	0.2	6,630	14	19	81	61
Argentina	−0.4	8,310	18	9	72	180
Spain	2.0	14,520	21	24	87	11
Madagascar	−2.4	640	11	23	14	16
Mauritius	3.1[e]	13,210	25	58	59	10[e]

Source: World Development Indicators 1997, tables 1.1, 1.3, 2.8, and 4.12, OUP, Oxford, 1997, and associated compact disc, from which the growth figure for Mauritius in the first column and the inflation figures in the last column were computed from data on GDP deflators, unless otherwise indicated.

[a] Based on the World Bank Atlas method, at constant 1987 prices.

[b] *Source*: International Monetary Fund, *International Financial Statistics Yearbook*, Washington, DC, 1997.

[c] 1970–94.

[d] *Source: World Development Report 1997*, table 7, OUP, Oxford, 1997.

[e] 1976–95.

dim these long-run prospects. All things considered, Thailand's economy seems basically sound. Exports and the quality of investment seem likely to benefit from the slump as time passes. The experience of Thailand and several other Asian countries shows that rapid growth over the long haul does not always have to be smooth.

Botswana, Nigeria, and Ghana

Let us now make a crossing to Africa, which is home to the country holding the current world record in economic growth over the past quarter century: Botswana. The story of Botswana merits consideration because Africa still tends to be synonymous with destitution, even despair, in the minds of many people.

But begin in Nigeria, where, in 1973–4, the first oil price increase in world markets triggered an unprecedented economic boom. National income per capita in this oil-producing nation increased fourfold or more from 1972 to 1980. Imbued with ambition and optimism, the Nigerian government built 31 universities throughout the country at huge expense. This was not a good investment, however, in a country where almost half of all adults still are illiterate and where less than a third of young people go to secondary school (Table 1.1).[15] Many other investment decisions in the wake of the oil boom were of a similar calibre. To make a long story short, this is why national economic output was bound to collapse after a while under the weight of unproductive capital. Now, 25 years later, Nigeria is basically back to square one (Figure 1.2). Almost all the windfall earnings from oil exports have gone with the wind. Investment, a respectable 17 per cent of GDP in 1970, before the upswing, briefly exceeded 30 per cent in the mid-1970s only to drop below 10 per cent in the 1980s, and has remained at or near that low level ever since (Table 1.1). To compound the problem, oil exports crowded out non-oil exports, which, in 1970, before the boom, amounted to more than 40 per cent of total exports, but fell to 4 per cent of the total in 1980 and to 3 per cent in 1990.[16] The example of Nigeria demonstrates how, without adequate economic policies and political safeguards, abundant natural resource wealth can turn out to be, at best, a mixed blessing.

Ghana has done slightly better, especially since the 1980s, when the country became a model client of the IMF and the World Bank, taking their advice on many aspects of economic policy and revising, or rather reversing, Nkrumah's economic development strategy by opening up the economy to increased foreign trade and investment. Over the whole period, 1970–95, Ghana's GNP per capita (in constant 1987 US dollars as in Figure 1.1) fell by about 1 per cent per year on average (Table 1.1); however, since 1982, it has grown by almost 1 per cent per year on average. In keeping with this, exports of goods and services first collapsed from 15 per cent of GDP in 1966 to 3 per cent in 1982, and then rose to 25 per cent in 1995 (Table 1.1). Investment displayed a similar pattern: it fell from 13 per cent of GDP in 1966 to 4 per cent in 1982, and then rose again to 19 per cent in 1995 (Table 1.1). Net foreign direct investment flowing into Ghana amounted to 3.6 per cent of GDP in 1995, compared with 2.4 per cent in Nigeria.[17]

This brings us to Botswana, whose GDP per capita (in constant 1987 US dollars) has increased by almost 7.5 per cent per year on average since independence in 1966. This means that, in real terms, income per head is now almost eight times as high as in 1966. Until 1985, Botswana and Nigeria developed roughly in tandem, as shown in Figure 1.2, but then their ways parted.[18] Both countries depend heavily on their natural resources: Nigeria on oil, Botswana on diamonds. Oil now accounts for over 90 per cent of Nigeria's total exports, 80 per cent of government revenue, and about a fifth of GDP, whereas diamonds make up 80 per cent of Botswana's total exports and

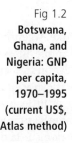

Fig 1.2
Botswana, Ghana, and Nigeria: GNP per capita, 1970–1995 (current US$, Atlas method)

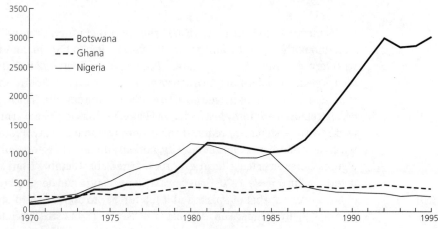

40 per cent of GDP. Botswana is democratic, even if the same political party has ruled the country without interruption since independence in 1966, whereas Nigeria has been ruled by its military for the most part since 1966. A crucial part of the explanation for their diverging economic performance appears to be this: Botswana has managed its resource wealth judiciously, using it, for example, to reduce illiteracy[19] to less than a third of the population, compared with almost a half in Nigeria, and to increase the secondary school enrolment rate above one half, compared with less than a third in Nigeria (Table 1.1).[20] Yet, Botswana's national income per capita was one-fourth less than that of Nigeria in 1970. This is how fast things can change.[21]

And then there is this: the rapid economic development of Botswana has been the most stable of the three, whether instability is measured by the standard deviation of economic growth from year to year in proportion to average growth over the whole period or, more simply, perhaps, by average inflation over the period. The former measure of instability is 1.0 for Botswana, 3.8 for Ghana, and 5.2 for Nigeria, based on the growth paths displayed in Figure 1.2. The average annual rates of growth of GNP per capita (in constant 1987 US dollars by the World Bank Atlas method, see Table 1.1) are 7.3 per cent in Botswana, −1.2 per cent in Ghana, and −0.9 per cent in Nigeria.[22] This is, of course, a small sample, but in this group of three, at least, the country with the least instability (Botswana) is the one with the highest rate of economic growth over the 25-year period. A comparison of inflation in the three countries tells a similar story. From 1970 to 1995, the average annual rate of inflation was 11 per cent in Botswana, 36 per cent in Ghana, and 19 per cent in Nigeria (Table 1.1). In this small group, the country with the least inflation (Botswana) is again the one with the highest rate of economic growth. We will revisit the linkages between price stability and growth in Chapter 4.

If the numbers shown in Figure 1.2 are adjusted for purchasing power, the World Bank's estimate of GNP per capita in Botswana in 1995 rises from US$ 3,020 to IUS$ 5,580; in Ghana, from US$ 390 to IUS$ 1,990; and in Nigeria, from US$ 260 to IUS$ 1,220 (Table 1.1).[23]

Uruguay, Argentina, and Spain

Let us move on, to South America. Earlier in this century, Uruguay, like Argentina, was among the richest countries in the world, ahead of Spain, for example. Blessed with fertile farmland, its agriculture flourished, and, due to its dedication to social security and social services, Uruguay became known as a South American welfare state. The government played an active role in economic affairs. Little by little, however, Uruguay's economy lost its forward-looking thrust. The government's attempts to protect the *status quo* reduced the economy's adaptability. Protectionism laid a paralysing hand on economic activity, not only domestic protectionism, but also foreign, because Uruguay's farm exports suffered considerably from agricultural protection in Europe. By 1970, Uruguay's GNP per capita had declined to the equivalent of 60 per cent of that of Spain, and it fell further to about a third of Spain's in 1995 (Figure 1.3). By comparison, Argentina's GNP per capita still exceeded that of Spain

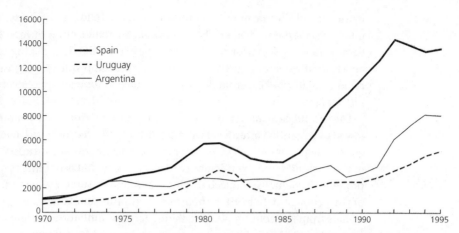

Fig 1.3
**Argentina,
Uruguay, and
Spain: GNP per
capita,
1970–1995
(current US$,
Atlas method)**

in 1970, but since then it has declined to about 60 per cent of the Spanish level. Meanwhile, having got rid of General Franco in 1976, democratic Spain made rapid progress, joined the European Union in 1986, and opened up its economy, expanding its exports from 14 per cent of GDP in the mid-1970s to 24 per cent in 1995 (Table 1.1).

The point of this comparison is that economic growth is relative. National economies rise and fall compared with others. From 1970 to 1995, the average annual growth rates of GNP per capita were −0.4 per cent in Argentina, 0.2 per cent in Uruguay, and 2.0 per cent in Spain (Table 1.1). Actually, the relative decline of Argentina and Uruguay has coincided with *rising* per capita incomes, i.e. positive per capita growth, in most years—specifically, in two of every three years in Argentina since 1970. The arguments of those who persistently warned against Argentina's decline and urged a change of economic policies to reverse the trend in the 1970s and 1980s could be countered by pointing to positive economic growth. Many were thus blinded to the gradual relative decline that was taking place. If two nations have the same income per head initially and their annual rates of per capita growth differ by 3 percentage points, then, in 60 years, the one with the faster growth will be six times as rich as the other. In Argentina and Uruguay, this is essentially what happened.[24]

What went wrong? There is no shortage of explanations.[25] Let us mention just three here.

First, Argentina's political development lagged behind its economic progress. A grossly uneven distribution of land holdings with monopolistic and protectionist proclivity to match set their mark on Argentina under Spanish rule, which ended in 1816. This situation did not improve much after Argentina gained independence. In effect, a small class of landowners ruled the country with an iron fist, and used its hold on power to block political decentralization, democratization, and economic diversification away from agriculture, which had been the driving force behind the economic upswing from 1895 to 1930. In Europe, by contrast, industry, trade, and services were given adequate elbow room in time to replace agriculture gradually as the mainstay of the masses. The political and also economic development of Argentina, unlike that of Europe, was marked by a hardening conflict between landowners and the emerging urban classes. Democratically elected leaders sometimes behaved like dictators. The gradual deterioration of living standards, triggered by the collapse of farm exports to Europe after 1930 and exacerbated by political underdevelopment, created the conditions for the election of Juan Perón as president in 1946, on a platform of higher wages, more public spending, and the nationalization of private industry. Not surprisingly, the result was high inflation and a rapid escalation of external debt. The military intervened in 1955 and drove Perón into exile.

The second explanation follows directly from the first. The economic policies followed by Argentina after 1930 were consistently flawed, despite frequent changes of government, sometimes by democratic means. Import substitution, overvaluation of the currency, and insufficient competition directed economic resources into unproductive channels, reduced foreign trade, and dragged down the living standards of the people. Civil disorder, inflation, corruption, and a massive exodus of professionals from the country all contributed to slow and uneven economic growth. Yet, it would be unwise to blame it all on Perón, even if his government caused considerable harm. No, one needs to wonder why Perón was elected by a landslide in the first place, not only in 1946, but then again in 1973. Perón's popularity was a direct consequence of political underdevelopment and of the wrong-headed economic policies of those who ruled Argentina before him. Perhaps the most serious mistake was the attempt to erect protective walls around domestic industries after 1930, when it had become clear that economic diversification away from agriculture was inevitable. Loss of foreign markets due to the Great Depression played a part in this, to be sure, but the protectionism remained in place even after the depression was over. To this day, Argentina is still a strikingly closed economy, with exports amounting to only 9 per cent of GDP in 1995 (up from 5 per cent in 1980), compared with an (unweighted) average export ratio of 38 per cent in the world as a whole.[26] Uruguay is also quite closed, for such a small country with only 3 million people: its export ratio in 1995 was only 19 per cent (Table 1.1).

The third possible explanation has to do with the long history of rampant inflation in both countries. In 1970–95, the average annual inflation rate was 180 per cent in Argentina and 61 per cent in Uruguay (Table 1.1). Since 1994, however, following radical economic reforms undertaken by the government of President Carlos Menem, inflation in Argentina has subsided, at least for the time being. Anyhow, it seems likely that rapid inflation over long periods, coupled with overvalued currencies and negative real interest rates, distorted trade and investment in both countries and thus impeded economic growth. In Uruguay, the inflation problem was virtually institutionalized by the coexistence of *two* central banks: one of the usual kind, operating on the time-honoured theory that excessive money creation leads to inflation, while the other, also a state bank with authority to issue money, went by the so-called real bills doctrine, which holds that printing money for productive purposes will not lead to inflation. The idea is simple: if the borrowers' enterprises are productive enough, the money issued to them will increase the supply of goods and services at least as much as demand, so that no extra inflation will ensue. As you would expect, the latter bank followed a more generous monetary policy than the former, with unsurprising consequences.

The moral of this short and selective account is that history matters for economic growth, and so does politics, even if their exact contribution in a given case may be hard to measure, let alone prove. Inflation may also matter for growth, not just inflation as such, but also the structure and functioning of the banking system and of public finances that produce the inflation.

Madagascar and Mauritius

For our last example, we now set sail for the Indian Ocean, where, off the east coast of Africa, there are two magnificent islands, among others.

Madagascar, which lies about 400 km. from the coast, is not exactly a household name in the annals of economics, but it is a huge place, the world's fourth largest island, the size of Texas, larger than France, Mauritius, which lies a bit farther east, is tiny, only about 2,000 sq. km. in area. Madagascar is sparsely populated, with 14 million people against 1 million in Mauritius. Madagascar was earlier a French colony, and gained independence in 1960. Mauritius was first under Dutch control, then French, then British, before gaining independence in 1968.

Figure 1.4 shows the path of GNP per capita in the two countries over the past 25 years. In Mauritius, GNP per capita (in constant 1987 US dollars) increased by 3 per cent per annum on average in this period, while in Madagascar, GNP per capita *decreased* by more than 2 per cent a year on average. In 1966 (not shown in the figure), income per head in Mauritius was about twice as large as in Madagascar. Until 1980, the centrally planned economy of Madagascar (the rulers themselves called it 'radical socialism') seemed perhaps to produce adequate results, even if they paled in comparison with the mixed economy of Mauritius, but then the two paths diverged, especially after the mid-1980s. Since 1980, income per head in Madagascar has actually fallen, while income per head in Mauritius has increased by leaps and bounds. With an adjustment for differences in purchasing power, the income gap between the two becomes larger: by this measure, income per head in Mauritius was more than twenty times as high as in Madagascar, or IUS$ 13,210 against IUS$ 640 in 1995 (Table 1.1). The growth differential between the two countries has been even larger since the mid-1980s, or almost 6 per cent average annual growth in Mauritius in 1985–95 compared with −2 per cent in Madagascar.

Fig 1.4
Madagascar and Mauritius: GNP per capita, 1970–1995 (current US$, Atlas method)

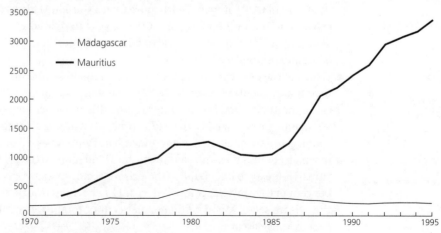

If this grossly different growth performance were all you knew about these two island states, what would you think about other aspects of their economic life?

- Which of the two has had more inflation? The answer is: Madagascar. Its inflation rate measured by the rate of change of the GDP deflator was 18 per cent per annum on average from 1976 to 1995, compared with 10 per cent a year in Mauritius (Table 1.1). More inflation went hand in hand with less growth.
- Which of the two is more dependent on exports of raw materials? Again, the answer is Madagascar. There primary exports, including food, account for about 80 per cent of total exports of goods and services compared with about a third in Mauritius, which has managed to diversify its economy away from its once overwhelming sugar industry.[27] This rhymes with the idea that abundant natural resources may be a mixed blessing, as in Nigeria, if, for example, the natural resource abundance bestows too much economic and political influence on a single dominant resource-based industry. Yet, its natural resources have clearly benefited Botswana, among others.
- Which of the two is more indebted abroad? Again, Madagascar, whose foreign debt/GNP ratio in 1995 was three times as high as that of Mauritius, or 142 per cent against 46 per cent.[28] Borrowed funds were allocated via public authorities to inefficient enterprises in Madagascar, thereby gradually reducing the productivity of capital and growth.
- Which of the two countries is more open to foreign trade and investment? The answer is now Mauritius, whose exports amounted to 58 per cent of GDP in 1995 against 23 per cent in Madagascar (Table 1.1). The difference was even larger earlier in the period. Moreover, net private capital flows into Mauritius amounted to US$ 304 million in 1995 compared with US$ 4 million in Madagascar. Foreign trade is good for growth, said Adam Smith; no surprise here.
- Which country invests more? The answer is again Mauritius, where investment equalled a fourth of GDP in 1995 compared with only 11 per cent in Madagascar (Table 1.1). Productive, market-oriented investment is a major source of economic growth, no less in remote islands than elsewhere.
- Which country is farther along on its way from agriculture to industry, trade, and services? The answer is still Mauritius, where agriculture accounts for only 9 per cent of GDP compared with more than a third in Madagascar. Mauritius receives almost a million foreign tourists a year compared with about 50,000 in Madagascar. Both countries are attractive tourist destinations, not least because of their exotic and varied nature.
- Which of the two sends more girls to school? Again, Mauritius, where all girls go to primary school compared with 72 per cent in Madagascar. This is relevant, because good education for girls improves health, increases longevity, and reduces population growth, and is, therefore, probably a prerequisite for growth in poor countries. More education goes hand in hand with less agriculture.
- In which country does the banking system lend more to the private sector? Mauritius. Domestic bank credit to the private sector in Mauritius amounted to 48 per cent of GDP in 1995 compared with 11 per cent in Madagascar. In Mauritius, the private sector stood behind 62 per cent of total investment against 53 per cent in Madagascar.

It hardly needs to be said that the above comparisons must not be taken too literally, for they are merely intended to highlight some of the aspects of economic growth that will be discussed in the chapters to follow. For one thing, it may be difficult to distinguish cause from effect in some cases. More and better education and extensive trade are both a cause and consequence of growth, for example. Moreover, it clearly takes more than just two countries, or a few pairs or clusters of countries, to reach firm conclusions about economic growth across countries. Even so, the examples reviewed above clearly have one thing in common: they all point to economic factors, including the economic system, institutions, and the orientation of economic policy, rather than exogenous technology as crucial determinants of economic growth. This is the fundamental message of the theory of endogenous growth. By 'endogenous' growth is meant that long-run growth depends at least in part on economic factors, including some that can be influenced by economic policy. 'Exogenous' growth, by contrast, is immune to economic influences in the long run. A good theory of economic growth must be able to explain why some countries grow apart while others grow together.

Economic growth is a complex and controversial phenomenon. This book attempts to illuminate and simplify the subject and thus make it accessible to laymen and students (a) by interpreting the theory of economic growth, old and new, in nontechnical language in order to identify the most important sources of growth; (b) by emphasizing the economic policy implications of the theory of growth and its empirical relevance; and (c) by demonstrating how, in theory and practice, economic growth, far from being beyond the reach of human control, depends crucially on choices that people make, individually and collectively. In the words of Arthur Lewis:

> Since the second world war it has become quite clear that rapid economic growth is available to those countries with adequate natural resources which make the effort to achieve it.[29]

The remainder of this introduction provides a brief preview of the book, chapter by chapter. The exposition is verbal throughout and illustrated with figures here and there, but the underlying algebra is confined to appendices at the end of the book.

Roots and branches

Chapter 2 provides a brief sketch of the doctrinal history of economic growth from Adam Smith to our times to lay a basis for an easy exposition of the theory of endogenous vs. exogenous growth. Special emphasis is laid on explaining how the major implications of endogenous growth theory can be traced to earlier writers, including Smith and his followers, and then Alfred Marshall, Arthur Lewis, Roy Harrod, and Evsey Domar. It is argued that Robert Solow's emphasis on technological progress as the key determinant of economic growth is consistent with endogenous growth, when technological progress is itself endogenous. The aim here is to provide the rudiments of a simple, unified framework in which economic growth rests on three key variables identified already by Smith: the saving rate, efficiency, and the depreciation of capital. These variables—efficiency, in particular—depend, in turn, on other things, including education, trade, inflation, natural resources, geography, governance, and so on. Several of these things, in their turn, can be influenced by economic policy. Thus a bridge is built from economic policy to economic growth.

Quantity and quality

Chapter 3 begins with endogenous-growth theory, summarizing some of its main implications in a few diagrams. The contributions of saving, efficiency, and depreciation to growth are explored both analytically and numerically so as to suggest an alternative to conventional growth accounting, whereby output growth is traced to the growth of individual inputs (labour, capital, etc.). Special emphasis is laid on the role of depreciation to drive home the point that gigantic investments, Soviet-style, are no guarantee for growth, if the capital resulting from these investments is of low quality, on the contrary. The recent controversy about extensive vs. intensive growth in Asia (i.e. whether growth in Asia can be attributed to more or better labour and capital) is discussed. The neoclassical growth model is also illustrated in a series of diagrams and shown to go a long way towards accounting for the differences in income per capita that are observed around the world. In the neoclassical model, economic growth is endogenous in the medium term, which actually turns out to span decades, even if growth is ultimately exogenous in the long run. A comparison of the two models, endogenous vs. exogenous growth, leads to the conclusion that their implications are qualitatively similar in the medium term, but quantitatively different. The chapter concludes with a discussion of optimal saving behaviour and illustrates its implications for economic growth and its interaction with the real rate of interest.

The importance of being efficient

Chapter 4 discusses convergence first, i.e. the extent to which economic growth differentials across countries can be traced to poor countries catching up with richer ones. The empirical evidence is shown to suggest absolute convergence, that is, narrowing national income gaps, among rich countries and possibly also divergence, that is, widening gaps, among poor countries. It is argued that the only way for poor countries to catch up with rich ones is for the poor countries either to save more or be more efficient than the rich countries. This leads to a discussion of poverty traps, that is, of circumstances which may make it difficult for poor countries to break out of perennial poverty. In general, poverty is not good for growth. This, in turn, leads to a closer scrutiny of the connection between saving, efficiency, and economic growth in an attempt to shed brighter light on the dependence of growth on some of its main potential determinants, not only national saving, but also (a) international trade and investment; (b) inflation; (c) private vs. public ownership; (d) education, health, and income distribution; and (e) natural resource endowments and geography. Here the reader is offered a glimpse of some of the recent empirical literature on the main sources of growth.

Reforms and growth

Economic and institutional reforms in order to increase efficiency will result in more rapid growth in the long run, but output may have to fall before it begins to rise more rapidly. Thus, in Chapter 5, at last, the linkages between unemployment and economic growth are discussed. The main point of the chapter, and of the book, however, is that, with appropriate economic policies and institutions, rapid economic growth is achievable almost anywhere. True, there are important natural and political obstacles to growth-friendly reforms, including conflicts, real or imagined, between economic growth and other policy objectives and also conflicts of interest between those who gain from reforms and those who lose. Even so, to grow or not to grow is in large measure a matter of choice.

Questions for review

1. Does economic growth matter? To whom? Why?
2. Consider two countries, A and B, with the same national income per capita in the year 2000. Suppose that in country A national income grows at 4 per cent a year on average and the population remains unchanged, whereas in country B national income grows by 2 per cent per year and the population increases by 1 per cent a year. If these growth rates continue indefinitely, what will the ratio of income per head in country B to that in country A be in 2025? What will it be in 2050?
3. In 1970, per capita GNP in the United Kingdom was about twice as high as that of Hong Kong. From 1970 to 1995, the annual average rate of growth of per capita GNP was 1.8 per cent in the United Kingdom compared with 5.8 per cent in Hong Kong. In 1995, the number of mobile phones per 1,000 people was 98 and 129 in the two countries. Do you want to guess which of the two countries had more mobile phones per capita?[30]

Notes

1. Adam Smith, *An Inquiry into the Nature and Causes of the Wealth of Nations* (Liberty Classics, Indianapolis, 1976), i. 342.

2. Thomas Malthus, *Essay on Population*, 5th edn. (London, 1817), 310.

3. See Armand Hammer, *Hammer: Witness to History* (Simon & Schuster, New York, 1987), 323.

4. See Paul Samuelson, *Economics*, 8th edn. (McGraw-Hill, New York, 1970), 831, Fig. 42–1.

5. Ragnar Frisch, 'Foreword' to Leif Johansen, *Norge og fellesmarkedet* (*Norway and the Common Market*) (Oslo, 1961), 9. Author's trans. from Norwegian. The italics are in the original.

6. But some did, and said so. Friedrich von Hayek, in his *Road to Serfdom* (1944), proved prophetic. For another example, Jan Winiecki published several articles in the 1980s explaining why the socialist system was bound to collapse before long. See Jan Winiecki 'Are Soviet-Type Economies Entering an Era of Long-Term Decline?', *Soviet Studies*, 38/3 (1986), 325–48, and 'Soviet-Type Economies: Considerations for the Future', *Soviet Studies*, 38/4 (1986), 543–61.

7. The phrase is from Solow, who used it in a different context. See W.W. Rostow, *Theories of Economic Growth from David Hume to the Present* (Oxford University Press, Oxford and New York, 1990), 373.

8. Adam Smith, *Wealth of Nations*, i. 111–12.

9. To wit, ch. III of Book I of *The Wealth of Nations* is entitled 'That the Division of Labour is limited by the Extent of the Market'.

10. Adam Smith, *Wealth of Nations*, i. 111–12.

11. It is useful—and, therefore, by now, common practice—to focus comparisons of national income across countries on differences in the purchasing power of households in order to avoid ascribing too high incomes and living standards to countries with high prices due to domestic inefficiency as well as to avoid exaggerating the income differences between rich and poor countries. When adjusted for purchasing-power differences, Russia's GNP per capita was one-sixth of that of the United States in 1995. The reliability of the purchasing-power-parity adjustment methods in use is, however, an unsettled issue.

12. See Dwight Perkins, 'Completing China's Move to the Market', *Journal of Economic Perspectives*, 8/2 (1994), 23–46, and Per Ronnås and Örjan Sjöberg, 'Economic Reform in Vietnam: Dismantling the Centrally Planned Economy', *Journal of Communist Studies*, 7/1 (1991), 7–19.

13. Because of recent problems with Burmese national income statistics, the World Bank does not report Burma's GNP per capita in US dollars in its 1997 issue of *World Development Indicators*. This is why the format of Figure 1.1 differs from that of the remaining figures in the chapter. In Figure 1.1, an attempt is made to describe the comparative per capita growth performance of Burma and Thailand 1960–94 based on the World Bank's *World Data* 1995, without, however, indicating the relative level of GNP per capita (in US dollars), which is arbitrarily set equal to 100 in 1960 in both countries. At the time of writing, 1994 was the latest year for which any national income statistics on Burma were available from the World Bank.

14. Specifically, the secondary and tertiary enrolment rates in Thailand were 37% (Table 1.1) and 19% in 1993, compared with 98% and 56% on average in high-income countries. Comparable information is not available for Burma. See also World Bank, *World Development Report 1997* (Oxford University Press, Oxford, 1997), table 7.

15. See World Bank, *World Development Report 1997* (Oxford University Press, Oxford, 1997), table 7.

16. See International Monetary Fund, *International Financial Statistics Yearbook*, Washington, DC, 1997.

17. See World Bank, *World Development Indicators 1997* (Oxford University Press, Oxford, 1997), table 5.1.

18. The three curves in Figure 1.2 would be flatter if GNP per capita were measured in US dollars at constant rather than current prices, but their relative positions would, of course, not change. The same applies to Figures 1.3 and 1.4 later in the chapter. US dollar values are obtained from domestic currencies by using a three-year weighted average of official exchange rates or an alternative conversion factor if necessary (i.e. if official exchange rates do not reflect the effective exchange rates applied to foreign transactions).

19. And so did Cuba, which remains utterly poor after 40 years of central planning. Increased literacy is a necessary, but not sufficient, condition for economic success.

20. See World Bank, *World Development Report 1997* (Oxford University Press, Oxford, 1997), table 7.

21. Yes, fast indeed. Botswana has been hit particularly hard by the aids epidemic, so that life expectancy has decreased from 60 years to 50 over the past few years. Even so, all three, Botswana, Ghana, and Nigeria, had the same population growth in 1985–95, or 3% per annum on average. The population of Botswana in 1995 was 1.5m, Ghana 17m, and Nigeria 111m.

22. The nominal rates of increase of GNP per capita implied by Figure 1.2 exceed the corresponding real rates because of inflation in the USA of about 5.3% per year on average during 1970–95, according to the US GDP deflator. The same applies to Figures 1.3 and 1.4.

23. By one international dollar (IUS$) is meant the amount of goods and services in the home country that one dollar would buy in the USA.

24. Not quite, because the income differences among the three countries may be exaggerated by not adjusting their national incomes for purchasing power parity. In 1995, Spain's PPP-adjusted GNP per capita was IUS$ 14,520, Argentina's IUS$ 8,310, and Uruguay's IUS$ 6,630 (Table 1.1).

25. See e.g. David Rock, *Argentina 1516–1987* (University of California Press, Berkeley, Calif., 1987).

26. The weighted average export ratio of the world as a whole, where each country is weighted by the size of its economy, is lower, or 22%, due to the weight of large countries which export relatively little, especially the USA and Japan.

27. See World Bank, *World Development Report 1997* (Oxford University Press, Oxford, 1997), table 15.

28. Ibid., table 17.

29. W. Arthur Lewis, *Some Aspects of Economic Development* (Ghana Publishing Corporation, Accra and Tema, 1968). In Ch. 4, we will take Lewis' statement a step further and argue that economic growth is available also to countries *without* natural resources.

30. The answer is Hong Kong. In 1995, Hong Kong also had more telephone mainlines per 1,000 people than the UK, or 530 compared with 502. On the other hand, the UK had far more television sets per 1,000 people than Hong Kong, or 612 against 359. In 1995, per capita GNP in Hong Kong exceeded that of the UK by about 20%, whether GNP is adjusted for purchasing power parity or not. See *World Development Indicators 1997*, table 1.1 and compact disc.

2

Roots and Branches

The proximate causes of economic growth are the effort to economize, the accumulation of knowledge, and the accumulation of capital.[1]

W. ARTHUR LEWIS

To change the rate of growth of real output per head you have to change the rate of technical progress.[2]

ROBERT SOLOW

The theory of economic growth has a long history that can be traced back at least to David Hume, who was Adam Smith's older friend and colleague. It is with Hume and then Smith that W.W. Rostow begins his prodigious book[3] on the doctrinal history and theory of economic growth, proceeding to the contributions of Thomas Malthus, David Ricardo, John Stuart Mill, and Karl Marx, who all were growth theorists. Each of them had his own special perspective on national economic prosperity and growth, among other things. Economic growth was at the very heart of classical economics.

Begin with Hume. In his rebellion against mercantilism, according to which a favourable balance of trade was a prerequisite for increased national wealth, Hume saw a clear connection from trade to prosperity and growth. He realized that it is not the trade *surplus* (excess of exports over imports) that matters most, but rather total trade as such (exports *plus* imports): 'If we consult history,' wrote Hume, 'we shall find, that in most nations, foreign trade has preceded any refinement in home manufactures, and given birth to domestic luxury.'[4] In Hume's view, not only exports, but also imports, are good for growth.

The first revolution: Adam Smith

Adam Smith took the argument a step further by making the links between the division of labour, efficiency, and the size of the market a central element in his wide-ranging theory of wealth creation, public policy, and economic growth. He may thus be said to have started the first revolution in growth theory. Like Hume, Smith regarded saving and investment both as by-products and precursors of domestic and foreign trade and, moreover, as a means of enlarging the market and increasing the division of labour and thereby also efficiency:

> The annual produce of the land and labour of any nation can be increased in its value by no other means, but by increasing either the number of its productive labourers, or the productive powers of those labourers who had before been employed. The number of its productive labourers, it is evident, can never be much increased, but in consequence of an increase in capital, or of the funds destined for maintaining them. The productive powers of the same number of labourers cannot be increased, but in consequence either of some addition or improvement to those machines and instruments which facilitate and abridge labour; or of a more proper division and distribution of employment. In either case an additional capital is almost always required. . . . When we compare, therefore, the state of a nation at two different periods, and find, that the annual produce of its land and labour is evidently greater at the latter than at the former, that its lands are better cultivated, its manufactures more numerous and more flourishing, and its trade more extensive, we may be assured that its capital must have increased during the interval between those two periods, and that more must have been added to it by the good conduct of some, than had been taken from it either by the private misconduct of others, or by the publick extravagance of government.[5]

Thus, it was Smith's view that high levels of saving and investment stimulate growth not only through the direct effects of the resulting accumulation of capital on output, but also through its indirect effects on labour productivity as well as its interaction with exchange and trade. Saving and investment encourage trade and vice versa, most obviously through foreign investment, which *is* trade in capital. Notice also Smith's reference to 'private misconduct' and 'the publick extravagance of government'. Smith made a clear distinction between quantity and quality: it takes either more or better capital (or labour or land, for that matter) to increase efficiency and economic growth. This distinction has not always been well understood, however. Nikita Khrushchev, for one, rationalized the Soviet Union's gigantic investment and industrialization efforts by saying that enough quantity insures quality.

We have already seen that Smith believed that foreign trade stimulates economic growth—see, for instance, his comment on the stagnation of China, quoted in the preceding chapter. Notice, however, that Smith's emphasis on the size of the market as a source of growth implies that, to increase growth, trade does not necessarily have to be with foreign countries, because a large domestic market can take the place of foreign markets.

Smith would thus not have been surprised to see how small countries in the modern world typically export and import more than large countries relative to their GDP. Hence, it stands to reason, according to Smith, that trade in the United States and Japan accounted for 24 and 17 per cent of GDP in 1995, respectively, while Belgium and Sweden, much smaller (i.e. less populous) countries, had much larger trade ratios (143 and 77 per cent, respectively). Trade within large countries generally enhances efficiency in the same way as trade between small countries and their foreign partners. In both cases, the effect is the same: to enlarge the market. Therefore, there is no reason to expect large (i.e. populous) countries with limited foreign trade to grow less rapidly than small countries with few people and, therefore, lots of trade with other countries. The link between trade and growth needs to be adjusted for country size.

Smith was also well aware of the mutual advantages of trade and growth and of their link to geography:

> The wealth of a neighbouring nation, however, though dangerous in war and politics, is certainly advantageous in trade. . . . A nation that would enrich itself by foreign trade, is certainly more likely to do so when its neighbours are all rich, industrious, and commercial nations. A great nation surrounded on all sides by wandering savages and poor barbarians might, no doubt, acquire riches by the cultivation of its own lands, and by its own interior commerce, but not by foreign trade.[6]

Smith's main point about the benefits from division of labour is general. If specialization increases efficiency and wealth and, thereby, economic growth, then just about *anything* that increases efficiency by the same amount, other things being equal, should be expected to have the same effect on growth. So, if foreign trade enlarges the market and thus facilitates further division of labour à la Smith, thereby increasing wealth and growth, then *all* other equivalent means of increasing the efficiency or quality of labour, capital, and land should be expected to affect economic growth in the same way. Because of its generality, this is perhaps the most fundamental implication of Smith's theory of growth, especially, as we shall see, for economic policy. This is what Arthur Lewis means by 'the effort to economize' in the quotation at the beginning of this chapter. Which brings us to the obvious question of the accumulation of knowledge—education.

What did Smith think of education, efficiency, and growth? Here the plot thickens a bit. It follows directly from his distinction between the quantity and quality of labour that Smith believed that education, by increasing labour productivity, is bound to increase also efficiency and growth. He was in favour of education, especially for

> the common people. They have little time to spare for education. Their parents can scarce afford to maintain them even in infancy. As soon as they are able to work, they must apply to some trade by which they can earn their subsistence. That trade too is generally so simple and uniform as to give little exercise to the understanding; while, at the same time, their labour is both so constant and so severe, that it leaves them little leisure and less inclination to apply to, or even to think of any thing else. . . . For a very small expence the publick can facilitate, can encourage, and can even impose upon almost the whole body of the people, the necessity of acquiring those most essential parts of education . . . to read, write, and account . . . [7]

Smith's views on education are relevant here, because he viewed division of labour as a bit of a mixed blessing and feared the economic, political, and social consequences of inferior education among the masses. Let him go on:

> The man whose whole life is spent in performing a few simple operations, of which the effects too are, perhaps, always the same, or very nearly the same, has no occasion to exert his understanding, or to exercise his invention in finding out expedients for removing difficulties which never occur. He naturally loses, therefore, the habit of such exertion, and generally becomes as stupid and ignorant as it is possible for a human creature to become. . . . Of the great and extensive interests of his country, he is altogether incapable of judging; and . . . equally incapable of defending his country in war. . . . His dexterity at

his own particular trade seems, in this manner, to be acquired at the expence of his intellectual, social, and martial virtues. But in every improved and civil society this is the state into which the labouring poor, that is, the great body of the people, must necessarily fall, unless government takes some pains to prevent it.[8]

Thus, even if he was quite critical of the public education institutions of his time, especially the universities, Smith favoured public support for education on the grounds that the benefits of education accrue not only to the educated classes, but to society at large. Even so, he thought that education could be improved through more private-sector involvement. In his words:

The expence of the institutions for education and religious instruction, is likewise, no doubt, beneficial to the whole society, and may, therefore, without injustice, be defrayed by the general contribution of the whole society. This expence, however, might perhaps with equal propriety, and even with some advantage, be defrayed altogether by those who receive the immediate benefit of such education and instruction, or by the voluntary contribution of those who think they have occasion for either the one or the other.

When the institutions or publick works which are beneficial to the whole society, either cannot be maintained altogether, or are not maintained altogether by the contribution of such particular members of the society as are most immediately benefited by them, the deficiency must in most cases be made up by the general contribution of the whole society.[9]

For this, of course, the government needed tax revenue. Smith devoted all of Book V of *The Wealth of Nations*, a third of the work, to tax matters and, soon after its publication, accepted an appointment as Commissioner of Customs in Scotland, a post he held until his death in 1790.

To sum up, then, Adam Smith attributed economic growth to an increase in the quantity and quality of the three main factors of production: labour, capital, and land. To this day, growth accounting—i.e. attempts to determine empirically the proportions in which economic growth can be traced to its proximate causes—is based on this classification. This, however, is perhaps not always the most helpful classification of the sources of growth, for two main reasons. First, the quantity of land is essentially fixed in most cases, even if its quality can be greatly enhanced, as occurred, for example, in the Green Revolution, which made India and many other developing countries self-sufficient in food. As the quotation from him on China in Chapter 1 shows, Smith was aware that 'soil, climate, and situation' contribute to growth through the quality of land.[10] Second, an increase in the labour force as such does not really count as a source of economic growth, because what matters for a nation's standard of living is not the growth of national economic output *per se*, but rather of output *per capita*.[11] Even so, Smith could explain how capital accumulation and trade increased the demand for labour, thus bidding up wages and augmenting the labour force along with capital by reducing child mortality and increasing longevity, among other things. Thus, with these provisos, we are left with (a) the increased quantity of capital through saving and investment and (b) the improved quality of labour, capital, and land as the two major sources of economic growth. And this is basically how modern growth accounting proceeds: it involves an attempt to establish the contributions of population growth and capital accumulation to output growth or, equivalently, of capital accumulation to output growth per capita, attributing the residual to total factor productivity (sometimes also called 'the measure of our ignorance')—i.e. to technological progress. In the United States, for example, growth accounting typically leads to a third of output growth being ascribed to population growth, roughly another third to capital accumulation, and the remaining third to technological progress.[12]

The following alternative classification of the causes of economic growth may be helpful, because it is more direct, and it may also do more justice to Smith's theory, as we—and he!—have described it above. Economic growth is driven forward by (a) the accumulation of capital through high levels of saving and investment and (b) increased efficiency through division of labour, increased foreign trade, more and better education, improved soil and climate (e.g. through air conditioning!), laws and institutions,[13] or any other means that increase the productivity of labour, capital, or land. If the accumulation of knowledge through education is counted as a separate item, we have the three-pronged classification offered by Arthur Lewis at the beginning of this chapter. Notice that the classical production function tracing national economic output to the inputs of labour, capital, and land lies behind both classifications.

It hardly needs to be said that, for simplicity, the above sketch has abstracted from various subtleties in Smith's account of the progress of wealth—i.e. economic growth—without, it is hoped, diluting or distorting his main message. *The Wealth of Nations* is an extremely rich, substantial, and wide-ranging book, blending as it does phenomenally far-sighted economic theory with countless empirical and practical examples and observations from afar and near as well as with the sometimes piercing personal opinions of the author.[14] 'I shall not mingle conjectures with certainties,' wrote Isaac Newton to a friend, but Adam Smith made no bones about such. Smith was familiar with Newtonian physics, of course, but *The Wealth of Nations* is nevertheless a completely non-mathematical book: it does not contain a single mathematical equation, not even a single graph.[15]

Adam Smith's followers

In essence, Adam Smith's theory of growth remained unchallenged for almost 200 years, except for the onslaught of Karl Marx. Smith's followers, especially Thomas Malthus, David Ricardo, and John Stuart Mill, added some details and changed emphases, but even so the broad contours of the theory remained essentially intact. One of Malthus's main interests was the question of population, which led him, early in his career, to predict that, because land is a fixed factor while population grows incessantly, economic growth would ultimately be stifled by insufficient food supplies for the people. His 'dismal science' earned Malthus and his views a reputation for pessimism, but later in life his outlook became more optimistic as he realized that the production of food depends not only on the quantity of land but also its quality, including fertility, among other things. Ricardo was more interested in the distribution of wealth than in its growth, but he nevertheless managed to strengthen the foundation of Smith's theory of growth, especially by providing a fuller explanation than Smith had done of the ways in which foreign trade increases efficiency and, thereby, economic growth. Mill, in his *Principles of Political Economy* (1848), which remained the definitive textbook of economics for half a century, rejected Malthus's prediction of stunted incomes and wealth with the argument that more and better education would restrain population growth. He reinstated production as the main focus of economics, likening the economic laws dictating production and the progress of wealth to those governing the expansion of gases in thermodynamics. Distribution, to Mill, was a different matter: if society did not like the distribution of income and wealth under *laissez-faire*, it could at will amend it by taxes and subsidies.

Marx disagreed. To him, the economic mechanisms driving production and distribution seemed closely related. He believed that the limits to growth first observed by Malthus were inescapable: economic growth, by raising wages, would induce profit-hungry capitalists to replace men by machines, thereby creating what John Maynard Keynes later called 'technological unemployment'.[16] Through repeated cycles of boom and bust, with each economic crisis somehow deeper than the preceding one, the capitalist system could not withstand the wrath of the jobless masses and would, therefore, eventually collapse. Marx did not see how workers rendered redundant by machines could be re-employed in new occupations.

Alfred Marshall was also a growth theorist, even if he is better known as the founding father of modern microeconomics. Marshall agreed with Smith on economic growth, adding organization as a fourth factor of production. 'Knowledge is our most powerful engine of production,' he wrote, and added: '. . . [o]rganization aids knowledge.'[17] Marshall thus made explicit the connection between education and growth that had only been implicit in *The Wealth of Nations*:

> There is no extravagance more prejudicial to growth of national wealth than that wasteful negligence which allows genius that happens to be born of lowly parentage to expend itself in lowly work. No change would conduce so much to a rapid increase of material wealth as an improvement in our schools, and especially those of the middle grades, provided it be combined with an extensive system of scholarships, which will enable the clever son of a working man to rise gradually from school to school till he has the best theoretical and practical education which the age can give.[18]

Marshall was also convinced that the distribution of income and wealth matters for efficiency and growth:

> The older economists took too little account of the fact that human faculties are as important a means of production as any other kind of capital; and we may conclude, in opposition to them, that any change in the distribution of wealth which gives more to the wage receivers and less to the capitalists is likely, other things being equal, to hasten the increase of material production, and . . . it will not perceptibly retard the storing-up of material wealth. . . . a slight and temporary check to the accumulation of material wealth need not necessarily be an evil, even from a purely economic point of view, if, being made quietly and without disturbance, it provided better opportunities for the great mass of the people, increased their efficiency, and developed in them such habits of self-respect as to result in the growth of a much more efficient race of producers in the next generation. For then it might do more in the long-run to promote growth of even material wealth than the great additions to our stock of factories and steam engines.[19]

And so the great debate on growth proceeded. Joseph Schumpeter, in his *Theory of Economic Development* (1911) and later works, directed the attention of growth theorists to technology through invention, innovation, and entrepreneurship. His entrepreneurs are rent-seekers, who are motivated by monopoly profits: they continue to invent and innovate as long as they can capture the rent from their patents. Schumpeter made the point that perfectly competitive markets, efficient as they may be from a static point of view, may not be very conducive to economic growth, because there is no rent to capture under perfect competition. Hence, static efficiency does not go along with dynamic efficiency.[20]

Keynes thought along partly similar lines and, in 1930, even as the world plunged into depression, expressed unbounded optimism about the future;

> From the earliest times of which we have record—back, say, to two thousand years before Christ—down to the beginning of the eighteenth century, there was no very great change in the standard of life of the average man living in the civilised centres of the earth. . . . This slow rate of progress, or lack of progress, was due to two reasons—to the remarkable absence of important technical improvements and to the failure of capital to accumulate.
>
> The modern age opened, I think, with the accumulation of capital which began in the sixteenth century. . . . From the sixteenth century, with a cumulative crescendo after the eighteenth, the great age of science and technical inventions began, which since the beginning of the nineteenth century has been in full flood—coal, steam, electricity, petrol, steel, rubber, cotton, the chemical industries, automatic machinery and the methods of mass production, wireless, printing, Newton, Darwin, and Einstein, and thousands of other things and men too famous and familiar to catalogue.
>
> What is the result? In spite of an enormous growth in the population of the world, which it has been necessary to equip with houses and machines, the average standard of life in Europe and the United States has been raised, I think, about fourfold. The growth of capital has been on a scale which is far beyond a hundredfold of what any previous age had known. And from now on we need not expect so great an increase of population. . . .
>
> At the same time technical improvements in manufacture and transport have been proceeding at a greater rate in the last ten years than ever before in history. . . . I draw the conclusion that, assuming no important wars and no important increase in population, the *economic problem* may be solved, or be at least within sight of solution, within a hundred years.[21]

Enter mathematics: Harrod and Domar

Adam Smith and his followers, until the second half of this century, stated their theory of economic growth in words, most in English. Alfred Marshall, in particular, wanted it that way: to him, mathematics in economics was as 'at best a useful piece of scaffolding, which should be removed in the presentation of final arguments'.[22] However, the use of mathematics became a permanent feature of analytical economics following the publication of Paul Samuelson's *Foundations of Economic Analysis* (1948), and was bound to have a great impact on growth theory in particular.

One growth-theoretical complication, which was not addressed explicitly by Smith and his followers, has to do with the dynamic interactions among macroeconomic variables and the associated distinction between flows (e.g. saving and investment, measured in, say, dollars or pounds *per year*) and stocks (e.g. capital, measured in dollars or pounds *at a point in time* such as the beginning of the year). To paraphrase Irving Fisher, a flow is as different from a stock as a waterfall is from sea level.[23] Because of the continuous movement involved, this distinction between flows and stocks is an inherently dynamic problem most easily dealt with by mathematics, which is confined to the appendices at the end of the book.

By definition, net investment equals the increase in the capital stock, net of depreciation due to physical or economic wear and tear.[24] This is why a *high* level of investment entails an *increasing* level of the capital stock. And this is, therefore, why high levels of saving and investment are good for growth even if they are stationary, that is, not increasing. High *and* rising levels of saving and investment are better still for growth, it is true, but that is another matter. The main point is that, by continuously augmenting the capital stock, even stationary levels of saving and investment relative to output drive the output higher and higher, thus generating economic growth. Without net investment, the capital stock would remain unchanged, so that, with given efficiency, economic growth would then also be nil. Negative net investment, which means that the capital stock is decreasing, because gross investment is not enough to keep up with the depreciation of capital, entails negative economic growth. Rapid depreciation due to investments of low quality is an important source of slow or even negative economic growth over long periods in many countries, especially in Sub-Saharan Africa.

The link between efficiency and growth is a bit more complicated. A high level of efficiency—for example, through vigorous foreign trade or high standards of education—stimulates growth by amplifying the effects of a given level of saving and investment on the rate of growth of output. An increase in efficiency will increase economic growth, yes, but output growth does not require a continuous increase in efficiency. All that is required is a steady accumulation of capital through saving and investment. A given level of efficiency, including the state of technology, will then translate the capital accumulation into economic growth.

Shortly before the middle of this century, Roy Harrod and Evsey Domar expressed the dynamic relationships described above in a simple equation, which neatly formalized, simplified, and summarized the essence of almost 200 years' theorizing about economic growth.[25] According to the Harrod–Domar model, economic growth depends on just three factors: (a) the saving rate, which is determined by households as they divide their income between consumption and saving; (b) the capital/output ratio, which reflects the way firms base their demand for capital on the amount of output they want to produce; and (c) the depreciation rate, which is partly a consequence of the quality of investment decisions in the past. Specifically, an increase in the saving rate increases the rate of economic growth. On the other hand, an increase in the use of capital relative to output reduces growth, because the need for more capital to produce a given level of output reflects reduced efficiency in the use of capital. An increase in depreciation also reduces growth, point for point, because it reduces the amount of saving available for net investment, i.e. for the accumulation of fresh capital. The more of its saving society has to set aside to replace worn-out or obsolete machinery and equipment, the less there remains to be invested in new capital. So, it is essentially all here, from Adam Smith onwards, in a single, simple equation: Growth depends on saving and efficiency, including depreciation.

As it began to gain currency in the 1950s as an elegant formalization of growth theory and a useful teaching device, the Harrod–Domar model came under attack, on two fronts at once. The model is based on two assumptions, one about the way households choose between consumption and saving and another about the way firms choose to adjust their capital stock to output. While the assumption that households want to save a fixed proportion of their income was and is not difficult to justify on the basis of both economic theory and empirical evidence, at least as a first approximation, the same cannot be said about the assumption that firms want to keep their capital stock in a fixed proportion to their output, which makes the capital/output ratio an exogenous behavioural parameter in the model: neither theory nor empirical evidence seemed to provide much support for that particular formulation. Therefore, a more convincing justification or, failing that, a more elaborate formulation of the link between capital and output was called for. Furthermore, the Harrod–Domar growth formula did not leave much room for the other crucial factor of production, labour. After all, population or labour-force growth is absent from the formula, which explains output growth solely by saving and efficiency. These weaknesses proved fatal to the Harrod–Domar model, as Robert Solow was to show in 1956,[26] or so it seemed.

The second revolution: The neoclassical model

Solow's point was really quite simple, and revolutionary. Suppose output is made by labour and capital under constant returns to scale, so that doubling both inputs doubles the output. This type of production function already had a long tradition in economics. Moreover, suppose capital grows at the same rate as output in the long run, as recently available economic statistics on the United States and other industrial countries compiled by Simon Kuznets and others seemed to show. Then, if we abstract for a moment from technological progress, output and capital must grow together at the same rate as labour.[27] Therefore, since population growth is basically a demographic phenomenon and, hence, exogenous from an economic point of view, it must follow that economic growth is also exogenous. Harrod knew this. He made a distinction between what he called the 'warranted' rate of growth, which depends on saving, efficiency, and depreciation, and the 'natural' rate of growth, which depends on population growth, noting that there was no automatic mechanism in place to guarantee that the two would converge. In particular, if warranted growth failed to keep up with natural growth, unemployment would ensue.

Economic growth remains exogenous when technological change is taken into account, for example in the form of increased labour productivity, which grows at an exogenously given rate. Now the constant-returns-to-scale production function relating output to labour and capital shifts out continuously at the rate of technological progress, because the same labour and capital make more and more output over time. In this case output and capital must grow in the long run at a rate that equals the sum of the rate of growth of the labour force (or population, if the labour-force participation rate is constant) and the rate of technological progress. Thus, according to Solow, saving behaviour was no longer relevant for long-run growth, nor was efficiency in a broad sense, except insofar as it mattered for technology. As population growth and technological progress were outside the purview of pure economics and thus outside the reach of economic policy, economic growth came to be widely seen as exogenous in the long run from an economic point of view, and hence immune to economic policy, good or bad, among other things. Even so, as we will see later on, in Solow's world saving and efficiency play an important role in the long run.

How did Solow reach this conclusion? He noticed that if the capital stock happens to be out of equilibrium, in the sense that its current value is either larger or smaller than its long-run equilibrium value (which grows over time in a growing economy), then the disequilibrium will set in motion a dynamic adjustment mechanism through which the capital stock will automatically move towards its long-run equilibrium value, gradually reducing the gap and ultimately closing it. The bottom line is a long-run steady-state equilibrium path along which output, capital, and quality-adjusted labour (measured in efficiency units to allow for increasing productivity) all grow at the same exogenously given rate. This means that the capital/output ratio remains constant over time, and output per head and capital per worker grow at the same exogenous rate as productivity. These properties of the model seemed to accord with the so-called 'stylized facts' of economic growth,[28] which Solow had set out to explain, prime among them the alleged constancy of the capital/output ratio over long periods. Solow showed how the capital/output ratio, rather than being exogenously fixed as in the Harrod–Domar model, is better viewed as an endogenous variable, which moves over time and ultimately reaches long-run equilibrium. Once attained, the long-run equilibrium is consistent with not only a constant capital/output ratio, but also with a constant rate of growth of output per capita, a constant rate of interest, and a constant distribution of national income between labour and capital, all of which seemed to apply to the so-called real world.[29] It is a rich and beautiful model.

Solow's contribution, which became known as the neoclassical model, spawned a large literature on economic growth. Following elaborate extensions of the neoclassical model in various directions in the 1960s, however, economic research on growth was reduced to a trifle in the 1970s, when macroeconomists began devoting most of their attention to short-run problems and policies. In the United States especially, a considerable part of the macroeconomic research agenda in the 1970s and early 1980s revolved around attempts to show that not only was economic growth in the long run immune to economic policy as shown by Solow, but unemployment in the short run was also immune to monetary and fiscal policy, because private economic agents with rational expectations could counteract all government attempts to change unemployment, or output for that matter, through policy.[30] Many thought that macroeconomics was dead.

The discovery that, after all, long-run economic growth depended on population growth and technological progress and nothing else created a problem for the Harrod–Domar view of growth, and not only Harrod and Domar, but almost all the classical economists from Adam Smith to Alfred Marshall, if not also Schumpeter and Keynes. Technically, Solow had rendered the Harrod–Domar model overidentified in the sense that a single variable, growth, was now being determined by two different equations, one explaining growth by saving, efficiency, and depreciation and the other, by population growth and technological progress. Mathematically speaking, one of these five fixed parameters had to be made endogenous, so that the two equations could be used to determine *two* variables, growth and one of the remaining five. Solow selected the capital/output ratio to solve the over-identification problem. He constructed his model in such a way that the capital/output ratio would gradually adjust through the dynamic mechanism described above so as not to violate the Harrod–Domar equation in the long run, even if growth is exogenous. Others went other routes, endogenizing either the saving rate,[31] population growth,[32] or technological progress.[33]

This is a bit technical, but try to look at it this way. In the Harrod–Domar model, the exogeneity of the capital/output ratio is what makes it possible to view growth as an endogenous variable: growth adjusts to the exogenously given capital/output ratio. What Solow did was reverse the roles of the rate of growth and the capital/output ratio: he treated the capital/output ratio as an endogenous variable that adjusts over time to the exogenously given growth rate of output—exogenous because its two underlying determinants, population growth and technological progress, are exogenous.

The third revolution: Endogenous growth

As the 1980s progressed, however, many economists became increasingly dissatisfied with what they perceived as the inability of the neoclassical growth model to answer several burning questions about economic growth. First, some began to doubt the wisdom of regarding technological change as exogenous from an economic point of view. The pace of technological progress, it was thought, is bound to have an economic explanation, at least in part. Second, many economists also felt increasingly frustrated by the exogeneity of long-run economic growth in the neoclassical model. If output per capita grows at a rate that depends solely on—in fact, is equal to—the rate of technological progress, then why is it that the growth performance of different countries differs so radically over long periods? Is the rate of technological progress really *that* different in different countries? Why is growth not more similar across countries? Does economics really have so little to say about these issues? And what does the neoclassical model tell us about relative growth performance anyway? In particular, do poor countries grow more rapidly than rich? What is the empirical evidence?

These concerns had not been completely neglected in the heyday of the neoclassical model. Standing on the shoulders of Simon Kuznets and others, Hollis Chenery and his associates at the World Bank continued among others to look for patterns in the economic growth of developing countries.[34] Meanwhile, although they did not have as many students as before, development economists continued to study economic aspects of economic development.[35] Even so, the new questions that were raised in the 1980s called for new thinking about economic growth.[36]

And thus a new view emerged, a new theory of growth. The key idea is quite simple: technology is probably not exogenous. More probably, it depends on economic factors, including, for example, the amount of capital available to workers, that is, the capital/labour ratio. The more capital workers have to work with, the more computers and so on, the more efficiently they will use the capital: they will learn by doing. If the dependence of technology on the capital/labour ratio is described in a particular, and admittedly somewhat arbitrary, way,[37] then, as Paul Romer showed— you probably guessed it!—the capital/output ratio turns out to be constant after all, as assumed by Harrod and Domar. Hence, economic growth has been freed to respond to changes in saving, efficiency, and depreciation, even in the long run. The Harrod–Domar model has thus been restored by stripping it of the drawbacks that led to its dismissal in the first place. Endogenous technology makes economic growth also endogenous. The theory of endogenous growth thus throws all windows wide open.

Summary

So this is where we stand at chapter's end. The theory of economic growth has deep roots that extend as far back in time as economics itself. The classical economists, from Adam Smith to at least Alfred Marshall, viewed economic growth as endogenous in the sense that it depends on economic factors—saving, efficiency, and depreciation, in particular. This view of growth was summarized in a simple equation by Harrod and Domar. An apparent inconsistency in Harrod and Domar's formalization led Solow to rebel and build a new model, which showed economic growth, surprisingly, to be exogenous in the long run, and thus independent of saving, efficiency, and depreciation, except in so far as efficiency affects technology. There was no discernible link between economic policy and long-run growth. Even so, empirically inclined economists at the World Bank and elsewhere continued to search for economic explanations of economic growth. Eventually, economic theorists went back to their drawing boards to see if it was not possible to restore the endogeneity of economic growth and re-establish the links between saving, efficiency, and growth. This enterprise has branched out over a wide field, to which we turn in the next chapter.

Questions for review

1. Suppose foreign trade stimulates economic growth as argued by Adam Smith, other things being equal. Does it follow that large countries with limited trade with the rest of the world should be expected to grow less rapidly than small countries with extensive foreign trade? Why not?
2. 'A high saving rate ensures rapid economic growth.' Is this statement true or false? Discuss.

3. Explain how more and better education affects (a) the level of per capita GNP in the long run and (b) its long-run rate of growth according to
   (i) the Harrod–Domar model;
   (ii) the Solow model;
   (iii) the endogenous-growth model.
4. Why does increased depreciation of capital reduce economic growth, other things being equal? Does it matter whether the depreciation is physical or economic?—i.e. whether it results from physical wear and tear or from low-quality investment decisions in the past.

Notes

1. W. Arthur Lewis, *The Theory of Economic Growth* (Allen & Unwin, London, 1955), 164.
2. Robert M. Solow, *Growth Theory: An Exposition* (Oxford University Press, Oxford, 1970), 77.
3. W.W. Rostow, *Theories of Economic Growth from David Hume to the Present* (Oxford University Press, Oxford and New York, 1990).
4. David Hume, *Writings on Economics*, ed. by Eugene Rotwein (University of Wisconsin Press, Madison, 1955), 13.
5. Adam Smith, *The Wealth of Nations* (Liberty Classics, Indianapolis, 1976), i. 343.
6. Ibid. 494–5.
7. Ibid., ii. 784–5.
8. Ibid., ii. 782.
9. Ibid., ii. 815.
10. This has recently inspired Jeffrey Sachs and his associates at the Harvard Institute for International Development to launch an ambitious empirical investigation into the links between geography and growth, as will be discussed in Ch. 4. See e.g. *Emerging Asia: Changes and Challenges* (Asian Development Bank, Manila, 1997), chs. 1 and 2, which were written by David Bloom, Jeffrey Sachs, and Steve Radelet.
11. Throughout the book, the terms per capita, per head, and per worker are used interchangeably to refer to both the labour force and population, because the labour-force participation rate is assumed to remain unchanged.
12. See Edward F. Denison, *Trends in American Economic Growth, 1929–82* (Brookings Institution, Washington, DC, 1982).
13. Again, see the quotation from Smith on China in Ch. 1.
14. E.g. Smith was not impressed by the young generation's propensity to travel abroad rather than study at home: 'Nothing but the discredit into which the universities are allowing themselves to fall, could ever have brought into repute so very absurd a practice as that of travelling at this early period of life.' Adam Smith, *Wealth of Nations*, ii. 774.
15. Some attempts have been made to translate Smith's account of economic growth into mathematics. See e.g. W.W. Rostow, *Theories of Economic Growth*, Appendix.
16. See John Maynard Keynes, 'Economic Possibilities for Our Grandchildren', in his *Essays in Persuasion* (W.W. Norton & Co., New York, 1963), 364. 'But this is only a temporary phase of maladjustment,' he added.
17. Alfred Marshall, *Principles of Economics*, 8th edn., (Macmillan, London, 1920), 115.
18. Ibid. 176.
19. Ibid. 191.
20. Recent work suggests, however, that static and dynamic efficiency can easily go hand in hand in Schumpeterian growth models, essentially because competition is good for growth. See Philippe Aghion and Peter Howitt, *Endogenous Growth Theory* (MIT Press, Cambridge, Mass., and London, 1998), ch. 7.
21. John Maynard Keynes, *Essays in Persuasion*, 360–3.
22. Attributed to Alfred Marshall by Mark Blaug, *Economic Theory in Retrospect* (Irwin, Homewood, Ill., 1962), 376.
23. See Irving Fisher, *The Rate of Interest* (Macmillan, New York, 1907), 270.
24. Physical depreciation is a technological phenomenon. A tractor gradually wears out with normal use, and ultimately breaks down because individual parts break or fail with time. By economic depreciation is meant obsolescence. Even if it may be technologically feasible to keep a tractor in running order for decades, it ceases to make economic sense at some point, because the upkeep ultimately becomes too expensive relative to the cost of a new and better tractor. For a good discussion of

depreciation, see Maurice Fitzgerald Scott, *A New View of Economic Growth* (Clarendon Press, Oxford, 1989), ch. 1.

25. See Appendix 2.1. See also Roy Harrod, *Towards a Dynamic Economics* (Macmillan, London, 1948), and Evsey D. Domar, 'Capital Expansion, Rate of Growth, and Employment', *Econometrica*, 14/2 (1946), 137–47.

26. Robert M. Solow, 'A Contribution to the Theory of Economic Growth', *Quarterly Journal of Economics*, 70/1 (1956), 65–94, and 'Technical Change and the Aggregate Production Function', *Review of Economics and Statistics*, 39/3 (1957), 312–20. See also Robert M. Solow, *Growth Theory: An Exposition* (Oxford University Press, Oxford, 1970).

27. See Appendix 2.2.

28. See Nicholas Kaldor, 'Capital Accumulation and Economic Growth', in Friedrich A. Lutz and Douglas C. Hague (eds), *The Theory of Capital* (St Martin's Press, New York, 1961), 177–222.

29. For more, see Appendix 2.2.

30. See e.g. Robert E. Lucas, Jr., 'Expectations and the Neutrality of Money', *Journal of Economic Theory*, 4/2 (1972), 103–24, and 'Econometric Policy Evaluation: A Critique', *Carnegie-Rochester Conference Series on Public Policy*, 1 (1976), 19–46.

31. See Nicholas Kaldor, 'Alternative Theories of Distribution', *Review of Economic Studies*, 23 (1955–6), 83–100.

32. See William H. Branson, *Macroeconomic Theory and Policy*, 3rd edn. (Harper & Row, New York, 1989), 593–4.

33. See Kenneth J. Arrow, 'The Economic Implications of Learning by Doing', *Review of Economic Studies*, 29/2 (1962), 155–73. For an easy introduction to some of the issues involved, see Paul M. Romer, 'The Origins of Endogenous Growth', *Journal of Economic Perspectives*, 8/1 (1994), 3–22, and Gene M. Grossman and Elhanan Helpman, 'Endogenous Innovation in the Theory of Growth', *Journal of Economic Perspectives*, 8/1 (1994), 23–44.

34. See Hollis B. Chenery and Moshe Syrquin, *Patterns of Development, 1950–1970* (Oxford University Press, London, 1975), and Hollis B. Chenery, Sherman Robinson, and Moshe Syrquin, *Industrialization and Growth, A Comparative Study* (Oxford University Press, New York, and the World Bank, Washington, DC, 1986).

35. Arthur Lewis concluded his presidential address to the American Economic Association in 1983 by claiming that 'Development Economics is not at its most spectacular, but it is alive and well.' See W. Arthur Lewis, 'The State of Development Theory', *American Economic Review*, 74/1 (1984), 1–10.

36. The theoretical literature on endogenous growth can be traced to Kenneth Arrow, 'The Economic Implications of Learning by Doing'. Important contributions were later made by Paul M. Romer, 'Increasing Returns and Long-run Growth', *Journal of Political Economy*, 94/5 (1986) 1002–37; Robert E. Lucas, Jr., 'On the Mechanics of Economic Development', *Journal of Monetary Economics*, 22/3 (1988), 3–42; and Gene M. Grossman and Elhanan Helpman, *Innovation and Growth in the Global Economy* (MIT Press, Cambridge, Mass., and London, 1991), among others. A different perspective on endogenous growth is provided in Maurice Fitzgerald Scott, *A New View of Economic Growth* (Clarendon Press, Oxford, 1989).

37. See Appendix 2.3.

3

Quantity and Quality

The practical question then for our consideration is, what are the most immediate and effective stimulants to the creation and progress of wealth.[1]

THOMAS MALTHUS

Why did development economics fade away? . . . the leading development economists failed to turn their intuitive insights into clear-cut models that could serve as the core of an enduring discipline.[2]

PAUL KRUGMAN

Saving behaviour and efficiency have always occupied a prominent place in economic theory. As we traced the twists and turns of the doctrinal history of economic growth in the preceding chapter, we saw that saving and efficiency were invariably viewed as crucial determinants of economic growth from the time of Adam Smith and onwards, until Robert Solow revolutionized growth theory in the 1950s by showing long-run per capita growth to be ultimately immune to all influences except technological progress, which was seen as an exogenous quantity from an economic point of view. And then, in the 1980s, growth theory was again revolutionized by the rediscovery that technological change and economic growth are both endogenous after all.

Let us now look at these developments in more detail by studying the two main theories of economic growth, the new theory of endogenous growth and the neoclassical theory of exogenous growth, and by comparing their answers to some key questions about growth, over time and across countries. Inevitably, the discussion to follow will be a bit technical in places: what you are about to be offered is 'textbook treatment' of the theory of economic growth. The most technical sections to follow are marked by an asterisk, and can be skipped or skimmed without significant loss of continuity.

Endogenous growth and technology*

We begin with endogenous growth where we left the subject towards the end of Chapter 2. We can summarize the main implications of endogenous-growth theory with the aid of a simple diagram. Figure 3.1 shows the rate of economic growth (i.e. the rate of growth of national economic output) on the vertical axis and the rate of technological progress (i.e. the rate of change of output *per capita*) on the horizontal axis. The line labelled G (for growth) describes the rate of growth of output, which depends on three key variables: the saving rate, efficiency, and depreciation, just as in the Harrod–Domar model. The G line is horizontal, because endogenous growth does not depend on technological progress. The 45° line labelled T (for technology) reflects the key property of the endogenous-growth model: that technological progress follows—in fact, equals—the rate of growth of output per capita through learning by doing, and not the other way around as in the Solow model. Thus, whenever growth increases or decreases, so does the pace of technological change. The point B, where the T line cuts the vertical axis, shows the rate of population growth. The point of intersection A of the two lines, G and T, describes the long-run equilibrium values of the rate of economic growth and the rate of technological advance.[3] At that point, economic growth is given by the distance OC along the vertical axis in the figure, of which OB is due to population growth and BC (= CA) is due to technological progress.[4]

Let us now experiment. Let us trace the effects of certain exogenous events on the rate of economic growth and technological progress, both of which are endogenous.

Experiment 1: The saving rate

What happens if the saving rate rises?—for example, because households become more optimistic about, or interested in, the future, and thus decide to reduce their consumption so as to be able to set aside more money for themselves or their off-spring to spend later. Alternatively, we could think of an increase in the saving rate as resulting from the government's decision to stimulate national saving by reducing government expenditure or increasing taxes (without creating growth-

Fig 3.1
Endogenous growth: Determination of economic growth and technological progress

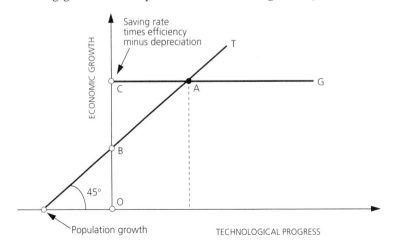

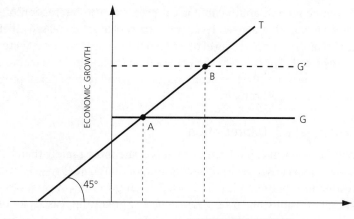

Fig 3.2
Endogenous growth: An increase in the saving rate or in efficiency increases economic growth and technological progress

ECONOMIC GROWTH

TECHNOLOGICAL PROGRESS

inhibiting distortions, which will be discussed in Chapter 4). In any case, an increase in the saving rate shifts the G line up to G′, as shown in Figure 3.2, so that the equilibrium point, where the two lines intersect, moves north-east from A to B, at which economic growth is faster than before, as is technological progress. Because population growth has not changed by assumption, the growth of output per capita increases as much (i.e. by the same percentage) as output growth. Economic growth increases because more capital is being accumulated and because technological progress accelerates through learning by doing: with more capital to work with, people learn how to use it more efficiently.

How fast does the economy move from A to B? The endogenous-growth theory we have outlined above[5] provides no answer to this important question, because no dynamic adjustment is involved in the theory. Additional considerations would have to be brought into the story to deal with the question of speed. This need not be a major handicap, however; after all, the theory of demand and supply does not address the question of speed of adjustment either. The dynamic deficiency of the endogenous-growth model actually has two dimensions: the model is silent on the time it takes the economy to move from one equilibrium to another and also about the stability of the growth equilibrium, that is, whether the economy, if shocked out of equilibrium by some external event, will automatically return to its initial position or not. The economy's move from the initial equilibrium at A to the new one at B can be either fast or slow; which, we do not know. If saving reacts slowly to increasing income, for example, the upward shift of the G line to G′ in Figure 3.2 will be slowed down, delaying the economy's move from A to B.

Experiment 2: Efficiency

What happens if efficiency increases?—where by efficiency is meant the amount of output that is being produced by using the existing stock of capital. An increase in efficiency can occur for any number of reasons. The liberalization of foreign trade, for example, increases efficiency, as has been known at least since the days of Adam Smith and David Ricardo. More and better education also increases efficiency, as was stressed so strongly and eloquently by Alfred Marshall.[6] Whatever its source, an increase in efficiency shifts the G line up to G′, as in Figure 3.2, thereby increasing both economic growth and technological progress. The interaction of saving and efficiency means that a given level of saving translates increased efficiency into more growth and that a given level of efficiency likewise translates increased saving into more growth. For this reason, increased saving and increased efficiency have qualitatively the same effect on economic growth and technological progress. Figure 3.2, therefore, covers both cases.

Experiment 3: Depreciation

What happens if capital begins to depreciate more rapidly than before? This could happen as a consequence of a deterioration in the quality—i.e. profitability—of investment. Suppose, for example, that a new government comes to power, nationalizes all the banks, and proceeds to allocate a greatly increased part of credit from the banking system to building up military defences against real and imagined enemies, building gigantic factories to make goods that nobody wants to buy, and erecting huge monuments to its leaders.[7] Even if not all such investment is completely wasted, you would expect that sort of build-up to result in a gradual deterioration of the capital stock, because the productive part of the capital stock is, by definition, the existing amount of machinery and equipment available for use as inputs into production of directly or indirectly saleable goods and services.

Whether the capital stock will rise or fall in such circumstances as have been described above depends on whether more has been 'added to it by the good conduct of some, than had been taken from it either by the private misconduct of others, or by the publick extravagance of government'.[8] While gross investment is never negative,[9] net investment can be negative, if gross investment does not suffice to make up for the wear and tear of existing capital. Therefore, if the depreciation of capital is sufficiently rapid, the capital stock will decline, so that output also declines: economic growth then becomes negative. Many countries have experienced negative economic growth over long periods. The World Bank reports negative growth of output in 12 countries from 1980 to 1990.[10] Many more countries have experienced negative growth of output per capita, which means that, even if the growth of output was positive, it did not keep up with population growth. The World Bank reports negative per capita growth in 45 countries in the period 1970–95.[11]

Let us return to the model. If the capital stock begins to depreciate more rapidly than before, the G line shifts down to G′ in Figure 3.3 and the growth equilibrium moves south-west from A to B. Economic growth slows down, and so does technological progress, because it follows per capita growth, and not vice versa, through learning by doing. More depreciation means less growth.

Experiment 4: Population growth

Our last experiment in this round is this: how does the economy react to an increase in population growth? In Figure 3.4, the T line shifts upwards and to the left to T′ because, with more population growth, a given rate of growth of output is consistent with less technological progress than before. The new T′ line cuts the vertical axis at point I, which lies above point H in the figure. The rate of population growth rises from OH to OI, but economic growth remains unchanged because the G line does not move (it moves only in response to changes in the saving rate, efficiency, and depre-

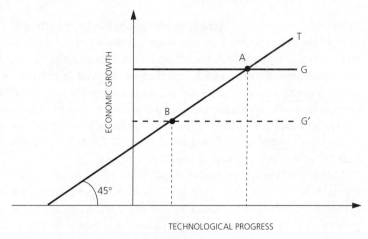

Fig 3.3
Endogenous growth: An increase in depreciation reduces economic growth and technological progress

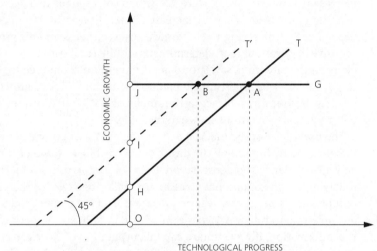

Fig 3.4
Endogenous growth: An increase in population growth reduces technological progress, but leaves economic growth unchanged

ciation, as in Figures 3.2 and 3.3). Consequently, the rate of growth of output per capita decreases from HJ to IJ in Figure 3.4. Presumably, this is what Thomas Malthus had in mind when he observed that 'the slowest progress in wealth is often made where the stimulus arising from population alone is the greatest'.[12]

Endogenous growth accounting

Figures 3.1–3.3 describe the qualitative reactions of endogenous economic growth and technological progress to changes in the three key determinants of growth: saving, efficiency, and depreciation. By assigning plausible values to the parameters of our simple model,[13] we can actually go a step further and get a glimpse of the likely quantitative responses of growth and technological progress to changes in the parameters. This amounts to growth accounting that differs from the conventional kind: rather than try to attribute economic growth to changes in the quantity and quality of labour, capital, and land, we now try to trace it to saving, efficiency, and depreciation.

Suppose for the purpose of the exercise that (a) the saving rate spans the range from 10 to 40 per cent of output, (b) efficiency (i.e. the output/capital ratio) is between 0.3 and 0.5, and (c) the rate of depreciation is 0.06, meaning that 6 per cent of the capital stock is effectively retired each year. In practice, the saving rate needs to be measured by the ratio of gross investment to GDP. Gross investment is financed not only by gross domestic saving, private and public, but also by foreign saving through borrowing abroad. For this reason, the gross investment rate provides a better measure of the ratio of total gross saving to GDP, which is our definition of the saving rate, than the gross domestic saving rate itself.

Table 3.1 indicates considerable sensitivity of the rate of economic growth to variations in its determinants. As saving rises from 10 per cent of GDP (which is not uncommon in parts of Sub-Saharan Africa) to 40 per cent (as in East Asia), annual output growth rises by 9 to 15 percentage points, depending on efficiency. Similarly, an increase in efficiency from 0.3 to 0.5 (which corresponds to a decrease in the capital/output ratio from 3.33 to 2), increases annual growth by 2 to 8 percentage points, depending on the saving rate. From this we see that economic growth is quite responsive to variations in its determinants within a realistic range. An increase in the depreciation rate from, say, 6 to 10 per cent per year, would reduce each growth figure in Table 3.1 by 4 percentage points. The annual rates of growth of output per head can be found by subtracting the annual rate of population growth from the annual growth rates of output shown in the table.

The usefulness of the method behind Table 3.1 as a growth-accounting device is understandably limited by the direct unobservability of two of the parameters involved—efficiency and depreciation. Even so, we can use this method to make the following rough conditional assessments. Take Togo, where the rate of growth of output was −1 per cent a year on average from 1970 to 1995 and where the saving (i.e. investment) rate was 15 per cent of GDP in 1970 and 14 per cent in 1995. From this information, if we assume a capital/output ratio of 2, we can conclude that the annual rate of depreciation of the capital stock must have been about 8 per cent. In this case, therefore, we conclude that while gross investment increased the capital stock by about 7 per cent a year, depreciation reduced it by about 8 per cent a year. Therefore, capital and output fell by 1 per cent per year on average.[14]

For another example, take Norway, where output grew by about 3 per cent a year on average from 1970 to 1995 and where the saving rate was 25 per cent of GDP on average over this period. From this, if the Norwegian capital/output ratio is 4, we impute a depreciation rate of 3.25 per cent per year. In this case, then, gross investment

Table 3.1 Economic growth as a function of the saving rate, efficiency, and depreciation, 1970–1995	Depreciation rate = 0.06	Efficiency = 0.30	Efficiency = 0.40	Efficiency = 0.50
	Saving rate = 0.10	−0.03	−0.02	−0.01
	Saving rate = 0.20	0.00	0.02	0.04
	Saving rate = 0.30	0.03	0.06	0.09
	Saving rate = 0.40	0.06	0.10	0.14

Source: Computations made on the basis of eq. (1) in Appendix 3.1, which states that the rate of economic growth equals the saving rate times efficiency minus depreciation.

increased capital by 6.25 per cent per year (i.e. one-quarter of 0.25), while deprecia-tion reduced capital by 3.25 per cent per year. This means that capital and output grew by about 3 per cent a year on average over the period. Alternatively, if the capi-tal/output ratio is 3, then the implicit rate of depreciation is 5.3 per cent a year.

Table 3.2 shows the results of a rough application of this accounting method to three regions: Sub-Saharan Africa, East Asia and Pacific, and the world as a whole. The first two lines show weighted average annual rates of growth of output in 1980–95 and weighted average saving rates over the same period.[15] The third line shows assumed values of the capital/output ratio: 2.5 in Africa and 3 in East Asia and the world. The capital/output ratio in Africa is lower than that in East Asia and the rest of the world, primarily because saving and investment rates in most African countries have, until recently, been much lower. This means that Africa produces more output per unit of capital. The annual average rate of depreciation is computed as a residual, which is more than three times as large in Africa as in East Asia. All things considered, Africa grew less rapidly than East Asia over the period in question as a result of a combination of less saving and more depreciation. Of the almost seven-point growth differential between Africa and East Asia shown in the top line of Table 3.2, 4 [= 0.33(0.34 − 0.22)100] percentage points can be traced to the higher sav-ing rate in East Asia and −1.5 [= 0.22(0.33 − 0.40)100] percentage points can be traced to the larger output/capital ratio for Africa, which leaves 4.5 [= 0.072 − 0.027)100] percentage points to be explained by more depreciation in Africa.[16] The table also suggests that if East Asia's capital/output ratio of 3 can be assumed to have been the same as that of the world at large, then 2.5 percentage points (i.e. the difference be-tween 0.052 and 0.027 in the bottom line) of the almost six-point growth differential can be traced to less depreciation in East Asia than in the world, which leaves the re-mainder, about 3.5 points, to be explained by East Asia's higher saving rate.

Table 3.3 shows an example of conventional economic growth accounting for com-parison. Here we divide output growth between the contributions of (1) capital growth through investment, (2) labour-force growth via population increase, and (3) a residual, which is attributed to total factor productivity growth, that is, to im-provements in the quality of capital and labour—in short, technological progress. We see in Table 3.3 that, in all three regions, about a half of the output growth is at-tributed to capital growth. Moreover, the residual is about the same in all three, im-plying an increase in total factor productivity of about 1.25 per cent per year on average. This means that technological progress has been relatively most important in the OECD region, accounting for a third of output growth compared with a fourth

Table 3.2 **Decomposition of growth in Sub-Saharan Africa, East Asia and Pacific, and the world, 1980–1995**	Sub-Saharan Africa	East Asia and Pacific	World
Growth, 1980–95	0.016	0.085	0.027
Saving rate, 1980–95	0.22	0.34	0.24
Efficiency (assumed)	0.40	0.33	0.33
Depreciation (residual)	0.072	0.027	0.052

Source: Computations made on the basis of eq. (1) in Appendix 3.1 and figures on growth and saving rates from the World Bank, *World Development Indicators 1997*, OUP, Oxford, 1997, tables 4.1 and 4.12.

	Seven OECD countries 1960–90	Four East Asian countries 1966–90	Seven Latin American countries 1940–80
Growth of output	0.039	0.088	0.049
Contribution of capital	0.021	0.044	0.024
Contribution of labour	0.005	0.032	0.013
Contribution of total factor productivity (residual)	0.013	0.012	0.012

Sources: For the OECD countries (Canada, France, Germany, Italy, Japan, the United Kingdom, and the United States), see Christopher Dougherty, *A Comparison of Productivity and Economic Growth in the G-7 Countries*, Ph. D. diss., Harvard University, 1991; for the East Asian countries (Hong Kong, Singapore, South Korea, and Taiwan), see Alwyn Young, 'The Tyranny of Numbers: Confronting the Statistical Realities of the East Asian Growth Experience', *Quarterly Journal of Economics* 110/3 (1995): 641–680; and for the Latin American countries (Argentina, Brazil, Chile, Colombia, Mexico, Peru, and Venezuela), see Victor J. Elias, *Sources of Growth: A Study of Seven Latin American Economies*, ICS Press, San Francisco, 1990.

in Latin America and one-seventh in East Asia. The flip side of this is that population growth has mattered much more in East Asia, where it has added more than 3 percentage points to the annual growth rate of output on average, against only a half of a percentage point in the OECD countries.

This output–input approach to growth accounting has led some observers to conclude that, for the most part, the spectacular growth performance of the East Asian economies since the mid-1960s has been achieved through the accumulation of more capital and through more labour as opposed to better, or more efficient, labour and capital.[17] Greater quantity has been the key, not better quality, the argument goes. The method of growth decomposition suggested in Table 3.2 shows this argument in a different light, even if it leads to a similar conclusion. Suppose the capital/output ratio has been the same in East Asia and Latin America—say, 3. We know from the World Bank that the saving rate in East Asia and Pacific was 0.34 on average in 1980–95, as shown in Table 3.2, and that the saving rate in Latin America and Caribbean in 1980–95 was 0.22 on average (same source). This means that of the 8.8 per cent annual economic growth in East Asia (Table 3.3), saving and efficiency together account for 11.2 percentage points (i.e. 0.34/3), which implies a depreciation rate of 2.4 per cent per year (because 11.2 − 8.8 = 2.4). Similarly, of the 4.9 per cent annual growth in Latin America shown in Table 3.3, saving and efficiency together account for 7.3 percentage points (i.e. 0.22/3), which again implies a depreciation rate of 2.4 per cent a year (because 7.3 − 4.9 = 2.4). From this we can conclude that saving matters significantly for explaining the difference between East Asian and Latin American growth.

But there is nothing particularly Soviet about saving behaviour in East Asia or about the way in which savings in the East Asian countries generally have been channelled into investment. Saving rates in East Asia have risen to their present high levels in response to a friendly, stable, generally market-oriented, and partly policy-induced climate for saving, including modest inflation, generally associated with positive real rates of interest and realistic real exchange rates. By realistic exchange rates is meant that persistent overvaluation of domestic currencies in real terms, with periodic bouts of capital flight as a consequence, generally was avoided in East Asia. Few of these conditions were met in much of Latin America, by contrast, until significant progress on the policy front began to be made there as well in the 1990s. Even so, the Asian crisis of 1997–8 is a useful reminder that not all of East Asia's savings have been well enough invested, as was mentioned in Chapter 1, mainly because the structure and functioning of the banking systems of several countries in the region have not been kept sufficiently separate from political considerations. In Chapter 4 we return to the links between inflation, instability, and economic growth.

The level of income per head with endogenous growth*

Ultimately, we are not interested mainly in economic growth as such, but rather in the fruits of growth, that is, the level of income and the standard of life it affords. So what does the theory of endogenous growth tell us about the level of output per head in the long run?

To answer this question, we first have to borrow the following result from production theory. Under fairly general conditions, inputs into production are employed up to the point where they earn the equivalent of their contribution to output, that is, where each factor of production is paid its marginal product, for this is how firms maximize their profit for the benefit of their stockholders. This means that each input is employed in proportion to the output, so that the proportion of input to output varies inversely with the input price. This is reasonable: it means that the typical firm's demand for each input varies (a) inversely with the price of the input and (b) directly with the output. This, in turn, means that if input prices are constant, then the input/output ratios are fixed.

Now consider Figure 3.5, where output per head is shown on the vertical axis and capital per worker is on the horizontal axis.[18] The figure shows two schedules. The straight line, labelled C, depicts a constant capital/output ratio, which results from assuming that the real interest rate, i.e. the rental price of capital, is constant. More precisely, the C line retains its given slope, shown by the angle between the C line and the horizontal axis, as long as the gross real interest rate—that is, the real interest rate plus depreciation, which is part of the cost of capital—does not move (and as long as the share of capital in national income, which we assume to be fixed throughout, does not move either). If either the interest rate or depreciation increases, capital becomes more costly to use, so that the capital/output ratio decreases; the C line then rotates counter-clockwise, widening the angle it forms with the horizontal axis.

The curve, labelled P, is the production function, which shows how output per head varies with capital per worker. The production function is curved because of decreasing returns to capital from the point of view of the typical firm: doubling the amount of capital per worker in the firm does less than double output per worker.

There is an externality involved here behind the scenes: the fact that learning by doing within each firm adds to knowledge, which benefits all firms, does not enter into the myopic individual firm's calculation of its costs and benefits of input use.

The intersection of the two schedules in Figure 3.5 describes the long-run equilibrium values of output per head and capital per worker. It actually describes their short-run equilibrium values as well, because there is no explicit dynamic adjustment involved here, as was mentioned before. This is not, however, a stationary equilibrium as it moves through time. Technological advance shifts the production function upwards over time, higher and higher. Consequently, the point of intersection between the two schedules drifts in a north-east direction along the C line at the rate of technological progress. This is how capital per worker on the horizontal axis and output per worker on the vertical axis increase with time. Keep this in mind when you view the figures to follow: you will be looking at snapshots of moving objects.

We are now in a position to start experimenting with Figure 3.5.

Experiment 1: The real interest rate

Suppose, first, that the real interest rate goes up (and suppose, for a moment, that there is no technological progress, so that the production function stays put; this allows us to talk about one thing at a time). In an open economy, an increase in the real interest rate could result from an increase in interest rates in world markets or from a government decision to adopt a more restrictive monetary policy stance at home. In any case, the increase in the interest rate reduces the capital/output ratio and thus shifts the C line counter-clockwise to C′, so that its intersection with the production function moves from point A to point B in Figure 3.6. The result is less capital per worker and less output per head. Therefore, if we now allow for technological progress, output per head will grow less than it did originally, at least as long as it takes the economy to move from the old equilibrium at A to the new one at B.

Once the new equilibrium position has been reached, at B, output will grow at the rate shown in Figure 3.1. The increase in the interest rate reduces the capital/output ratio, as we have said, and thus increases efficiency, and thereby increases economic growth as in Figure 3.2. This means that the production function in Figure 3.6 will be

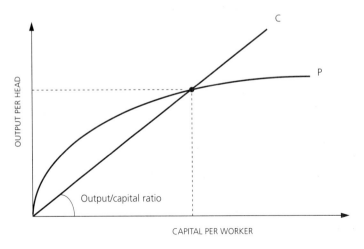

Fig 3.5
Endogenous growth: Determination of capital per worker and output per head

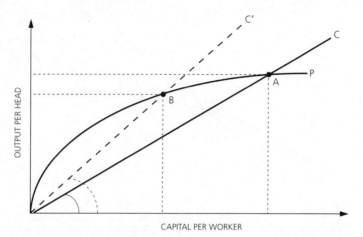

Fig 3.6
Endogenous
growth: An increase
in the real interest
rate or in
depreciation
reduces capital per
worker and output
per head

drifting upwards more rapidly than before (you have to imagine this, because it is not shown in the figure). The positive effect of a higher interest rate on growth will be stronger still, if the increase in the interest rate increases the saving rate, as it might.[19] Here we have an example of an event which reduces the level of output per head and increases its rate of growth. No contradiction is involved. Think of a runner, who takes a rest for a minute. At the end of the break, the distance he has covered per minute since he started, his average speed, has decreased, but when he starts running again, his new speed may well be higher than before the break. We will encounter more such examples as we proceed farther.

Experiment 2: Depreciation

Suppose next that depreciation increases. This also causes the cost of capital to rise, so that the effect will be qualitatively the same as that of an increase in the interest rate: the capital/output ratio falls, and so do both capital per worker and output per head. Figure 3.6 covers this case as well. Here, however, the interpretation is a little different. Increased depreciation is likely to reflect, at least in part, a deterioration in the quality and profitability of investment decisions. A reduction in the quality of investments reduces not only the level of output per head as in Figure 3.6, but also its rate of growth as in Figure 3.3. Here we have a case where the level and the rate of growth of output per capita move in the same direction.

Experiment 3: Efficiency

Now suppose static efficiency increases. By this is meant that the level of output per head increases once and for all for any given amount of capital per worker, while we still abstract initially from technological progress, which involves increased dynamic efficiency. Therefore, the production function shifts upwards from P to P′ in Figure 3.7. The result is an increase in both capital per worker and output per head. Even so, the capital/output ratio remains unchanged, because the C line does not move. Economic growth per capita must increase at least temporarily as the economy moves from A to B in Figure 3.7. Referring back to Figure 3.2, we recall that increased efficiency also increases long-run growth. This means that the production function in Figure 3.7 will be drifting upwards more rapidly than before (not shown).

Fig 3.7
Endogenous
growth: An increase
in static efficiency
increases capital
per worker and
output per head

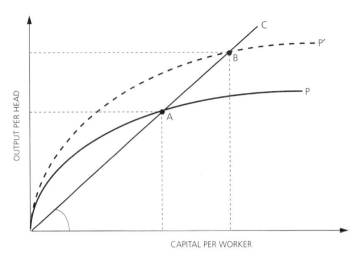

Fig 3.7
Endogenous growth: An increase in static efficiency increases capital per worker and output per head

Here we have a case where an external event increases both the level and rate of growth of output per capita. Increased static efficiency increases also dynamic efficiency. We will see in Chapter 4, however, that this is not always the case with increased efficiency: sometimes it reduces the level of output—workers are temporarily dislodged by increased foreign competition following trade liberalization, for example, or by new owners of formerly state-owned enterprises following privatization—while laying the basis for more rapid growth of output in the long run.

In sum, we have now identified three important determinants of income per head, our main measure of the standard of living: the real interest rate, depreciation, and efficiency. Specifically, we have seen that income per capita is inversely related to real interest and depreciation (Figure 3.6) and directly related to efficiency (Figure 3.7). Now you must be wondering: what became of the saving rate? Why has it disappeared from the story? Does the saving rate not matter for the level of income per head in this endogenous-growth framework?—even if it matters for economic growth, as we saw in Figure 3.2. But don't worry: the saving rate does, in fact, lie buried below the surface of the story that we have just told. To dig it up, we have to look more closely at the relationship between the saving rate and the interest rate. An increase in the saving rate involves the accumulation of capital, which tends to drive its price—i.e. the real interest rate—down, other things being equal. Hence, our experiment behind Figure 3.6, where we saw that an increase in the real interest rate reduces output per capita, is equivalent to an experiment that tests the reaction of output per head to a decrease in the saving rate. We will make that experiment in a short while. Notice, again, that no inconsistency is involved. It is perfectly possible for an increase in the real rate of interest to increase the saving rate, other things being equal, and for an increase in the saving rate—induced, for example, by more favourable tax treatment of savings—to reduce the real interest rate.

But first we must ask: what if there is no learning by doing? The elimination of learning by doing from the story we have just told—without introducing some other mechanism, such as research and development, that would preserve the endogeneity of technological progress[20]—takes us back to the neoclassical world of exogenous growth, to which we now return.

The neoclassical model again*

In order to assess fully the upshot of the endogenous-growth story we have told thus far, we have to compare and contrast it with its predecessor, the neoclassical model of exogenous growth. So let us now describe the workings of the neoclassical model in a few figures, focusing first on the level of output per capita and capital per worker and then on the rate of growth of output per head and efficiency. This will enable us to explore in more detail the qualitative and quantitative differences and similarities between endogenous and exogenous economic growth.

Figure 3.8 is identical to Figure 3.5. It shows a production function relating output per capita to capital per worker with diminishing returns. It also shows a straight line representing the capital/output ratio, which Solow treated as a crucial endogenous variable in his model and found to be fixed in the long run. Let us very briefly recapitulate the history of the capital/output ratio in growth theory. Harrod and Domar assumed the capital/output ratio to be fixed, without an adequate explanation. Their growth model was overdetermined: it had two equations and only one unknown or endogenous variable. Then Solow came along and made the capital/output ratio endogenous through the automatic adjustment of the capital stock to any discrepancy between the actual addition to capital taking place through saving and investment and the addition that would be necessary to keep capital growing at the same pace as output and the labour force, including labour productivity. Solow showed that when the capital stock increases more than is necessary for it to keep up with population growth, productivity gains, and depreciation, then the capital/output ratio increases. In this process, however, output increases more slowly than capital because of diminishing returns to capital. Therefore, the capital/output ratio slows down little by little until it stops when the long-run equilibrium growth path has been reached. Along this path, output, capital, and labour in efficiency units all grow at the same rate, which is exogenously given by technological progress. This means that the level of saving and investment forthcoming is just sufficient to keep capital growing at the same pace as output and quality-adjusted labour—i.e. to keep up with population growth, productivity growth, and depreciation.

Fig 3.8

Exogenous growth: Determination of capital per worker and output per head

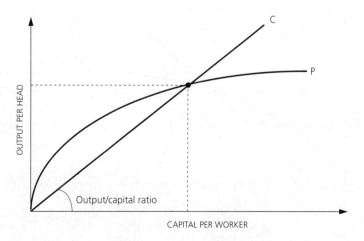

In Figure 3.8, we assume that this adjustment process has been completed, so that the C line reflects a constant capital/output ratio in long-run equilibrium. The point of intersection between the production function and the C line shows the corresponding long-run equilibrium values of output per head and capital per head. By contrast, you remember, the equilibrium point in Figure 3.5 reflects both short-run and long-run equilibrium.

Let us now experiment.

Experiment 1: The saving rate

How do output per head and capital per worker react to an increase in the saving rate? Because saving equals investment, an increase in the saving rate leads the capital stock to begin to rise more rapidly than before, that is, more rapidly than is necessary for it just to keep up with population, productivity growth, and depreciation, which are all unchanged by assumption. For this reason, the capital/output ratio begins to increase. This is illustrated by the clockwise rotation of the C line to C' in Figure 3.9. This happens gradually: the capital/output ratio decelerates until it finally stops moving. Consequently, the economy moves gradually from its initial long-run equilibrium point A in the figure to its new long-run equilibrium point B, where output per head and capital per worker are larger than before.

The distinction between the short run and the long run is important here. In the short run, an increase in the saving rate, by reducing consumption, reduces aggregate demand and thereby also the level of output. In this light it stands to reason that the economy's movement from A to B in Figure 3.9 takes time. Output needs time to fall as a result of an increase in the saving rate, before it begins to rise towards its new long-run equilibrium. But when the new long-run equilibrium has been reached, the growth of output per head is again equal to the rate of technological progress, which is exogenous here by assumption. The stimulating effect of an increase in the saving rate on growth is, therefore, temporary: output grows more rapidly than before as long as it takes the economy to move from the old to the new long-run equilibrium, but thereafter economic growth will be the same as it was before the increase in the saving rate, which started the process.

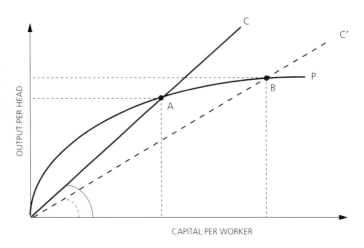

Fig 3.9
**Exogenous growth:
An increase in the
saving rate
increases capital
per worker and
output per head**

Experiment 2: Efficiency

In the next experiment, we investigate the effects of an increase in static efficiency, that is, an increase in the output produced from given inputs. This shifts the production function upwards (Figure 3.10), so that output begins to rise. It also increases saving and investment and, just as in the preceding experiment, leads the capital stock to begin to rise more rapidly than before, that is, more rapidly than is necessary for it just to keep up with population, technical progress, and depreciation, which are still unchanged by assumption. The result is, therefore, similar as before: output per head and capital per worker both increase from the original long-run equilibrium A in the figure to the new long-run equilibrium B, except now the capital/output ratio stays put. The increase in static efficiency provides a temporary boost to economic growth, for output per head must grow more rapidly than before in order to increase from A to B, but once point B has been reached, per capita growth is again constrained by the exogenously given rate of technological progress. Point B drifts north-east along the C line at the rate of technological progress, just as point A was adrift in the same direction along the same C line before the experiment began.

Experiment 3: Population growth

Next we ask: How do output per head and capital per worker react to an increase in population growth? Suppose the economy is originally in long-run equilibrium at point A in Figure 3.11, and then the labour force begins to rise more rapidly than before. This means that the current level of saving and investment is no longer enough to maintain the same amount of capital per worker as at point A. Therefore, the capital/labour ratio begins to fall, so that output per capita and capital per worker also begin to fall towards point B in the figure. Because of the curvature of the production function (i.e. because of diminishing returns to capital), output per head falls less than capital per worker, so that the capital/output ratio increases. This is shown by the counter-clockwise rotation of the C line to C' in Figure 3.11. As before, this occurs gradually. As long as it takes the economy to move from A to B in the figure, output has to grow less rapidly than the labour force to make it possible for output per worker to decrease. If we take technological progress into account, output has to

Fig 3.10

Exogenous growth: An increase in static efficiency increases capital per worker and output per head

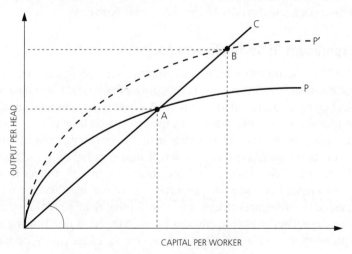

CAPITAL PER WORKER

Fig 3.11

**Exogenous growth:
An increase in
population growth
or in depreciation
reduces capital per
worker and output
per head**

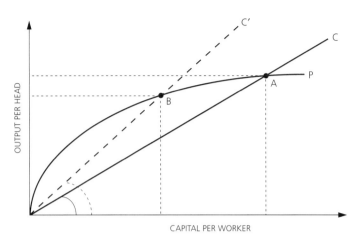

grow less rapidly than the labour force in efficiency units (i.e. including improved labour productivity) to complete the process of adjustment from A to B. But once the adjustment has been completed, the rate of growth of output equals the rate of population growth plus the exogenous rate of technological progress. Output therefore grows more rapidly than before because population growth has increased, but the rate of growth of output per head is unchanged because technological progress is given.

Experiment 4: Depreciation

Suppose now that the capital stock begins to depreciate more rapidly than before. Now the current level of saving and investment is no longer enough to keep the capital stock per worker intact. The subsequent course of events is the same as in the preceding experiment, when the population began to grow more rapidly. More depreciation and more population growth both render the current level of capital formation insufficient to maintain the existing capital/labour ratio: more depreciation erodes the numerator of the ratio over time, while more population growth accelerates the denominator. In either case, the capital/labour ratio begins to decline, and output per head also falls. Figure 3.11 covers both cases.

Experiment 5: Technological progress

Our last experiment in this round involves increased dynamic efficiency, by which is meant an increase in the rate of change of technological know-how. Suppose technology begins to advance at a faster pace than before. This affects capital per worker and output per head in two ways. First, the production function begins to drift upwards at faster pace than before. If we freeze the system for an instant, this means that the production function at that instant will be at P′ rather than P in Figure 3.12. Second, the current level of saving and investment no longer suffices to maintain capital in its original equilibrium proportion to labour in efficiency units, because the quality, i.e. efficiency, of labour is now improving more rapidly than before. Therefore, capital per worker in efficiency units falls, other things being equal. Notice the symmetry: if population growth, depreciation, or technological progress increase,

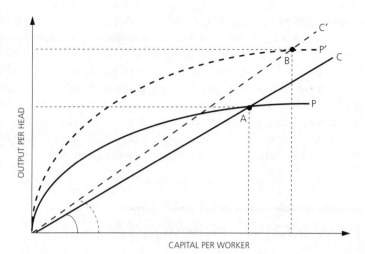

Fig 3.12

Exogenous growth: An increase in dynamic efficiency (technological progress) increases capital per worker and output per head

then the current amount of saving and investment needed to maintain capital in its original equilibrium proportion to labour in efficiency units increases, leaving less for the accumulation of fresh capital, which means that the capital/output ratio declines. Therefore, the C line rotates counter-clockwise to C′ in Figure 3.12. But in the case of increased technological progress, the production function also shifts from P to P′, so that a new equilibrium is ultimately reached at point B, which then continues to drift north-east along the new C′ line. In the end, therefore, increased dynamic efficiency increases both capital per worker and output per head.

We can now summarize the results from our five foregoing experiments on the neoclassical model as follows:

■ An increase in the saving rate increases output per head (Figure 3.9);
■ An increase in static efficiency increases output per head (Figure 3.10);
■ Increased depreciation reduces output per head (Figure 3.11);
■ Increased population growth reduces output per head (Figure 3.11);
■ An increase in dynamic efficiency increases output per head (Figure 3.12).

The striking thing about these results is that the long-run equilibrium level of output per capita depends on the saving rate, static efficiency, depreciation, and population growth as well as on dynamic efficiency, even if the long-run equilibrium rate of growth of output per head depends solely on dynamic efficiency—i.e. technological progress. In other words, even if a higher saving rate and so on has no effect on the long-run rate of growth of output, it does affect the level of output in the long run. This raises two questions.

First, how sensitive is the level of output per head to variations in the saving rate, static efficiency, depreciation, and population growth? Is it, in particular, sensitive enough for us to be able on that basis to account for the observed differences in living standards across countries? If it is, this means that economic performance over long periods depends after all on economic variables in addition to technological progress, which, if true, makes the exogeneity of economic growth in the long run according to the Solow model less binding than it otherwise would be. Second, and this question is closely related to the first, if an increase in the saving rate or in static efficiency or a decrease in depreciation provides only a temporary boost to economic growth, and thus increases economic growth per capita only in the medium term, i.e. as long as it takes the economy to reach long-run equilibrium anew, then how long does it take? How long is the medium term? The point is this: if the medium term proves to last long—say, decades—then the neoclassical conclusion that economic growth is independent of the saving rate, static efficiency, and depreciation in the long run becomes less arresting than it otherwise would be. For the concept of long-run equilibrium to be interesting and relevant from an economic point of view, it must not be too remote. The longer the road to the long run, in other words, the more it matters what happens along the way at a given speed.

How strong? How long?

It is good to know that an increase in, say, the saving rate lifts income per head in the long run, but it is not enough, for we must also know by how much. If the effect is small, then, perhaps, it is not particularly interesting. Accordingly, the quantitative question we now must ask is this. How large are the effects of more saving, more efficiency, and less depreciation on output per capita likely to be?—under realistic assumptions about the range of the relevant parameters. To put the same question differently, how far can the Solow model take us towards a full accounting for the differences in income per head that can be observed in the world?

First we must establish the observed income differences that we want to explain. According to the World Bank, Switzerland had the world's highest GNP per capita in 1995 (US$ 40,630) and Mozambique had the lowest (US$ 80).[21] When measured in 1995 US dollars, the difference between the two countries' GNP per capita is more than 500-fold. When adjusted for differences in prices and hence purchasing power, however, the Swiss figure drops to IUS$ 25,860 and the figure for Mozambique rises to IUS$ 810, which leaves us with a 32-fold difference between the two countries. By this purchasing-power-parity-adjusted measure, it was actually the United States that had the world's largest GNP per capita in 1995 (IUS$ 26,980), while Ethiopia had the smallest GNP per capita (IUS$ 450), a 60-fold difference. These numbers give us an idea of the size of the income gap that we need to understand. So, we want our model to be able to explain, say, 30-fold to 60-fold differences in the level of output per capita across countries. Can the Solow model do this?

Table 3.4 shows how output per head varies with the saving rate and with general efficiency,[22] including technology, for given rates of population growth, technological progress, and depreciation.[23] In the table, we assume the population to grow by 1 per cent per year, technology to progress also by 1 per cent per year, and the capital stock to depreciate by 8 per cent per year. On these assumptions, the table shows how output per head varies as the saving rate rises from 10 to 40 per cent of output and as general efficiency rises from 1 to 4. We use the term general efficiency here rather than efficiency, because efficiency was used before to refer to the output/capital ratio.[24] Table 3.4 shows that output per head doubles as the saving rate quadruples at a given level of general efficiency. It also shows that output per head rises by a factor of eight as general efficiency increases by a factor of 4, given the saving rate.

Table 3.4
How output per
head varies with
the saving rate and
general efficiency

Depreciation rate = 0.08	Saving rate = 0.1	Saving rate = 0.2	Saving rate = 0.3	Saving rate = 0.4
General efficiency = 1	1.00	1.41	1.73	2.00
General efficiency = 2	2.83	4.00	4.90	5.66
General efficiency = 3	5.20	7.35	9.00	10.39
General efficiency = 4	8.00	11.31	13.86	16.00

Source: Calculation based on eq. (4) in Appendix 3.2 on the assumption that population growth and technological progress are each 1 per cent per year and the rate of depreciation of capital is 8 per cent per year. Notice that the term 'general efficiency' refers to the ratio of output to the bundle of labour and capital used to produce it, and differs from efficiency, which refers to the output/capital ratio as in Tables 3.1 and 3.2.

Combining the two, we see that output per head increases by a factor of 16, when both the saving rate and general efficiency increase by a factor of 4.

We can get more variation in output per head by allowing also population growth and depreciation to vary. Suppose that we let population growth stretch from 1 to 4 per cent per year and the depreciation rate stretch from 4 to 20 per cent per year, keeping the annual rate of technological progress constant at 1 per cent throughout. When we do this, the ratio between the highest possible output per head and the lowest rises to almost 33. The range more than doubles, from a high/low ratio of 16 to almost 33, because more population growth and more depreciation reduce output per head in the long run. The range widens even further if we allow capital to account for a greater share of output than the one-third that we have assumed throughout this discussion. By increasing the share of capital from 1/3 to 40 per cent,[25] the ratio of the highest possible level of output per capita to the lowest increases from almost 33 to 66 on the premises stated above. This redoubling occurs because a higher share of capital in output makes output more sensitive to variations in capital through saving, efficiency, and depreciation. The share of capital in output can be raised even higher—say, up to two-thirds—by broadening the concept of capital to include human capital.[26] When this is done, the contribution of education to economic growth and output per head, which we will discuss in Chapter 4, is channelled through this broad measure of capital rather than through general efficiency.

We can conclude from this that the Solow model, as we have described it, is versatile enough to be able to account for at least a good deal of the income differences that we observe around the world. And notice that the figures in Table 3.4 and the surrounding text refer to long-run equilibrium levels of output per capita. Insofar as individual countries have yet to reach their long-run equilibrium, their current income differences may be larger than those which ultimately will emerge in the long run.

This brings us to the next question. How long does it take a country to reach its long-run equilibrium? Specifically, how long does it take the capital stock, and hence also output and the capital/output ratio, to move to the long-run equilibrium identified by Solow?—if the economy happens initially to be out of equilibrium or it is thrown out of pre-existing equilibrium by some exogenous event, say, a change in the saving rate or a technological innovation. What then?

It turns out that the adjustment mechanism is rather slow. It takes a long time—decades!—for the economy to travel to its new long-run equilibrium. This result holds for a wide range of reasonable estimates of the exogenous parameters of the Solow model.

Let us take an example. Suppose that (a) people save 24 per cent of their income; (b) the labour force grows by 1 per cent per year; (c) labour productivity also grows by 1 per cent per year; (d) depreciation amounts to 4 per cent of the capital stock every year; (e) the share of capital in national income is one-third; and (f) the capital stock is initially at one-half of its long-run equilibrium level. In this case, the capital/output ratio needs to rise from 2.52 to 4 to reach equilibrium, and output per capita must increase by a bit more than 25 per cent. In this example, it takes the capital/output ratio and output per head 16 years to travel half the distance to their long-run equilibrium, 32 years to travel three-quarters of the way, and 54 years to travel 90 per cent of the way. After 72 years, 5 per cent of the gap will still remain. Figure 3.13 shows the path of the capital/output ratio in this example.[27] Clearly, the speed of adjustment is quite slow. Specifically, the gradual increase in output per head reduces the remaining gap by about 4 per cent or so per year.

If we replace the last assumption above by the assumption that the capital stock is initially one-quarter of its long-run equilibrium level, which implies an initial capital/output ratio of 1.59 compared with the long-run equilibrium rate of four, the numbers change a little, but not much. In this case, it still takes 16 years to close the gap between the initial capital/output ratio and its long-run equilibrium value in half, and 56 years to close 90 per cent of the gap. After 72 years, 5 per cent of the gap still remains.

The time it takes for the economy to settle down in long-run equilibrium in Solow's world has a fundamental implication. When, for example, the saving rate rises and the capital stock accordingly begins to rise to a new, higher equilibrium level, output also begins to rise. Together, output and capital keep rising as long as it takes the adjustment mechanism to be completed. We are talking here about decades. This means that, after all, increased saving is capable of stimulating economic growth for a long time, even if, ultimately, per capita growth depends solely on technological progress. The same applies to an increase in static efficiency or a de-

Fig 3.13
It takes a long time: The evolution of the capital/output ratio in the Solow model

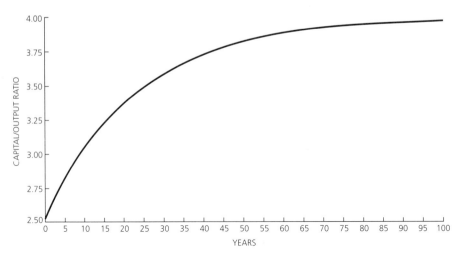

crease in depreciation: their effects on economic growth can last a long time, even if they peter out in the end.

Consequently, the almost exclusive focus of the practitioners of the Solow model from the 1950s to the 1980s on technological change as the sole driving force of economic growth in the long run was clearly misplaced. Saving behaviour, efficiency, and depreciation can matter greatly for economic growth and for the consequent income differences across countries around the world over long periods, once the Solow model is viewed in this light.

Exogenous growth illustrated*

Earlier in this chapter, we presented endogenous-growth theory in a series of figures to illustrate its implications for economic growth (Figures 3.1–3.4) and for the attendant level of output per capita (Figures 3.5–3.8). We have also illustrated the implications of exogenous-growth theory for the level of output per capita (Figures 3.9–3.12). Now, to close the circle, it remains to describe the determination of economic growth in the Solow model in a few figures.

Figure 3.14 depicts the determination of economic growth and efficiency, that is, the output/capital ratio. The upward-sloping G line (G for growth) reflects the Harrod–Domar equation. Its slope (i.e. the angle it forms with the horizontal axis) is the saving rate. The higher the saving rate—i.e. the steeper the G line—the more a given hike in efficiency increases economic growth, other things being equal, at least for a time. The G line cuts the vertical axis below the horizontal axis at a point that indicates the rate of depreciation. This reflects the fact that if neither the saving rate nor efficiency made any contribution to economic growth, then output growth would be negative: output would fall at the same rate as the capital stock, i.e. at the rate of depreciation. The horizontal S line (S for Solow) cuts the vertical axis at a point showing the sum of population growth and technological progress, and reflects the long-run equilibrium condition that economic growth must equal that sum. The broken vertical E line (E for efficiency) shows the level of efficiency, that is, the

Fig 3.14
Exogenous growth: Determination of economic growth and efficiency

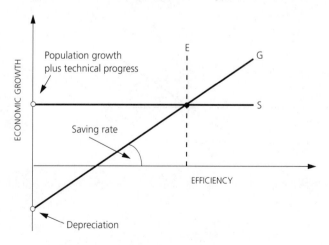

output/capital ratio, which is a key endogenous variable in the Solow model. Medium-run equilibrium is shown by the intersection of the G line and the E line. Long-run equilibrium is shown by the intersection of all three lines in the figure: G, E, and S. The transition from medium-run to long-run equilibrium takes place through the automatic attraction of the E line to the point of intersection between the G line and the S line through the dynamic adjustment process discovered by Solow.

Let us now experiment.

Experiment 1: The saving rate

First, suppose an increase in the saving rate (Figure 3.15). This rotates the G line counter-clockwise from G to G', because the slope of the G line equals the saving rate. At the initial capital/output ratio, economic growth increases from point A to point B in the figure. The medium-term equilibrium at point B will not last, however, because the increase in the saving rate triggers a gradual increase in the capital/output ratio—i.e. a decrease in the output/capital ratio, or efficiency; see Figure 3.9—which makes the E line begin to drift to the left towards E'. This process takes time, as we saw in the preceding subsection. But it will continue as long as it takes the economy to travel from the medium-run equilibrium at B to the new long-run equilibrium at C, where all three schedules intersect again and economic growth again equals population growth plus technical progress. This confirms our earlier result that an increase in the saving rate increases economic growth in the medium term, which typically lasts a long time, as we have seen, but that the effect weakens over time and vanishes in the end.

Experiment 2: Depreciation

What if depreciation increases? Then the G line shifts down and to the right to G', with its slope unchanged, so that economic growth decreases from A to B at the original level of efficiency (Figure 3.16). More depreciation increases the erosion of the capital stock, the capital/output ratio begins to fall, as we saw in Figure 3.11, and thereby efficiency begins to rise. Therefore, the E line begins to move to the right to-

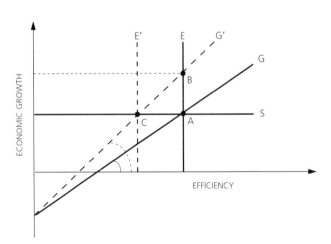

Fig 3.15
Exogenous growth: An increase in the saving rate increases economic growth for a long time, but not forever

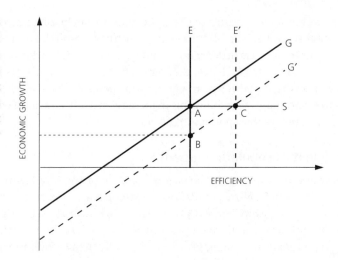

Fig 3.16
Exogenous growth: An increase in depreciation reduces economic growth for a long time, but not forever

wards E′. As a result, the decrease in economic growth is reversed as growth edges back towards the new long-run equilibrium at point C, where economic growth has been restored to its initial rate, equal to the rate of population growth plus technological progress, and the capital/output ratio has finally come to rest.

Experiment 3: Static efficiency

Next, we study the effect of an increase in static efficiency (Figure 3.17). Suppose, for example, that foreign trade is liberalized, so that, with increased specialization, more output can be produced per unit of capital. The economy becomes more efficient, and the E line shifts to the right to E′. This means that economic growth increases from A to B in the figure, but the increase will not last. Point B is not a long-run equilibrium point, because it does not lie on the S line, which has not moved. We saw in Figure 3.10 that an increase in static efficiency leaves the capital/output ratio unchanged in the long run. This means that the E line must shift back from E′ towards its initial position. The mechanism is the same as we have encountered before. The initial boost to efficiency increases the level of saving and investment, so that the capital stock begins to rise more rapidly than before.

Fig 3.17
Exogenous growth: An increase in static efficiency increases economic growth for a long time, but not forever

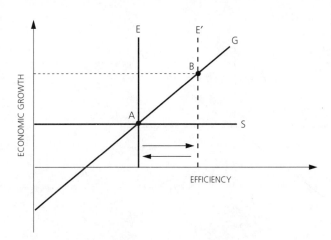

Therefore, output also begins to rise more rapidly than before, but less rapidly than the capital stock because of diminishing returns to capital. So, the capital/output ratio begins to increase little by little, and efficiency drifts back from E′ to its initial level at E in Figure 3.17. Hence, economic growth is restored to its original exogenous rate at the initial long-run equilibrium point A. Even so, the medium-term boost to economic growth following an increase in static efficiency will typically last a long-time, before it evaporates in the end.

Experiment 4: Population growth

Suppose now that the population begins to grow more rapidly (Figure 3.18). Then the S line shifts up to S′. More population growth increases the output/capital ratio, i.e. efficiency, as we saw in Figure 3.11, so that the E line drifts to the right to E′. A new long-run equilibrium is ultimately established at point B, where all three lines, G, S′, and E′, cross again and output grows more rapidly than before; after all, once again, output growth equals population growth plus technological progress.

Experiment 5: Technological progress

Which brings us to the last experiment in this round: what if technological progress speeds up? Figure 3.18 covers this case as well. The S line shifts up to S′. Increased technological progress raises the output/capital ratio, as we saw in Figure 3.12, so that the E line drifts to the right towards E′. At the end of the day—a long day!—a new long-run equilibrium is reached at point B in Figure 3.18.

How much to save

We have seen from our experiments in this chapter that saving is good for growth, at least in theory (how good it is in practice we will study in Chapter 4). The theory of economic growth that we have reviewed predicts that the larger the share of their

Fig 3.18
Exogenous growth: Increased population growth or dynamic efficiency (technological progress) increases economic growth forever

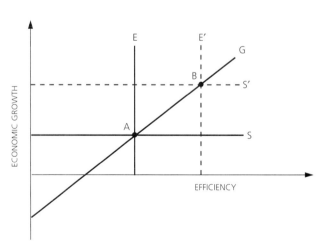

incomes that households devote to saving and firms to investment, the higher will be the level of output per head, other things being equal—and hence also its rate of growth over extended periods, if not *ad infinitum*. Does this mean that the more people save, the better? No, because saving incurs a cost in terms of current consumption forgone. It is, therefore, not a coincidence that no country saves, say, 50 per cent of its national income, even if some individuals may do so.[28] And so the question arises as to how much a country should save.

The best answer is probably this: the optimal share of saving in national income is that which allows the citizens as much consumption as possible in the long run, because the objective of saving (as well as of all other economic activity, when you think about it) is ultimately consumption—but later. Too little saving results in too little output and thereby also too little scope for consumption in the long run. Too much saving, on the other hand, while generating a large output per capita, leaves too small a share of that output for consumption. So we must look for an optimum somewhere between too little saving and too much.

The quest for the optimal amount of saving involves choosing the optimal path of consumption over time. A country with a given earnings potential faces a choice between consuming more or less today (or in this generation) than tomorrow (or the next generation). By consuming more today and saving less, the country can maintain a higher current standard of life than otherwise at the cost of a lower standard later. Conversely, by consuming less today and saving more, the country lays the ground for a higher future standard of life at the cost of a lower current standard. Most of us face decisions like these in our every day lives, and so do whole nations.

So what should the optimal path of a nation's consumption look like? It may help here to consider the following example. Take a farmer who needs to decide what is the best time to fell a tree, which grows most rapidly at first and then, as time passes, less and less rapidly as it approaches full maturity. This problem has a simple solution. The best time to fell the tree and sell it is when its rate of growth has slowed down to the point where it is equal to the real rate of interest that the farmer can get on his money in a bank (or elsewhere, for that matter). As long as his tree grows more rapidly than his money in the bank, it pays the farmer to let the tree keep growing. But as soon as the tree begins to grow more slowly than money in the bank, it pays to fell it and sell it and deposit the money rather in the bank, where it will grow at the real rate of interest. Hence the rule: one should not accept growth that does not at least keep up with the real interest rate.

Actually, the appropriate benchmark for optimal growth in the above rule is not the real rate of interest stripped bare, but rather the real interest rate net of the subjective rate of time preference, a concept launched long ago by Irving Fisher.[29] The idea is this: If you are offered a choice between a million today and two million in a year's time, you will almost surely prefer the latter (assuming no inflation), because the possibility of earning 100 per cent real interest in a year with certainty is remote in most cases. But if you are offered a choice between a million today and 1.08 million in a year, you will perhaps take the first option. This is where Fisher's concept of subjective time preference enters the picture: most people are impatient by nature. They prefer money now to money later. The intensity of this preference is indicated by the subjective rate of time preference—the discount rate, in short. If your personal rate of discount is 10 per cent per year, this means that you are indifferent between a million now and 1.1 million next year, if the real interest rate is zero. In this case, anything less than 1.1 million in a year's time is inferior to a million today. This explains why you would then prefer one million at once to 1.08 million in a year, if the real interest rate is zero.

Suppose now that the real interest rate is not zero, but 4 per cent per year. How would you then weigh one million now against 1.06 million next year? You would presumably be indifferent under the assumptions stated above. This is because one million today is subjectively equivalent to 1.1 million next year, given a 10 per cent discount rate, but it will grow to 1.04 million in a year, given a 4 per cent rate of real interest. This means that *not* taking the one million now would confer a net loss of 6 per cent, that is, the real interest rate minus the discount rate. Hence the indifference between one million now and 1.06 million a year from now.

These considerations apply also to countries—not that countries can or deserve to be closed down the way trees are felled if they fail to grow fast enough, but, even so, consumption and consumer welfare can be shown to reach a sustainable maximum over the long run, when the rate of growth of consumption and output per capita equals, or is at least proportional to, the real interest rate adjusted for impatience. This condition for optimal growth actually makes saving directly proportional to output, as we have assumed throughout.[30] It follows that consumption is also proportional to output, because consumption plus saving equals output, so that consumption, output, and capital must all grow at the same rate in equilibrium.

In sum, then, it is in the interest of consumers to save that proportion of their income that maximizes their consumption over time. The optimal saving rate thus chosen from a wide range of available possibilities influences capital accumulation and hence also the equilibrium levels of capital per worker and output per head (recall Figure 3.9). If the optimal saving rate exceeds the current saving rate, then the increase in the saving rate necessary to reach the optimal level affects economic growth as was shown in Figures 3.2 and 3.15. The result that maximum saving is not a sensible economic objective (because it would mean zero consumption!) means that maximal economic growth is not a desirable or sensible objective either. Rather, economic growth should be sustained at that rate which permits maximal consumption in the long run. This can be achieved by setting the saving rate right.

Let us take a concrete example. Consider a consumer who is also an investor—for example, a co-owner or stockholder in a firm. Then, if maximal consumption over time is his objective, he should accumulate capital as long as the accumulation increases his consumption—that is, as long as it adds more to output than it does to investment. This is because output is equal to consumption plus investment, by definition. When the accumulation of capital adds as much to investment as to output, consumption is at a peak; at that point, further accumulation of capital does not pay. This peak can be reached by following the so-called golden rule of capital accumulation, which exists in several guises.[31] In its simplest guise, the rule states that maximum sustainable consumption is achieved by saving capital income (i.e. investing profits) and consuming labour income.[32]

How high does the saving rate have to be for growth to be optimal? Our formulae for the optimal saving rate[33] can be used to quantify optimal saving strategies and to assess whether saving rates observed around the world are optimal or not or close to being so, in the sense of being consistent with as much consumption as possible over time. Suppose now that (a) the share of capital in national income is one-third; (b) output growth equals the real interest rate; and (c) the discount rate equals the rate of population growth. Then output per head grows at the rate of real interest adjusted for impatience, as optimal growth requires. In this case, the optimal saving rate equals the share of capital in national income and is, therefore, one-third according to the golden rule.

Very few countries actually save and invest that much of their income. In 1995, only Thailand (where gross domestic investment was 43 per cent of GNP), China (40 per cent), Indonesia (38 per cent), Korea (37 per cent), Hong Kong (35 per cent), and Singapore (33 per cent) reached or surpassed that level. Does this mean that consumers do not maximize their consumption over time? No. Suppose instead of assumptions (b) and (c) in the preceding paragraph that economic growth is, say, 3 per cent per year, the real interest rate is 6 per cent,[34] and depreciation is 4 per cent. Then our formula[35] yields an optimal saving rate of 23 per cent, which equals the weighted world average saving (i.e. investment) rate in 1995. The comparable weighted average was 27 per cent for low- and middle-income countries and 21 per cent for high-income countries.[36]

Optimal growth in figures*

We can now describe the consequences of optimal saving behaviour for economic growth.

Begin with exogenous growth. Figure 3.19 illustrates the determination of optimal exogenous growth and the real rate of interest. The G line reflects the rule of optimal growth, which must equal the real rate of interest adjusted for impatience and population growth. The G line forms a 45° degree line with the horizontal axis, because an increase in the real interest rate increases optimal growth point for point.[37] Increased impatience—i.e. less willingness to save—shifts the G line downwards, which increases the real interest rate compatible with a given growth rate or, equivalently, reduces the optimal growth rate consistent with a given real interest rate. The horizontal S line, like its namesakes in Figures 3.14–3.18, expresses the Solow

Fig 3.19
Exogenous growth with optimal saving: Determination of economic growth and the real interest rate

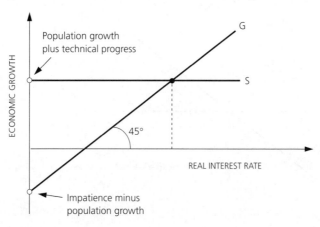

condition that economic growth equals population growth plus technological progress.

Experiment 1: Technological progress

Suppose now that technology begins to progress at faster pace. Then the S line shifts up to S′ and economic growth increases from A to B in Figure 3.20, as in Figure 3.18. As efficiency increased in Figure 3.18, so the real rate of interest also rises in Figure 3.20, because an increase in the real interest rate reduces the capital/output ratio, which means more efficiency. A higher real interest rate thus goes hand in hand with increased efficiency. Capital per worker and output per head increase as in Figure 3.12.

Experiment 2: Population growth

Next, suppose that population growth increases. Now both the S line and the G line shift up by the amount of the population growth increase to S′ and G′, so that their intersection point moves straight north from A to B in Figure 3.21. Therefore, economic growth increases by as much as the labour force, but the real interest rate remains unchanged, as does the rate of growth of output per capita. Figures 3.11 and 3.18 apply as before.

Fig 3.20
Exogenous growth with optimal saving: Increased technological progress increases economic growth and the real interest rate

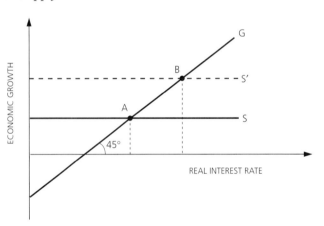

Fig 3.21
Exogenous growth with optimal saving: An increase in population growth increases economic growth, but leaves the real interest rate unchanged

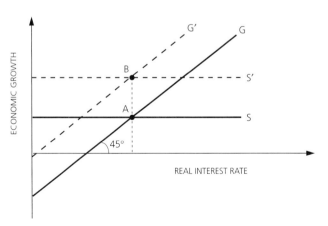

Experiment 3: Depreciation

In the two experiments illustrated in Figures 3.20–3.21, the real interest rate and efficiency moved in tandom or stayed put, because the two are directly related for given depreciation. To study the effects of increased depreciation, however, we need to add a new line to Figure 3.19, a vertical R line (R for real interest) that passes through the point of intersection of the S line and the G line (Figure 3.22). This addition is necessary, because increased depreciation drives a wedge between real interest and efficiency. More depreciation reduces the real interest rate that is compatible with a given level of efficiency at maximum profit (or, equivalently, increases the level of efficiency that is compatible with a given real interest rate). An increase in deprecation thus shifts the R line in Figure 3.22 to the left to R', so that economic growth and the real interest rate both decline from A to B for given efficiency. The new equilibrium at B is not sustainable, however, for it does not satisfy the condition that economic growth equals population growth plus technological progress. Efficiency begins to adjust in the background because increased depreciation reduces the capital stock more than it reduces output (due to diminishing returns to capital), so that the capital/output ratio decreases (i.e. efficiency increases) little by little. The gradual increase in efficiency causes the R' line to drift back towards its original position at R. This process ends when the original equilibrium at point A is restored. Therefore, economic growth is ultimately independent of depreciation as in Figure 3.16.

Experiment 4: Impatience

Now suppose people suddenly become less impatient and thus more willing to save. This shifts the G line up and to the left to G' in Figure 3.23. Economic growth increases as the economy moves from A to B. However, more saving depresses the real rate of interest, so that the R line drifts to the left to R'. To remain optimal, economic growth must follow the real interest rate downwards as the economy drifts on from B to C in the figure. Economic growth in the long run remains the same as before, because it is exogenous, after all, i.e. immune to all but technological growth and population growth. Growth does, however, increase for a (long) while, as in Figure 3.15. The effects of increased patience on capital per worker and output per capita are the same as in Figure 3.9.

Fig 3.22
**Exogenous growth
with optimal
saving: Increased
depreciation
reduces economic
growth for a time,
but not forever**

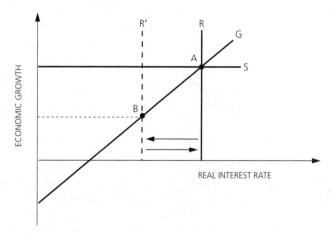

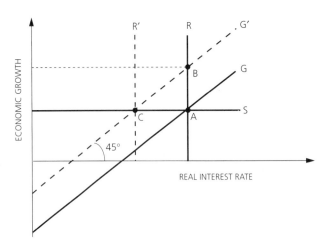

Fig 3.23
Exogenous growth with optimal saving: Increased patience increases economic growth for a time, reduces the real interest rate, and leaves growth ultimately unchanged

The determination of optimal endogenous growth and the real interest rate is illustrated in Figure 3.24. The G line you have already met in Figures 3.19–3.23. The R line shows the real interest rate that is consistent with maximum profit. The R line shifts to the right with increased efficiency because of the inverse relationship between the capital/output ratio and the real interest rate, and to the left with increased depreciation because depreciation drives a wedge between the real interest rate and efficiency: more depreciation calls for more efficiency at a given real rate of interest and hence also for a lower real rate of interest at a given level of efficiency.[38]

Experiment 5: Static efficiency

Figure 3.25 shows the reaction of optimal economic growth to an increase in efficiency. The R line shifts to the right to R′, so that the real interest rate rises from A to B in the figure. Economic growth also rises, as in Figure 3.2, except here the reason is that the growth rate must keep up with the real interest rate to remain optimal. Capital per worker and output per head increase as in Figure 3.7.

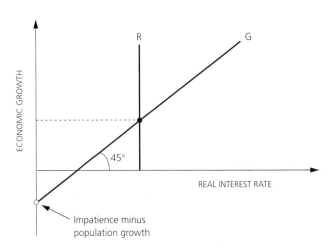

Fig 3.24
Endogenous growth with optimal saving: Determination of economic growth and the real interest rate

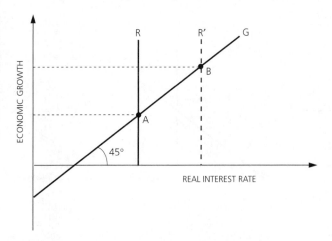

Fig 3.25
Endogenous growth with optimal saving: An increase in efficiency increases economic growth and the real interest rate

Experiment 6: Depreciation again

Figure 3.26 shows the effects of increased depreciation. Now the R line shifts to the left to R′ and the real interest rate decreases from A to B, and so does economic growth, as in Figure 3.3. Capital per worker and output per head decrease as in Figure 3.6.

Experiment 7: Impatience again

Figure 3.27 illustrates at last the effects of increased patience, i.e. an increase in the propensity to save. The G line shifts upwards and to the left to G′. Economic growth increases from A to B, as it did in Figure 3.2, but the real interest rate remains unchanged.

Experiment 8: Population growth again

Figure 3.27 also covers the case of increased population growth: output growth increases from A to B, but the growth of output per capita and the real interest rate stay the same.

 These results are summarized in Table 3.5. Notice that the medium-term effects

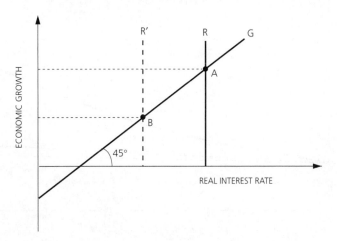

Fig 3.26
Endogenous growth with optimal saving: An increase in depreciation reduces economic growth and the real interest rate

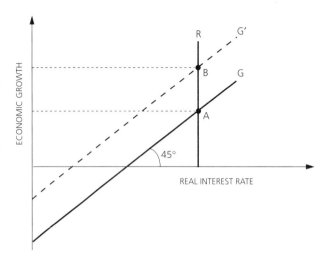

Fig 3.27
Endogenous growth with optimal saving: Increased patience or population growth increases economic growth, but leaves the real interest rate unchanged

with exogenous growth are qualitatively the same throughout as the long-run effects with endogenous growth. Quantitatively, however, they are quite different. Figure 3.28 displays the path of output per capita for 20 years following an increase in the saving rate from 15 to 30 per cent, other things being equal. The grey curve at the bottom of the figure shows how output per head would have evolved with the saving rate stuck at 15 per cent, assuming the labour force and labour productivity to grow by 1 per cent each per year. The depreciation rate is assumed 4 per cent per year. These figures imply a capital/output ratio of 2.5 in long-run equilibrium.[39] Now suppose the saving rate rises to 30 per cent in year 1. The broken black curve shows the path of output per capita with exogenous growth. After 20 years, the broken black curve has risen 24 per cent above the grey curve on its way to a long-run equilibrium position 41 per cent above the grey curve—this is because the saving rate has doubled and the square root of 2 is 1.41.[40] In the long run, the doubling of the saving rate doubles also the capital/output ratio, from 2.5 to 5.

The solid black line in the figure shows the path of output per head with endogenous growth. In this case, the increase in the saving rate stimulates economic growth by increasing the rate of technological progress by 6 percentage points, from 1 to 7

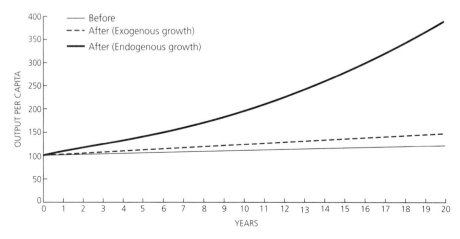

Fig 3.28
The first twenty years: The path of output per capita before and after an increase in the saving rate from 15 to 30 per cent

Table 3.5
Optimal economic growth: Overview of results

	Economic growth	Real interest rate	Reference
Exogenous growth			
Saving rate	Zero/plus	Minus/zero	Figure 3.23
Efficiency (dynamic)	Plus	Plus	Figure 3.20
Depreciation	Zero/minus	Zero/minus	Figure 3.22
Population growth	Plus	Zero	Figure 3.21
Endogenous growth			
Saving rate	Plus	Zero	Figure 3.27
Efficiency (static)	Plus	Plus	Figure 3.25
Depreciation	Minus	Minus	Figure 3.26
Population growth	Plus	Zero	Figure 3.27

Note: The table shows the long-run effects of increases in the variables listed in the first column of the table on economic growth and on the real rate of interest. Zero/plus means that the long-run effect is zero, while the medium-term effect is positive, and so on.

per cent per year. Why 6 per cent? This is because the capital/output ratio remains unchanged at 2.5 when growth is endogenous, so that efficiency, i.e. the output/capital ratio, stays at 0.4. An increase in the saving rate by 15 percentage points then translates into a six-point increase in growth (because 0.4 times 15 equals 6).[41] It is precisely the constancy of efficiency that gives increased saving its great power to increase economic growth in the endogenous-growth model. With exogenous growth, by contrast, the effect of increased saving on growth is weakened by the consequent increase in the capital/output ratio, which entails reduced efficiency.

Summary

This has been a long chapter, not least if you have worked your way through the three appendices as you went along, and it has been a bit technical in some places. The main message of the chapter is nonetheless quite simple and can be summarized as follows. There is not much qualitative difference between endogenous and exogenous growth. In either case, economic growth depends crucially on the macroeconomic variables emphasized by Adam Smith and many others ever since. These variables are saving, efficiency (including technology), and depreciation, as outlined by Harrod and Domar. These linkages are explicit in the theory of endogenous growth (hence the name) and implicit in the theory of exogenous growth. In the latter case, however, it is technically true that long-run growth is immune to all influences other than population growth and technological progress, but life is long: it takes a long time to reach the long-run steady-state equilibrium where the growth effects of increased saving and efficiency have at last died out, leaving further economic growth in a state of immunity from all economic influences. In other words, the time span (it has been called the medium run) over which saving and efficiency exert a potentially strong influence on economic growth seems long enough to be interesting and relevant from an economic point of view. Even so, when we look at numbers and simulate hypothetical growth paths, the capacity of increased saving to increase economic growth is much larger when growth is endogenous rather than exogenous. The main reason for this is the power of compound growth as well as the decoupling of efficiency from the saving rate in the endogenous-growth model. When economic growth is endogenous, an increase in the quantity of capital through saving and investment does not reduce its quality, as it does automatically in the exogenous-growth model.

Which of the two determinants of economic growth, saving or efficiency, quantity or quality, is the most important? Keynes answered this question as follows:

> It has been usual to think of the accumulated wealth of the world as having been painfully built out of that voluntary abstinence of individuals from the immediate enjoyment of consumption, which we call Thrift. But . . . mere abstinence is not enough to build cities or drain fens. . . . It is Enterprise which builds and improves the world's possessions. . . . If Enterprise is afoot, wealth accumulates whatever may be happening to Thrift; and if Enterprise to asleep, wealth decays whatever Thrift may be doing.[42]

The next chapter is devoted to what Keynes called Enterprise—that is, efficiency and economic growth.

Questions for review

1. Does the rate of growth of output per head depend on population growth? Does the answer to this question depend on whether economic growth is exogenous or endogenous? How? Illustrate your answers with diagrams. Does your analysis imply that countries with small populations ultimately become more—or less?—affluent per capita than large (i.e. populous) countries?

2. Consider a country that is exposed to an adverse external shock—a lasting decline in the price of its main exports, for example. This shock lowers the standard of living, and people decide to consume more and save less out of current income, other things being equal. If this change is permanent, how would you expect it to influence (i) the rate of growth of output per capita in the long run and (ii) the level of income per capita in the long run?

3. Consider a country whose capital stock is greatly reduced because of a natural calamity or war, for example. What additional information do you need in order to be able to assess the likely consequences of the reduction in the capital stock for the level and rate of growth of per capita GNP in the long run?

4. 'An increase in the propensity to save increases economic growth only temporarily. Therefore, government policies aimed at stimulating saving are not well suited to improving the standard of living in the long run.' Evaluate this statement in view of the theories of (a) exogenous economic growth and (b) endogenous growth.

5. 'A nation dedicated to the maximum welfare of its citizens should aim for as rapid economic growth as possible.' True or false? Why?

Notes

1. Thomas Malthus, *Essay on Population*, 5th edn. (London, 1817), 310.
2. Paul Krugman, *Development, Geography, and Economic Theory* (MIT Press, Cambridge, Mass., and London, 1995), 23–4.
3. The labels of the points of intersection in the figures are not to be confused with the variables and parameters that bear some of the same labels in the appendices.
4. The equations behind the two lines, G and T, are presented in Appendix 3.1, which picks up the thread from Appendix 2.3 in Ch. 2.
5. See also Appendix 3.1.
6. In Chapter 4, we will argue on similar grounds that successful privatization and price stabilization appear likely to increase macroeconomic efficiency—privatization by improving the quality of corporate management under new, private ownership, and stabilization by removing the distorting influence of inflation on the choice of firms between real capital and financial capital (i.e. money) as inputs in production.
7. Enver Hoxha had 700,000 concrete bunkers built all across Albania, where they still litter the landscape, 24 per sq. km. It would be extremely costly to demolish them all. For comparison, the population of Albania in the 1940s, when Hoxha came to power, was about 1.5m.
8. Adam Smith, *The Wealth of Nations* (Liberty Classics, Indianapolis, 1976), i. 343.
9. The lowest gross investment/GDP ratio on record in 1995 is Haiti's 2%, down from 17% in 1980. See World Bank, *World Development Indicators 1997* (Oxford University Press, Oxford, 1997), table 4.12.
10. The countries with negative GDP growth in 1980–90 are Argentina, Haiti, Iraq, Jordan, Libya, Mozambique, Nicaragua, Niger, Peru, Saudi Arabia, Trinidad and Tobago, and the United Arab Emirates. See *World Development Indicators*, table 4.1.
11. Ibid., table 1.3. The 45 countries with negative growth of output per head in 1970–95 are Argentina, Armenia, Bahrain, Bolivia, Central African Republic, Chad, Comoros, Côte d'Ivoire, El Salvador, Estonia, Gabon, Georgia, Ghana, Guatemala, Guyana, Haiti, Iran, Jamaica, Kuwait, Liberia, Libya, Madagascar, Malawi, Mauritania, Mozambique, Nicaragua, Niger, Nigeria, Peru, Qatar, Rwanda, São Tomé and Principe, Saudi Arabia, Senegal, Sierra Leone, Somalia, South Africa, Sudan, Togo, Trinidad and Tobago, the United Arab Emirates, Venezuela, Zaire, Zambia, and Zimbabwe. Notice the number of oil producers in the group, including Bahrain, Gabon, Iran, Kuwait, Libya, Qatar, Saudi Arabia, the United Arab Emirates, and Venezuela. We will discuss the relationship between natural resources and economic growth in Ch. 4. The countries with positive per capita growth over the same period, 1970–95, are twice as many as those with negative per capita growth, or 91.
12. Thomas Malthus, *Essay on Population*, 5th edn. (London, 1817), 310.
13. See Appendix 3.1.
14. We could also conduct the experiment in a different order. Suppose we have reason to believe that the annual rate of depreciation is 8%. This means that the saving rate times the output/capital ratio must be 7%. Therefore, with a saving rate of 14%, the output/capital ratio must be 0.5, which implies a capital/output ratio of 2. If, instead, the depreciation rate was 10%, then, by the same argument, the implicit output/capital ratio would be 0.64. The accounting method entails a trade-off between the two types of inefficiency: the larger the extent to which inefficiency is assumed to manifest itself through large depreciation, the smaller is the extent to which it will appear in a low output/capital ratio.
15. The growth rates and saving rates are weighted by the size of the economies in question, so that in the world column, for example, the United States weighs a good deal more heavily than Luxembourg.
16. The basis for this decomposition is provided in the last paragraph of Appendix 3.1.

17. 'Asian growth,' says Paul Krugman, 'like that of the Soviet Union in its high-growth era, seems to be driven by extraordinary growth in inputs like labour and capital rather than by gains in efficiency.' See Paul Krugman, 'The Myth of Asia's Miracle', *Foreign Affairs* (Nov.–Dec. 1994), 69–70.

18. Recall that throughout the book, the terms per capita, per head, and per worker are used interchangeably to refer to both the labour force and population, because the labour-force participation rate is assumed to remain unchanged.

19. Does an increase in real interest rates stimulate saving? The empirical evidence on this question is mixed. For a brief overview of the evidence, see Thorvaldur Gylfason, 'Optimal Saving, Interest Rates, and Economic Growth', *Scandinavian Journal of Economics*, 95/4 (1993), 517–33, table 1.

20. See Appendix 3.1.

21. World Bank, *World Development Report 1997* (Oxford University Press, Oxford, 1997).

22. By general efficiency is meant the ratio of output to the bundle of labour and capital used in its production.

23. The computation is based on eq. (4) in Appendix 3.2.

24. Here the capital/output ratio is proportional to the saving rate in the long run by equation (2) in Appendix 3.2, and increases from 1 to 4 as the saving rate increases from 0.1 to 0.4.

25. A capital share of about 40% has been reported in several studies. Summarizing a number of works, one study reports an average capital share of 38.5% for 12 industrial countries, of 45.3% for 20 developing countries, and of 40% for 7 centrally planned economies. See Hollis B. Chenery, Sherman Robinson, and Moshe Syrquin, *Industrialization and Growth: A Comparative Study* (Oxford University Press, Oxford, 1986), table 2-2.

26. See Robert E. Lucas, Jr., 'On the Mechanics of Economic Development', *Journal of Monetary Economics*, 22/3 (1988), 3–42, and N. Gregory Mankiw, David Romer, and David N. Weil, 'A Contribution to the Empirics of Economic Growth', *Quarterly Journal of Economics*, 107/2 (1992), 407–37.

27. The calculation behind Figure 3.13 is based on the adjustment eq. (13) in Appendix 2.2 with the parameter assumptions stated in the text.

28. The highest saving rates on record are those of some of the oil-producing countries following the oil-price increases of the 1970s. For example, Saudi Arabia's gross domestic saving was 62% of GDP in 1980, compared with 30% in 1995. Even so, gross domestic investment in Saudi Arabia was 22% in 1980 and 20% in 1995. The huge gap between saving and investment in 1980 was matched by an approximately equally large surplus on the current account of the balance of payments. The world's highest gross domestic saving rate in 1995, 48%, belongs to Gabon, another oil producer. See World Bank, *World Development Report 1997*, table 13.

29. See Irving Fisher, *The Theory of Interest* (Macmillan, New York, 1930), ch. 4.

30. In other words, the simple assumption that the saving rate is fixed turns out to be fully compatible with rational consumer behavior, as is shown in Appendix 3.3.

31. This is shown in Appendix 3.3.

32. See eq. (17) in Appendix 3.3.

33. See Appendix 3.3.

34. This means that impatience exceeds population growth by 3%.

35. See eq. (13) in Appendix 3.3.

36. See *World Development Report 1997*, table 13.

37. See Appendix 3.3.

38. See eq. (12) in Appendix 3.3.

39. See eq. (2) in Appendix 3.2.

40. See eq. (4) in Appendix 3.2.

41. See eq. (24) in Appendix 3.1.

42. John Maynard Keynes, *Treatise on Money* (London and New York, 1930).

4

The Importance of Being Efficient

There are only two qualities in the world: efficiency and inefficiency, and only two sorts of people: the efficient and the inefficient.[1]

GEORGE BERNARD SHAW

A people among whom wealth is well distributed, and who have high ambitions, are likely to accumulate a great deal of public property.[2]

ALFRED MARSHALL

Economic growth is important. It is actually hard to think of other things that might be more important, if you happen to live in places like Bangladesh, Bolivia, or Burundi, where, for most people, life is a constant struggle against economic and other hardships.[3] Money isn't everything, it is true, as the philosopher said, but if you have enough of it, you can usually buy the rest. Even in the so-called industrial countries, a significant part of the population finds it difficult to make ends meet: poverty, unemployment, homelessness, the list goes on—the economic problem is far from having been finally solved even in the most affluent countries. So economic growth, while not a cure-all, matters to them, too.

This is probably even more obvious than it seems. Yet the importance of economic growth was not always a foregone conclusion. In the early 1970s, for example, an international group of (mostly) natural scientists associated with the Massachusetts Institute of Technology issued a famous report called *The Limits to Growth*.[4] The authors argued that continued economic growth was not only well-nigh impossible, because the earth's natural resources like oil and minerals are finite, but that growth was probably also outright undesirable, because it constituted a grave threat to the natural environment through the overexploitation and looming ultimate exhaustion of nature's bounties and other forms of pollution.

This was the heyday of the neoclassical growth model, which taught that economic growth in the long run is exogenous—predetermined, if you prefer. To inhibit per capita growth, dwindling oil and mineral supplies somehow had to reduce the rate of technological progress. To many economists at the time, however, this did not seem to be a likely outcome. On the contrary, it should probably have seemed more likely, if anything, at least if you look back, that the threat of exhaustion of important natural resources would stimulate technological innovation and progress.[5] Anyhow, today, a quarter of a century after the publication of *The Limits to Growth*, oil reserves appear to be as plentiful as ever, and the price of oil is accordingly low, at least by recent historical standards.[6] And output per head in the world economy as a whole has increased by almost a half since 1970. We return to the relationship between natural resources and economic growth towards the end of the chapter.

Pessimism about the world's economic prospects was not confined to natural scientists in those years. In 1968, when the East Asian countries had already embarked on their phenomenal journey from rags to relative riches, Gunnar Myrdal, the Nobel-prize winning Swedish economist, published a 2,300-page tome, *The Asian Drama*, where he argued that economic growth in Asia, though highly desirable, was improbable if not impossible for all kinds of reasons.[7] But let us not get into that, now that we think we know better.

Even when it is adjusted in keeping with purchasing power, GDP is not a perfect measure of national economic output and welfare, for at least two reasons. First, GDP reflects output without regard to the inputs that are used or even depleted in the production process. Some nations work longer hours than others to maintain a comparable standard of life. Others run down their natural resources for the same purpose, as will be discussed at the end of the chapter. Second, GDP does not reflect various kinds of economic activity such as home production. This makes a difference when, for example, you compare the GDP of two nations, one of which cares for its young and old 'for free' at home, while the other does it through paid service, public or private. The latter country will then register a larger GDP than the former, other things being equal, without necessarily being better off.

To most people, economic growth is important for the obvious reason that only through growth can we expect a higher level of income at the end of the day and a better standard of life. This, however, is not the only reason. Most of us care not only about absolute economic growth, but also about relative growth, that is, our country's economic growth performance relative to that of other comparable countries. Most Swedes, for example, were reasonably satisfied—and some still are!—with their economy's growth performance since 1970, until it dawned on them that several other OECD countries had been growing more briskly: Sweden had been falling down the international income ladder rung by rung, from third place in 1970 to 16th in 1994.[8] The Irish, whose once-impoverished economy grew by more than 5 per cent per year in per capita terms from 1985 to 1995—a European record, by the way—celebrated with spectacular fireworks, when it became known that, in 1996, their purchasing-power-parity-adjusted GDP per capita had overtaken that of the mother country across the channel, according to the OECD, a big change from having been 44 per cent below the British level in 1970. Likewise, the impressive growth record of the East Asian countries since 1965 has sent a powerful message not only to other parts of Asia, but to Africa and around the world.

Now we must ask: Do poor countries grow more rapidly than rich? Will the poor ultimately catch up? Or will the income gap separating them from the rich countries perhaps grow wider over time?

Growing together? Or growing apart?

Remarkable as it may seem in retrospect, these questions did not arise, at least not in macroeconomic circles, in the 1960s, when the neoclassical growth model took macroeconomic theory by storm, and not in the 1970s either. There appear to be two main reasons for this.

First, because economic growth was deemed exogenous in the long run, as we have described in earlier chapters, perhaps there may not have seemed to be much point, at least not from the perspective of empirical economists, in bothering about different rates of technological progress in different places, if nothing could be done about them anyway.[9] The short run seemed to many to be a more interesting and potentially fruitful perspective from the point of view of empirical research, because the short run was at least within the shooting range of macroeconomic policies. Some reacted by turning away from macroeconomics. The idea that it might take a long time to reach long-run equilibrium, where growth is exogenous, had not yet been born, let alone the idea that economic growth in the long run might be endogenous after all.

In the second place, the information necessary to address the question of convergence vs. divergence was not yet at hand. In the 1960s, the countries of Africa, for example, had only recently become independent. So, in the years following independence, the macroeconomic performance of these countries, not to speak of their long-run growth, could not be subjected to empirical scrutiny by the statistical methods, including regression analysis, commonly applied to industrial countries, simply because the necessary data were not available. Today, economists studying the former republics of the Soviet Union have the same problem: in newly independent States, it typically takes many years for reliable statistical estimates of macroeconomic relationships and, especially, measures of long-run growth to become available.[10]

This changed in the 1980s. By then, international organizations, especially the World Bank and the International Monetary Fund, had amassed a wealth of economic data from the national governments of their member countries, data that could be used for assessing economic growth across countries and over time. Moreover, academic researchers under the auspices of the United Nations had by then prepared a comprehensive and user-friendly set of purchasing-power-parity-adjusted measures of GDP, which appeared to provide a better basis for cross-country comparisons of incomes and living standards than the raw figures from the national income accounts.[11] Shortly thereafter, the World Bank also began publishing purchasing-power-parity-adjusted measures of GNP in most of its member countries.

The timing here is probably not a pure coincidence. The endogenous-growth revolution took place just as the fresh data with which to test the ideas derived from the new theory were becoming available. If this was not a coincidence, it was not the first time: the Keynesian revolution coincided with the invention of national income accounting, which provided the quantitative framework needed for the empirical implementation of Keynesian analysis of national income and employment in the years after the Second World War.

What are the facts of the matter? Does economic growth across countries converge?

Figure 4.1 shows GDP per capita in 1992 on the vertical axis, country by country, and the level of each country's GDP per capita in 1970 on the horizontal axis. Both measures are adjusted for purchasing power parity and expressed in constant 1987 prices. The figure spans the world economy as a whole—that is, the 128 countries for which the requisite information is available in the Penn World Tables.[12] Each country's experience is summarized by a single observation. Economic growth is shown by the distance of each observation from the 45° line. Dots above the 45° line indicate positive economic growth from 1970 to 1992, dots below the line show negative growth. As you can see, the regression line through the scatterplot is approximately parallel to the 45° line. There is thus no discernible relationship between per capita growth and initial income per head, neither convergence nor divergence.

Figure 4.2 shows the same variables, except now only for the 23 countries classified by the World Bank as high-income countries.[13] Now a clear pattern emerges: you

Fig 4.1
The world economy: No convergence

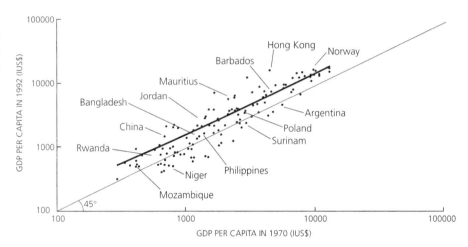

Fig 4.2
The high- income countries: Convergence

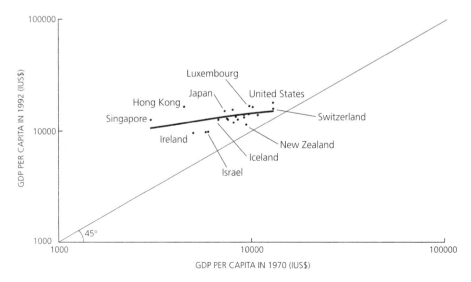

can see a tendency for the lowest incomes in the group to be associated with the highest growth rates and vice versa. The regression line through the scatterplot is significantly flatter than the 45° line. There seems to be a clear tendency towards convergence within the high-income group.[14] Similarly, several studies have reported evidence of convergence of different regions within countries and continents (the states of the United States, the provinces of Canada, the prefectures of Japan, the states of India, the regions of Europe, the communes of Sweden).[15]

For statistical reasons, however, the pattern displayed in Figure 4.2 should probably be taken with a grain of salt. For a given level of income in 1992, a high level of income in 1970 entails a low growth rate from 1970 to 1992 by definition.[16] This creates a danger that statistical errors of measurement will be mistaken for a sign of economic convergence. Suppose our measures of income in 1970 are subject to greater errors than our income measures for 1992, not an unreasonable assumption. Such statistical errors will exaggerate the variation in the observed initial income levels and will, therefore, bias the slope of the regression line through our scatterplot in Figure 4.2, making the line look flatter than it really is.[17]

You can see this in Figure 4.3, where initial income per head (say, in 1870 or 1970) is shown on the horizontal axis and current income per head (say, in 1992) is on the vertical axis. Convergence means that the regression line AB is flatter than the 45° line, which can be interpreted in two ways: (a) the rate of growth, reflected by the distance between the two lines (e.g. the distance EF), declines as initial income increases and (b) the range of current incomes, measured by the vertical distance between points A and B in the figure, is narrower than the range of initial incomes, which is measured by the horizontal distance between A and B—i.e. the distribution of incomes across countries is more even than before. Therefore, if the observed range of initial incomes is exaggerated through errors of measurement, the true (but unobserved) range is smaller than the observed range. Suppose the true range of initial incomes is shown by the horizontal distance between C and D in the figure, and that current incomes were correctly measured all along, so that the vertical distance between C and D is the same as that between A and B. The unbiased regression line CD must then be steeper than the biased regression line AB. If the bias is large enough, the CD line may have a slope of one, as the 45° line, which means neither

Fig 4.3
Errors of measurement of initial income may create an illusion of convergence

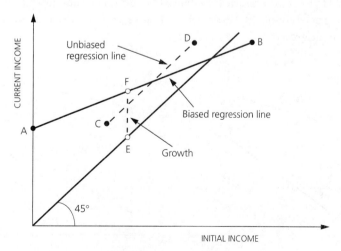

convergence nor divergence (this is the case shown in the figure), or it may even be steeper still, which means divergence.[18]

The two interpretations of convergence described above have names, but they are not particularly descriptive. The first type of convergence, by which is meant that economic growth is related to initial income (the lower the level of income, the higher the rate of growth), has been called 'beta convergence', because the slope co-efficient of a bivariate regression is often denoted by beta. The second type of convergence, by which is meant that the distribution of national incomes per head becomes more even across countries over time, has been called 'sigma convergence', because sigma is most often used to denote standard deviation, a common measure of dispersion. The two types of convergence are closely related, but they are not identical. In particular, beta convergence tends to generate, but does not necessarily guarantee, sigma convergence. The dispersion of GNP per capita across countries may become less even over time for various reasons, even if economic growth is inversely related to initial income *per se*.

Figure 4.4 demonstrates the distinction. In Panel A, the poor countries grow more rapidly than the rich countries, and the distribution of incomes between them becomes more equal over time, as indicated by the narrowing gap between the two paths in the panel. In this case, beta convergence generates sigma convergence. In Panel B, the poor countries are exposed to an adverse shock, which shifts their income path downwards. Therefore, even if the poor countries grow more rapidly than the rich ones, the distribution of incomes between the two groups becomes less equal over time, as is indicated by the widening gap between the two groups in Panel B. This is a case where beta convergence does not generate sigma convergence.

Figure 4.5 shows the relationship between GDP per capita in 1992 and initial GDP per capita (i.e. in 1970) in the low- and middle-income countries, according to the World Bank's classification. The figure covers those 105 countries from Figure 4.1 which were excluded from Figure 4.2. Because the low- and middle-income countries are so much more numerous than the high-income countries in the sample as a whole, it is not surprising, perhaps, that Figure 4.5 makes the same overall impression as Figure 4.1. Here, again, we seem to have neither convergence nor divergence.

In sum, then, subject to the qualifications that have been stated above, there seems to be some empirical evidence of convergence among rich countries, but not among poor countries. How do these findings rhyme with our two main theories of economic growth?

Fig 4.4
Beta convergence does not necessarily generate sigma convergence

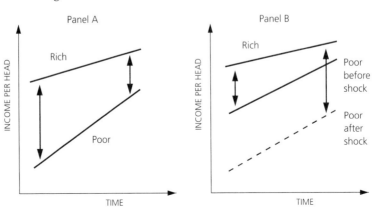

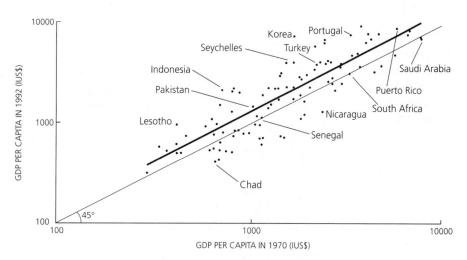

Fig 4.5
The low- and middle-income countries: No convergence

Absolute vs. conditional convergence

Let us begin with exogenous growth. If our data reflect output per capita in long-run equilibrium, then the Solow model predicts neither convergence nor divergence. In Solow's model, long-run growth of output per capita depends solely on technological progress, a wholly exogenous phenomenon from our economic point of view.

If, on the other hand, our data describe countries at different stages on their dynamic adjustment path towards the Solovian long-run equilibrium, then the plot thickens a bit. Suppose, to paraphrase Ernest Hemingway, that the only difference between rich countries and poor is that the rich have more capital per worker than the poor. This, of course, is too simplistic, because in reality rich and poor countries differ in more ways than one, but, for the sake of the argument, let us assume this for a moment. Then, if rich countries and poor are identical in all other respects, have the same saving rates, the same population growth, the same rate of technological progress, and so forth, they will ultimately have also the same output per capita.[19] This means that the poor countries must converge on the rich. Another way to see this is by noticing that if the poor countries initially have less capital per worker and hence also less output per capita than the rich (this is what makes the poor poor), and if they will end up with the same output per capita, then they will have to grow faster in the meantime to catch up. This phenomenon is called absolute convergence—i.e. convergence no matter what.

Figure 4.6 illustrates the point. If two countries are exactly the same except for their income per capita, they will both end up at the long-run equilibrium point E in the figure. Therefore, if the poor country's initial income per head is OA, which is below the rich country's income per head, OB, then, clearly, the poor country must grow more rapidly than the rich country for both of them ultimately to achieve the common level of income per head, OC. But this result, again, is based on the unrealistic assumption that rich and poor countries are identical in all respects but one, the initial stock of capital. Therefore, the failure of the poor countries to converge on the

Fig 4.6
Absolute convergence: Poor countries grow more rapidly than rich ones in the medium run

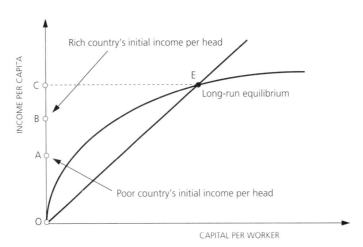

rich evident in Figure 4.1 does not by itself constitute a valid refutation of the medium-term implications of the Solow model.

To test the validity of the medium-term dynamic implications of the Solow model for convergence (i.e. the implications of the model as countries traverse towards their long-run equilibrium growth paths), one must allow for the possibility that the rich and poor countries differ in more ways than one. They may, for example, have different saving rates. Their standards of efficiency may also differ, for many reasons, as may their population growth rates and depreciation. Suppose we now correct for all these differences by regressing the rate of growth of output per capita across countries on all these potential determinants of growth, and then ask whether poor countries grow more rapidly than rich countries, other things being equal—i.e. after all these other differences have been taken into consideration. If the answer is yes, we have what is called conditional convergence. Poor countries then converge on rich countries on the condition that they have the same saving rates, the same efficiency, and so on.

Looking back at Figure 4.1, we see immediately that there is no evidence of absolute convergence in the world as a whole. No regression analysis is required to reach that conclusion, even if the virtually parallel regression line through the scatterplot in the figure helps confirm the impression. On the other hand, detailed regression analysis is required for studying conditional convergence. Several empirical studies have shown that, when the necessary adjustments have been made, the rate of growth of output per capita is inversely related to the initial level of output per capita in an economically and statistically significant way. Specifically, a doubling of income per head has typically been found to reduce per capita growth by about one percentage point, sometimes a bit more, sometimes less.[20]

Does this finding of conditional convergence help us discriminate among competing explanations of economic growth? No, not really. Conditional convergence is consistent with the medium-term dynamic implications of the neoclassical model, it is true, as has been stressed by Robert Barro among others, but in the long run, according to that model, all countries bump against the same ceiling. 'Basically,' says Barro, '2 per cent per capita growth seems to be as good as it gets in the long run for a country that is already rich.'[21] Yet, Hong Kong and Singapore are already rich, and they show various signs of continuing to grow quite rapidly in the years ahead despite the setbacks of 1997–8. Clearly, their growth performance is no longer a question of catching up with Western Europe and North America. Singapore, for example, is the only major city in the world that regulates its road traffic mostly by price—i.e. by a system of general road fees, by far the most efficient method of keeping traffic under control.[22] Unsurprisingly, Singapore is also one of the least congested of the world's major cities, which almost surely provides a significant boost to the city state's overall efficiency. This is mentioned here only as an example of the ability of the Singaporeans to get many things right ahead of others. To take another example, Ireland is no longer a poor European country catching up with its rich partners in the European Union. No, Ireland is probably better described as a European sputnik, whose output per capita continues to grow at over 5 per cent per year, even if its income per head is now above average in the European Union. This is what you can expect from a country which, despite a population of only 3.5 million, has in a relatively short time become a major magnet for foreign investment and a giant in the computer industry, for instance: nearly a half of all software in use in computers in European homes and offices is made in Ireland.

But even if conditional convergence is consistent with the medium-term dynamic implications of the Solow model, it is not necessarily incompatible with the theory of endogenous growth in the long run. You will recall from the last part of Chapter 3 that the theory of exogenous growth in the medium term—i.e. when countries are still on their way towards long-run equilibrium—and of endogenous growth in the long run are qualitatively similar, even if they are quantitatively different. Therefore, we must ask: what does the theory of endogenous growth tell us about the relative economic growth of rich and poor countries?

Because endogenous economic growth depends solely on the saving rate, efficiency, and depreciation, as we saw in Chapters 2 and 3, the theory of endogenous growth predicts that poor countries will grow faster than, and thus converge on, richer countries, if and only if the poor countries either save a higher proportion of their incomes than the rich, are more efficient (i.e. produce more output per unit of capital), or have less depreciation.

Take saving. There may seem to be reasonably good grounds for believing that saving rates tend to be directly related to incomes per capita. When you are poor, you sometimes feel that you cannot afford to save much, because of your immediate consumption needs. When your income rises and more of your most urgent consumption needs can be met, the scope for saving increases. This, in fact, is the essence of the short-run Keynesian consumption function: an individual's or a nation's consumption increases with income, but less than dollar for dollar or pound for pound, as shown in Figure 4.7. This means that the ratio of consumption to income, shown by the angle between the rays from the origin and the horizontal axis in the figure, decreases as income rises from A to B in the figure. This, in turn, means that the saving rate increases with income. This phenomenon has been widely observed in studies of consumer behaviour in the short run and across households. The long-run consumption function generally does not have this property, however, for consumption tends to be roughly proportional to income in the long run: the saving rate is then independent of income.[23]

Figure 4.8 shows the average saving (i.e. investment) rates of 161 countries

Fig 4.7
**Why the saving rate
varies directly with
income**

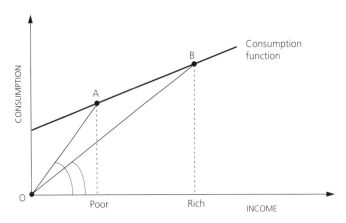

Fig 4.8
**The saving rate
varies directly with
income**

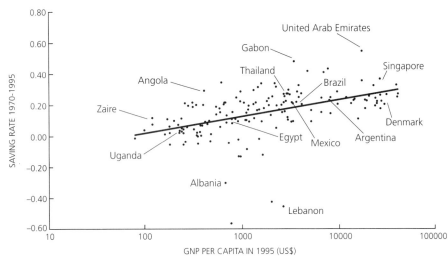

reporting to the World Bank over the period 1970–95 on the upright axis and their GNP per capita in 1995, measured in US dollars, on the horizontal axis.[24] Each country is represented by a single data point. If you like, you can view the 1995 level of a country's GNP per head as a cumulative measure of its past economic growth or of its stage of development over the period as a whole.[25] The regression line through the scatterplot shows that an increase in income per head from, say, US$ 3,000 to US$ 6,000 (i.e. a 100 per cent increase) is associated with an increase in the saving rate from 18 to 21 per cent (i.e. a 17 per cent increase). This example implies an elasticity of the saving rate with respect to income per head of about 0.17 (= 17/100).

This correlation need not be a sure sign of causation, however. We have seen before that the saving rate is one of the main determinants of income per capita in the long run. Therefore, Figure 4.8 may simply be telling us that the more countries save in proportion to their incomes, the higher their incomes will be. This interpretation seems natural when the level of GNP per capita in 1995 is being compared with the average saving rate over the past 25 years. Suppose that this is what the picture is telling us. Then the regression line through the scatterplot shows that an increase in the saving rate from, say, 20 to 25 per cent of output (i.e. a 25 per cent increase) is associated with an increase in GNP per capita from USD$ 4,800 to US$ 14,100 (i.e. a 192 per cent increase). This implies an elasticity of income per head with respect to the saving rate of almost 8, which is much larger than what the Solow model predicts in the long run.[26] Most probably, though, the pattern in the figure reflects both phenomena: that saving rates depend on income per capita and vice versa. In any case, we have no basis here for believing that poor countries save more and, therefore, grow faster than rich countries. On the other hand, saving rates have increased in several developing countries in recent years in response to more efficient financial intermediation and higher rates of return, which conform more closely to the scarcity value of capital than before.[27]

Poverty traps

Notice now the following implication of the foregoing discussion. A poor country may become stuck in perennial poverty, precisely because it is so poor that it cannot afford to save as much of its income as would be necessary for its income to rise. If you are living on less than a dollar a day, as almost 1½ billion people do today, a quarter of mankind, then your personal scope for current sacrifice for future gain is severely constrained, to say the least. This could be part of the reason why many poor countries have remained poor. They have been unwilling or unable to accept the reduction in consumption in the short run that is necessary to increase saving enough to lay a basis for more rapid economic growth in the medium or long run, other things being equal. This is changing, however. Consumption in low-income countries decreased from a weighted average of 66 per cent of GDP in 1980 to 59 per cent in 1995, while their saving (i.e. investment) rate increased from 24 to 32 per cent. The pattern is uneven: in Sub-Saharan Africa, consumption actually rose from a weighted average of 60 per cent of GDP in 1980 to 67 per cent in 1995, while the saving rate fell from 23 to 19 per cent. Yet, several African countries are now consuming less and saving and investing more than they used to. Take Ghana, for example, where consumption decreased from 84 per cent of GDP in 1980 to 77 per cent in 1995, while the saving rate jumped from 6 to 19 per cent of GDP. Mauritius is another case in point: there consumption fell from 75 per cent of GDP in 1980 to 65 per cent in 1995, while the saving rate rose from 21 to 25 per cent. In Uganda, consumption fell from 89 per cent of GDP to 83 per cent between 1980 and 1995, while the saving rate rose from 6 to 16 per cent. This list of examples could be extended.

But their unwillingness or inability to save more so as to invest more is not the only possible reason why countries get caught in poverty traps. There are at least three other potentially important additional explanations for this.

The first concerns population growth. In poor countries, through the ages, the sole form of social security was communal and familial care: grown children, some of them at least, took care of their aged or infirm parents. To secure themselves in old age parents therefore produced many children, in the hope that at least one would stay behind with them. This is still the way it is in many parts of the world. This is one reason why population growth is much more rapid in poor countries than rich. For example, from 1980 to 1995 the annual average rate of population growth was 2.8

per cent in Sub-Saharan Africa and 2.1 per cent in South Asia, the two regions where most of the world's poor are concentrated, compared with 0.7 per cent population growth in the high-income countries.[28]

Figure 4.9 confirms this pattern. It shows the annual average growth of population from 1970 to 1995 on the vertical axis, country by country, and each country's GNP per head in 1995 on the horizontal axis. As in Figure 4.8, each country is represented by a single pair of observations. The regression line through the scatter shows that an increase in income per head from, say, US$ 3,000 to US$ 6,000 (i.e. a 100 per cent increase) is associated with a decrease in population growth from 1.8 to 1.6 per cent (i.e. a 10 per cent decrease or thereabouts). This implies an elasticity of population growth with respect to national income per head of about −0.1.

As before, however, this correlation need not indicate causation. We have seen before that population growth is one of the main determinants of the level of output per capita in the long run.[29] To refresh your memory, if need be, take a look at Figure 4.10, which simulates the effects of an increase in population growth from 1 to 3 per cent per year on output per capita with exogenous growth (the broken black curve) and with endogenous growth (the solid black curve), compared with no change (the solid grey curve). The simulation is in other respects based on the same premises as the one displayed in Figure 3.28 in Chapter 3: the saving rate is 15 per cent by assumption, the rate of technological progress is 1 per cent per year, and the rate of de-

Fig 4.9
Population growth varies inversely with income

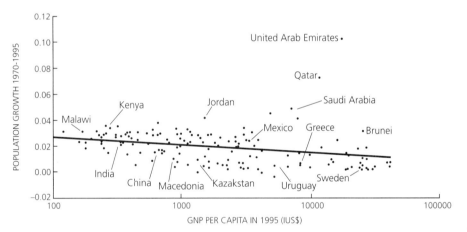

Fig 4.10
The first twenty years: The path of output per capita with and without an increase in population growth from 1 per cent per year to 3 per cent

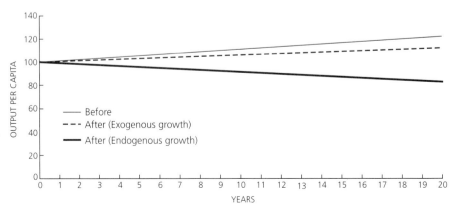

preciation is 4 per cent per year. As you can see, Figure 4.10 shows that, after 20 years, income per head is about 10 per cent to a third lower than initially as a result of more rapid population growth.

Viewed in this light, Figure 4.9 may simply be telling us that more rapid population growth results in less income per head rather than the other way round. If that is what is going on in the picture, then the downward-sloping regression line through the scatterplot shows that an increase in population growth from, say, 1.5 to 2 per cent per year (i.e. a 33 per cent increase) goes hand in hand with a decrease in GNP per capita from US$ 10,200 to USD 1,500 (i.e. an 85 per cent decrease!). This example implies an elasticity of output per head with respect to population growth of about −2.5, which, again, is much larger than what the Solow model predicts.[30] All things considered, it seems reasonable to conclude that the pattern displayed in Figure 4.9 mirrors both possibilities: that population growth depends on income per capita and vice versa.

The second explanation has to do with externalities (due, for instance, to increasing returns to scale), imperfect competition, and the possibility of low-income-slow-growth equilibria—i.e. poverty traps—resulting from such phenomena. Imagine a country whose entrepreneurs would be glad to launch a modern sector, if only they thought there was a local market for the output of that sector. And why may there not be a market for the modern output? Precisely because the modern sector is too small. Specifically, if there are fixed costs of production in the modern sector and hence increasing returns to scale, production in that sector will be too costly, and hence not competitive, unless sufficiently many producers simultaneously set up shop in the modern sector to keep costs down. Therefore, no single entrepreneur wants to make the move from the traditional to the modern sector on his own, for alone he would be doomed to failure. But if many entrepreneurs moved together, they could all profit.[31] This may be another part of the reason why many poor countries have failed to industrialize and have instead become mired too long in too much agriculture and perpetual poverty.

The third and last possible explanation for poverty traps and the absence of a Big Push for rapid growth in many developing countries has to do with education. It has been argued above that many poor countries, or at least many families in those countries, cannot afford to save as much of their incomes as rich countries, which tends to impede growth. In the same way, many people in poor countries cannot afford to send as many of their children to school or to keep them in school as long as is customary and affordable in rich countries. Education is just another form of investment, but in human rather than in real or financial capital. Therefore, if abject poverty restricts the accumulation of real and financial capital, it would seem likely to restrict also the accumulation of human capital in a comparable way.

Figure 4.11 seems to support this hypothesis. It shows primary-school enrolment rates for both sexes in 1993 on the vertical axis and GNP per capita in 1995 on the horizontal axis. As before, the experience of each country is summarized by a single point in the figure. You see that there is a clear tendency for primary-school enrolment rates to be lower in low-income countries than in high-income countries, even if the figure does not reflect the frequently long lags involved: it takes time for investment in education to bear fruit. The regression line through the scatterplot shows that an increase in income per head from, say, US$ 3,000 to US$ 6,000 (i.e. a

Fig 4.11
Primary-school enrolment varies directly with income

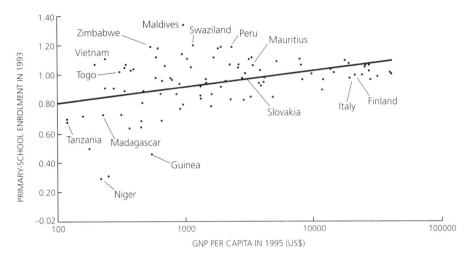

100 per cent increase) is associated with an increase in primary-school enrolment from 97 to 100 per cent (i.e. by about 3 per cent). This example implies an elasticity of primary-school enrolment with respect to national income per head of about 0.03.

Once again, this correlation need not necessarily imply causation, even if a causal relationship seems likely, because schooling is a potentially important determinant of economic efficiency and hence also of income per capita. Most likely, one presumes, the pattern observed in Figure 4.11 reflects both effects: education depends on income and the other way round. In any case, this seems to show that at least one aspect of economic efficiency is less favourable in poor countries than in rich countries, which, like less saving, would lead us to expect poor countries to grow less rapidly than rich countries, other things being equal.

But other things are not equal. Economic efficiency depends on a host of factors, to which most of the rest of this chapter is devoted. There is no way *a priori* to tell how, when all is said and done, economic efficiency varies with income per capita. Consequently, there is no way either *a priori* to tell whether poor countries can be expected automatically to catch up with the rich countries or not. But this is not necessarily a gloomy conclusion, not at all. On the contrary, it should become increasingly clear as the chapter progresses that 'rapid economic growth is available to those countries with adequate natural resources which make the effort to achieve it', in the words of Arthur Lewis, written 30 years ago.[32]

We now have to take a long and hard look at economic efficiency, not primarily to see if poor countries are likely to be more or less efficient than rich countries, in the sense that they produce more output per unit of capital, but also because economic efficiency is a crucial determinant of economic growth, with or without convergence.

We now proceed to deal with various aspects of economic efficiency, case by case. By efficiency is meant, as before, the amount of national economic output that is being produced with given inputs or, in a narrower sense, with a given stock of capital at full employment. This concept of efficiency is static. It means that, in order to enhance efficiency, it is necessary either to increase the output that can be squeezed out of given resources or to reduce the inputs necessary to make given output. Our motive should be obvious: together with saving, efficiency is the *primus motor* of economic growth, whether it is medium-term growth à la Solow or long-run growth according to the endogenous-growth model. To reiterate our interpretation of Adam Smith's view of economic growth from Chapter 1, whatever is good for economic efficiency is also good for growth.

Case 1: Liberalization

Let us start with foreign trade. Our strategy involves three steps. First, we demonstrate the qualitative efficiency-enhancing effects of increased trade with the rest of the world. Then we ask the quantitative question: how large are these effects likely to be? At last, we attempt also to quantify the links between trade and growth through efficiency, and report recent empirical evidence.

Reallocation

Consider a country with two sectors of economic activity: one traditional, one modern. In Figure 4.12, the production possibilities, given the county's fixed endowment of labour, capital, and land, are described by the production frontier DEFG, which describes the different bundles of traditional and modern output that can be produced by the available labour, capital, and land. On the frontier, all the factors of production are fully employed. The frontier is concave due to diminishing returns to factor use (i.e. diminishing marginal productivity): the more resources that are transferred from the traditional sector to the modern sector, the less will be the addition to modern output resulting from a given transfer of resources.

Suppose the government protects the traditional sector at the outset by restricting the imports of goods that compete with traditional output by imposing a tariff on such imports. This raises the relative price of traditional output and attracts more resources to the traditional sector at the expense of the modern sector than otherwise would be the case. The domestic price ratio, distorted by the tariff, is shown by the

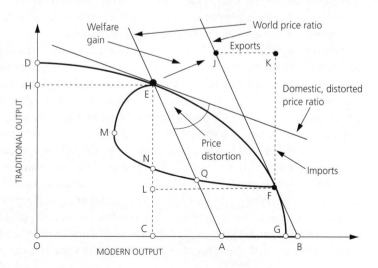

Fig 4.12 Liberalization increases economic efficiency: The reallocation effect

price line that just touches without penetrating the production frontier at point E in the figure. At this ratio of prices of traditional and modern output, it is most profitable for domestic producers to produce OH units of traditional output and OC units of modern output. But this price ratio is, as we have said, distorted by the tariff. The world price ratio is shown by the slope of the steeper line EQA. The distance CA on the horizontal axis shows the amount of traditional output produced at point E, measured in units of modern output,[33] and the sum of modern and traditional output, OC plus CA, that is, OA, equals total national output by definition.

Now the government decides to liberalize trade by removing the tariff on traditional output. The distorted price line is no longer relevant to domestic producers, who must now compete in world markets. The price ratio that matters to them under free trade is the world price ratio. Therefore, it no longer pays for them to produce at the old equilibrium point E in the figure. Now that the protection of the traditional sector has been withdrawn and the relative price of traditional output has fallen accordingly, it pays to transfer resources from the traditional sector to the modern sector, whose output has increased in price relative to the traditional sector. This reallocation of resources continues until the new equilibrium point F is reached, where the world price line touches the production frontier. At this point, F, national output has increased by the maximum possible amount, shown by the bold segment AB on the horizontal axis in Figure 4.12, that is, from OA to OB. Traditional output has decreased by EL in the figure, and modern output has increased by LF. If, for some reason, the reallocation stopped short of point F or went beyond it, then national output would be less than at F. Hence the optimality of just that point of tangency, F.

It should be clear from the figure that the larger the initial price distortion resulting from the restriction on foreign trade, the more costly the distortion will be in terms of total output foregone and, therefore, the larger will be the output gain from eliminating the distortion. Actually, the output gain from liberalization, i.e. the distance AB in the figure, is directly proportional to the square of the original price distortion, which is shown by the angle between the domestic, distorted price line and the world price line.[34] Specifically, if we denote the expansion of output by e, the multiplicative proportionality factor by m, and the constant original trade distortion by c, then we have, simply put, $e = mc^2$. The multiplicative factor reflects the share of the modern sector in total output after the liberalization.

Three more points need to be made. In the first place, national output at full employment has been increased by a change in economic policy—by the abolition of a prohibitive tariff in this case. This has been accomplished not by increasing the amount of labour, capital, or land used in production, but by using the available factors of production more efficiently. The country has managed to squeeze more output out of given inputs, which is the hallmark of increased efficiency.

Second, foreign trade allows consumption to differ from production, thus enabling the country to reach beyond the confines of its own production possibilities. Even if the country produces at point F in Figure 4.12 under free trade, it is free to consume at, say, point J. This means that JK of modern output (i.e. production at F less consumption at J) is exported abroad and FK of traditional output (i.e. consumption at J less production at F) is imported. Because the slope of JF equals the world price ratio by construction, the value of exports equals the value of imports, so that trade is balanced.[35] Notice also that the new consumption point J lies to the north and east of the original consumption (and production) point E. Thus, a more efficient allocation of resources at full employment under free trade allows a country to consume more of everything, including, in particular, the commodity whose domestic production has decreased. The welfare gain from liberalization is shown by the distance from E to J, while the output gain is shown by the distance AB. The two are only loosely related: by sliding point J up or down the line JFB, you can see that the welfare gain changes, even if the output gain remains the same.

Third, there is no presumption that the transition from the original pre-trade equilibrium at point E in Figure 4.12 to the final free-trade equilibrium at point F will be painless. On the contrary, it is likely in most cases that the initial contraction of traditional output is accompanied by job losses in the traditional sector, because the modern sector cannot immediately absorb all those who are thrown out of work in the traditional sector. For one thing, the workers dislodged from the traditional sector may need to be retrained, before they can be gainfully employed in the modern sector. For another, the contraction of employment and incomes in the traditional sector may be contagious: it may cause a contraction also in the modern sector, because those who have lost their jobs in the traditional sector have less to spend on modern output. Therefore, output may follow a path such as EMNQF in Figure 4.12. At point M, the modern sector bottoms out and begins to recover, as resourceful entrepreneurs find ways to re-employ labour and capital that have become redundant in the traditional sector. At N, modern output is restored to its initial level. At Q, national output is restored to its initial level. Finally, at F, the gains from free trade are reaped in full and full employment is restored.

The path of output following economic liberalization is shown in Figure 4.13. National economic output (i.e. GNP) is stagnant until time t_1, when the liberalization effort is launched. Output decreases initially from its initial equilibrium level at E, and then moves via M, N, and Q to a new equilibrium at F, where the output is larger than it was initially at E. The shaded area EMNQ indicates the cumulative, short-term output loss from liberalization. Even so, because the liberalization increases economic efficiency by increasing the amount of output produced by given inputs, it will also boost economic growth. Therefore, output grows more rapidly from point F, that is, from time t_2, onwards than it did before the story began at E. Hence, the path of

Fig 4.13
The path of output following economic liberalization is shaped like a sickle

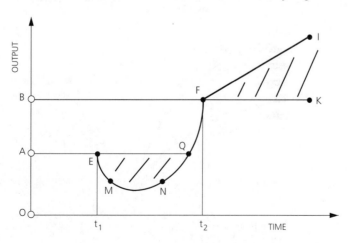

output is EMNQFI rather than EMNQFK. The growth bonus is shown by the shaded triangle FIK.

Reorganization

We have thus far described the reallocation effect of liberalization, that is, the output gain from allocating existing resources as efficiently as possible between alternative uses in view of world market prices. This is not the end of the story, however, for the liberalization may induce firms in the previously protected industry to reorganize their production by economizing in various ways, adopting new and better techniques of production, and so on.[36]

This reorganization effect is described in Figure 4.14 by an upward shift of the production frontier from DEFG to JHG. Production now takes place at point H rather than F. The total output gain is now shown by the bold segment AC on the horizontal axis, of which AB is the gain from reallocation as in Figure 4.12 and BC is the additional gain from reorganization.[37] More is consumed of everything than before, as can be seen by comparing the new consumption point J with the old one E, as in Figure 4.12, to gauge the total welfare gain. The trade triangle JKH in Figure 4.14 has the same interpretation as the trade triangle JKF in Figure 4.12. Further, more is now produced of both types of output: the new production point H lies to the north and east of the original production point E. This, by the way, seems to have occurred in agriculture in New Zealand after its radical liberalization in 1984. A few years later, the country's farm sector was larger than before the liberalization took place and its farmers fewer, yes, but stronger.[38]

Empirical evidence

How large are the output gains from liberalization? Our simple formulae[39] permit us map the magnitude of the output gains as a function of just two variables: the original price distortion and the share of the modern sector at the end of the day. Suppose domestic relative prices initially are out of line with world market prices by a factor of 2, 3, 4, or 5. These numbers correspond to implicit initial tariff rates of 100, 200,

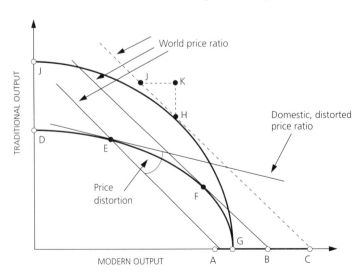

Fig 4.14
Liberalization increases economic efficiency: The reorganization effect

300, and 400 per cent. These numbers should not be taken literally as tariffs, but rather as indications of the price distortions that can result from tariffs and other barriers to trade.[40] Suppose, further, that the share of the modern sector in total output following the liberalization will be in the range from 50 to 90 per cent. The output gains that follow from these assumptions are shown in Table 4.1.

According to Table 4.1, the static output gains from liberalization can be quite large. The reallocation effect alone ranges from 7 to 40 per cent of output given the range of the underlying parameters shown in the first column and the first row of the table. When the reorganization effect is added, the total effect ranges from 12 to 73 per cent of output. For comparison, even the lowest figure in the table, 7 per cent in the top left corner, exceeds the rough estimates of the permanent static output gains of 4–5 per cent which were originally expected to emerge gradually from the market unification of Europe after 1992.[41] Implicit in the above exercise is an elasticity of 1 of modern output with repect to its relative price.[42] A more elastic supply response would yield larger output gains than those shown in Table 4.1.

Table 4.2 shows the rate of growth of output resulting from different values of the saving rate and the output/capital ratio (i.e. efficiency), given a 5 per cent annual rate of depreciation. From these numbers we can deduce some examples of the dynamic output gain—that is, the growth bonus—associated with the static efficiency gains reported in Table 4.1. Suppose the saving rate is 0.20 and that efficiency (i.e. the output/capital ratio) increases by a third, a mid-range figure from Table 4.1 (say, from 0.25 to 0.33). Then the rate of growth of output increases from 0 to 1.7 per cent per year by Table 4.2. The higher the saving rate, the larger the dynamic output gain resulting from a given increase in efficiency through liberalization.[43] These numbers indicate that liberalization can have substantial effects on economic growth over time.

Table 4.1 **Static output gains: The proportional once-and-for-all increase in total output resulting from liberalization (%)**

Panel A. Gains from reallocation

No gain from reorganization	Modern-sector share = 0.5	Modern-sector share = 0.7	Modern-sector share = 0.9
100% tariff	7	10	13
200% tariff	13	18	25
300% tariff	16	25	34
400% tariff	19	29	40

Panel B. Gains from reallocation and reorganization

Productivity rises by 90% of distortion	Modern-sector share = 0.5	Modern-sector share = 0.7	Modern-sector share = 0.9
100% tariff	12	17	23
200% tariff	23	33	45
300% tariff	30	44	61
400% tariff	34	52	73

Source: Author's computations based on eqs. (11) and (20) in Appendix 4.1, with k = 0.0 in Panel A and k = 0.9 in Panel B.

Table 4.2 **Dynamic output gains: The growth of output increases with increased efficiency through liberalization (output growth in %)**

Depreciation rate = 0.05	Efficiency = 1/4	Efficiency = 1/3	Efficiency = 1/2
Saving rate = 0.1	−2.5	−1.7	0.0
Saving rate = 0.2	0.0	1.7	5.0
Saving rate = 0.3	2.5	5.0	10.0
Saving rate = 0.4	5.0	8.3	15.0

Source: Author's computations based on eq. (6) in Appendix 2.3.

How do these hypothetical results square with hard empirical evidence of the links between trade and growth? Look first at Figure 4.15. It shows GNP per capita in 1995 on the vertical axis and an index of countries' openness to external trade in 1994 on the horizontal axis. This index is defined as the ratio of exports of goods and services to GNP in per cent, adjusted for country size by regressing the export ratio on the population and subtracting the predicted value from the regression from the actual export ratio to find a measure of openness.[44] This adjustment is necessary because, as we discussed briefly in Chapter 2, large countries are typically less dependent on trade than small countries. This means that a large country with a modest export ratio (like China, with an export ratio of 26 per cent in 1994 and a population of 1.2 billion) may be considered relatively more open to trade than a much smaller country with a larger export ratio (like, for example, Kenya, with an export ratio of 38 per cent in 1994 and a population of 26 million). Because the regression predicts export ratios of 7 per cent in China and 29 per cent in Kenya, the values of the openness index are 19 (= 26 − 7) for China and 9 (= 38 − 29) for Kenya. To take another example, the regression predicts an export ratio of 27 per cent in Argentina (population 34 million), whereas the actual ratio in 1994 was only 7 per cent. Therefore, the openness index for Argentina is −20. Thailand (population 59 million), on the other hand, is assigned an openness index of 15, because the regression predicts an export ratio of 24 per cent, while the actual ratio in 1994 was 39 per cent.

Figure 4.15 displays a tendency for GNP per capita and openness to go hand in hand. The regression line through the scatterplot indicates that a swing in openness from −20 to 20 is associated with more than a doubling of GNP per capita, from US$

Fig 4.15 **Increased openness goes along with higher income**

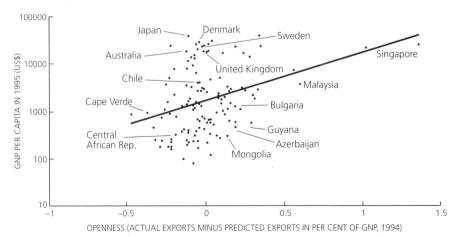

1,100 to US$ 2,800, other things being equal. The four outliers far to the right in the figure (Singapore, Hong Kong, Malaysia, and Bahrain) do not have to be excluded from the regression because, believe it or not, the regression is essentially the same with them and without. We cannot, however, exclude the possibility that the relationship is reciprocal, that is, that openness is good for growth and vice versa.

In any case, the regression line must not be taken too literally, for it is only intended to allow the raw data to provide a rough impression of the pattern that would be expected to emerge in the absence of any other influences on income per head and openness, or if all such influences happened to cancel out. A conclusive demonstration of a positive empirical relationship between income and openness would require detailed econometric scrutiny where other relevant explanatory variables would be taken into account. This qualification applies to all the empirical figures in this chapter. There is a substantive issue involved here. Income per head and openness are both endogenous variables. In principle, they can move in the same direction or in opposition directions, depending on the nature of the exogenous influences that impinge on them. Economic theory predicts that an exogenous increase in tariff protection would reduce both income per head and openness in the long run (see Figure 4.12), thereby giving rise to a positive relationship between income and openness, other things being equal. A simultaneous increase in the saving rate and in tariff protection, on the other hand, might very well yield a different pattern, where higher incomes (due to more saving outweighing increased protection) seemed to go along with less openness (due to higher tariffs). Thus, anything is possible.

Thus far, though, and this may be a bit surprising in view of the potential importance and time-honoured history of the subject, relatively few econometric studies have reported significant effects of freer trade on economic growth. Jeffrey Sachs and associates define openness as 'the fraction of years during which the country is rated as an open economy', a complicated composite criterion, which reflects (a) black-market foreign-exchange premia, (b) whether the country was socialist or not, (c) the scope of its export marketing board, and (d) the coverage of quotas on imports of intermediate and capital goods.[45] They report a strong, positive effect of openness, thus defined, on economic growth: the growth rate of GDP per capita was 2½ per cent higher in fully open economies than in completely closed ones from 1970 to 1989, other things being equal. A few others have also reported similar results for developing countries, that is, that economic growth is related to measures of outward orientation, price distortions, tariffs, and other trade interventions:[46] more openness and less distortions mean more growth.

The gains from trade are not confined to goods and services. Vigorous trade in capital produces comparable efficiency gains and growth effects as other trade, at least in principle, not only through capital imports, but also, like all other trade, through better access to new ideas and state-of-the-art technology. And in practice? Figure 4.16 shows a scatterplot of GNP per capita in 1995 and average foreign direct investment over the period 1970–95. The regression line through the plot indicates a positive relationship between foreign direct investment and income per head. Specifically, an increase in inward foreign direct investment from 0 to 5 per cent of GNP is associated with a doubling of GNP per capita from US$ 800 to US$ 1,600. As always, though, it seems likely that the benefits are mutual, that is, that foreign investment is good for growth and vice versa.

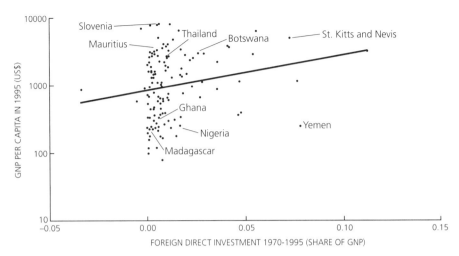

Fig 4.16
**More foreign
investment goes
along with higher
income**

One last point before leaving this case. The argument that tariff distortions reduce efficiency and economic growth applies not only to international trade, but also, *pari passu*, to public finance. Domestic tax distortions—for example, the tax wedges resulting from high marginal income tax rates—entail significant efficiency losses, and thus seem bound to impede economic growth. The similarity goes farther: the welfare gain from removing a tax distortion is proportional to the square of the initial distortion, a well-known result in welfare economics.[47] The square of the distortion enters the formula because the welfare gain is measured by an area enclosed by a right triangle whose short sides are both proportional to the tax rate.

Case 2: Stabilization

We can approach inflation in much the same way as we did trade restrictions in Case 1, because inflation, especially when it is rapid or variable, also creates economic distortions, at least in production (and perhaps in consumption as well, as we will see). This perspective provides a convenient starting point.

Consider a country whose producers use two types of capital, real capital and financial capital, i.e. money. We have encountered real capital before: by this is meant machinery, equipment, factories, and such. Financial capital, on the other hand, is essentially cash, which is useful to have on hand in order to keep production going smoothly. You can think of a farmer who borrows money in a bank at the beginning of the production period to purchase fertilizer and other inputs, and then repays the bank at the end of the period, when the harvest is in. Or you can think of a farmer who needs to have cash on hand in order to buy spare parts or fuel for his tractor—his real capital!—to keep it in running order.

Inflation punishes the producer for keeping cash because its value erodes as prices rise, while the value of the tractor and other real capital is basically immune to inflation. Therefore, inflation tends to distort the farmer's use of inputs: he is tempted to replace financial capital by real capital in order to protect himself against inflation. But this has a cost. If the farmer has too little cash on hand, he may lack the funds needed to replace broken parts of his tractors or even to buy fuel. This is probably part of the reason why idle tractors sometimes litter the landscape in high-inflation countries. And this creates inefficiency, which impedes economic growth.

Figure 4.17 illustrates the point. The initial equilibrium point of the typical profit-maximizing producer is E, which is where the price line EH touches the isoquant connecting E and G. The isoquant, by definition, shows how a given quantity of output can be made from different combinations of real capital on the vertical axis and financial capital on the horizontal axis; hence the name. The slope of EH reflects a price ratio of sorts, that is, the price of financial capital relative to that of real capital, and can be measured by one plus the rate of inflation.[48] The higher the inflation rate, the steeper is the price line and the farther to the north-west along the original iso-quant lies the original equilibrium point E, indicating that financial capital is being replaced by real capital.

Suppose the government now eliminates inflation. This changes the factor price ratio to one-to-one, as shown by the 45° line DEFB. Price stability makes it profitable for producers to increase their cash holdings from E to F, which enables them to re-duce their use of real capital accordingly, and move onto a higher isoquant, which touches the new price line at F. Total output is now OB along the horizontal axis in the figure, compared with OA before, as can be seen by noticing that the points E and G are on the same isoquant, which represents initial output, before inflation was stamped out.

You may now realize that you have seen this before, for this is virtually the same story as the earlier one about liberalization (Figure 4.12), except the names of the variables have been changed.[49] The inflation distortion is shown by the angle be-tween the new price line and the old one in Figure 4.17. The output gain from eco-nomic stabilization, which is measured in units of financial capital by the bold segment AB on the horizontal axis, turns out to be directly proportional to the square of the inflation distortion, just as in the case of the trade distortion.[50] It is the same story.

And so, by increasing the amount of output produced by a given bundle of inputs,

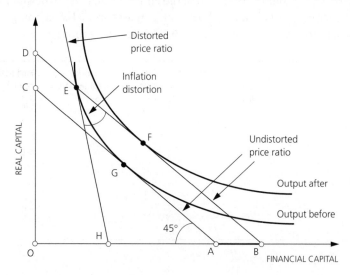

Fig 4.17
Stabilization increases economic efficiency

represented by the original equilibrium point E in Figure 4.17, stabilization increases economic efficiency and thereby also economic growth. Notice, however, that less inflation mean less inflation tax revenue to the government. If the revenue shortfall is met by cuts in wasteful spending, the efficiency gains from stabilization will be greater still. But if the government chooses to meet the inflation tax revenue shortfall by increasing other taxes, such as the income tax or the value added tax, then one tax distortion is being replaced by another, presumably smaller one—smaller because high inflation is a particularly blunt and inefficient method of taxation.[51] Notice, further, that the use of money as an input in production the way we have described it gives rise to an inverse relationship between the real rate of interest and the rate of inflation. Increased inflation induces firms to switch from money to real capital, which reduces the marginal product of capital and hence also the real rate of interest. This effect is frequently compounded by capital market imperfections, which decrease real interest further, sometimes far below zero, in the wake of increased inflation.

Empirical evidence

How large are these effects? Table 4.3 shows the proportional increase in output resulting from the elimination of inflation, when (a) inflation was initially 20, 50, 100, or 200 per cent per year and (b) the ratio of financial to real capital is 0.11, 0.25, 0.5, or 1.0, after the inflation has been stopped.[52] For example, bringing inflation down from 50 per cent a year to zero increases GNP by 1.5 to 4 per cent once and for all, depending on the ratio of financial to real capital, when inflation is zero. The more money is used in production and the more severe the initial inflation problem, the larger will be the output gain from eliminating inflation.

The numbers shown in Table 4.3 are smaller than those in Table 4.1, but, even so, they are not trivial. Think of it this way. During 1990–95, 27 countries had annual inflation of more than 50 per cent per year, and 49 countries had inflation of more than 20 per cent per year.[53] If stabilization can be expected to increase GNP permanently by 1–2 per cent, to take the lowest (and probably also the most plausible) figures in the table, it is almost surely worth the effort. An increase in output for given inputs, and thereby in efficiency, by 2 per cent increases annual economic growth by 0.4 percentage points, if the saving rate is 0.2 (because 0.02 times 0.2 is 0.004), other things

Table 4.3 **Static output gains from stabilization (%)**	Financial/real capital ratio = 0.11	Financial/real capital ratio = 0.25	Financial/real capital ratio = 0.5	Financial/real capital ratio = 1.0
20% inflation	0.8	1.3	1.9	2.1
50% inflation	1.5	2.7	3.7	4.2
100% inflation	2.2	4.0	5.6	6.2
200% inflation	3.0	5.3	7.4	8.3

Source: Author's computations based on eqs. (10) and (12) in Appendix 4.2.

being equal. This increase in growth will, in 30 years, lift the level of GNP per capita by 12.5 per cent above the level it would otherwise attain, other things being the same. And 12.5 per cent of any country's GNP is a large number.

What is the empirical evidence on inflation and growth? Table 4.4 reviews the results of ten recent econometric studies by showing their prediction of the effect of (almost) eliminating 50 per cent annual inflation on growth. These studies are based on large samples of countries, either cross-sections, where each country is represented by a single pair of observations on inflation and growth (and other relevant variables), or panel data, where each country is represented by several observations for different subperiods (typically of 5 or 10 years). The general conclusion from these studies is that a 45-point drop in inflation from 50 per cent to 5 per cent a year increases the rate of growth of output per capita by 1–2 percentage points. These numbers are higher than those deduced from Table 4.3 in the preceding paragraph, because those estimates were confined to the cost of inflation as a production distortion. But inflation may have other effects as well—on consumption and saving, for example. Experience thus seems to indicate that high inflation hurts growth, but where the threshold between high and low inflation lies in this context—at 40 per cent per year? 20 per cent? 10 per cent?—is not yet known.[54]

Figure 4.18 conveys a similar impression as Table 4.4. In the figure, GNP per capita in 1995 is on the vertical axis and the average inflation distortion, defined as the inflation rate divided by one plus the inflation rate, in 1970–95 is on the horizontal axis.[55] The inflation distortion index lies between 0 (when inflation is zero) and 1

	No. of countries	Period	Data	Effect on growth (%)
Fischer (1991)	73	1970–85	Cross-section	2.1
Gylfason (1991)	37	1980–85	Cross-section	2.0
Roubini and Sala-i-Martin (1992)	98	1960–85	Cross-section	2.2
De Gregorio (1993)	12	1950–85	Cross-section	0.7
Fischer (1993)	80	1960–89	Cross-section	1.8
Barro (1995)	100	1960–90	Cross-section	1.0–1.5
Gylfason and Herbertsson (1996)	145–170	1960–92	Panel data	0.6–1.3
Barro (1997)	80–87	1960–90	Panel data	1.3–1.8
Bruno and Easterly (1998)	97	1961–92	Panel data	1.2
Gylfason (1999)	160	1985–94	Cross-section	2.4

Table 4.4
The effect on economic growth per capita of a decrease in inflation from 50% to 5% per year

Sources: Robert J. Barro, 'Inflation and Economic Growth', Bank of England *Quarterly Bulletin*, May 1995: 166–76; Robert J. Barro, *Determinants of Economic Growth*, MIT Press, Mass., 1997; Michael Bruno and William Easterly, 'Inflation Crises and Long-Run Growth', *Journal of Monetary Economics* 41/1 (1998): 3–26; Julio De Gregorio, 'The Effects of Inflation on Economic Growth: Lessons from Latin America', *European Economic Review* 36/2 (1992): 417–25; Stanley Fischer, 'Growth, Macroeconomics, and Development', NBER *Macroeconomics Annual* 1991: 329–64; Stanley Fischer, 'The Role of Macroeconomic Factors in Growth', *Journal of Monetary Economics* 32/4 (1993): 485–512; Thorvaldur Gylfason, 'Inflation, Growth, and External Debt: A View of the Landscape', *World Economy* 14/3 (1991): 279–98; Thorvaldur Gylfason and Tryggvi Thor Herbertsson, 'Does Inflation Matter for Growth?', CEPR Discussion Paper 1503, 1996; Thorvaldur Gylfason, 'Exports, Inflation, and Growth', *World Development* 27 (1999); and Nouriel Roubini and Xavier Sala-i-Martin, 'Financial Repression and Economic Growth', *Journal of Development Economics* 39/1 (1992): 5–30.

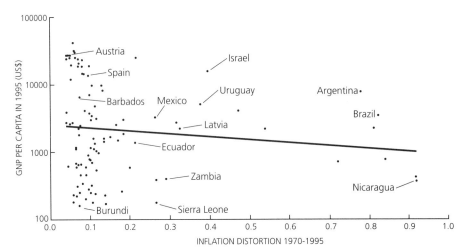

Fig 4.18
More inflation goes along with lower income

(when inflation is infinite). This is, in this context, probably a better measure of the cost of inflation than the inflation rate itself. Suppose inflation drops by 45 percentage points. Then it will most likely matter whether we are dealing with a reduction from 545 to 500 per cent a year or from 50 to 5 per cent, for in the latter case we are likely to see a more positive effect on economic growth. In percentage terms, you see, the first drop in inflation (from 545 to 500) is one of 8 per cent and the second (from 50 to 5) is 90 per cent.

The regression line through the scatterplot in Figure 4.18 is significantly negatively sloped, which confirms our impression of an inverse relationship between inflation and growth. This result depends on the inclusion of high-inflation countries in our sample. Specifically, a decrease in inflation from 50 per cent a year to 5 per cent, which means that the inflation distortion decreases from 0.333 to 0.048, is associated with an increase in GNP per head by a third, or from US$ 1,800 to US$ 2,400. Once again, however, we cannot be sure of the direction of the causal relationship involved. It is quite possible that slow growth tends to increase inflation and also that low-income countries, which are the majority of the countries in the sample, have characteristics—e.g. immature financial markets—which are in themselves conducive to both slow growth and high inflation. We will return briefly to both of these points a little later in this section.

A simple model of inflation and growth

Let us now take a closer look at the linkages between inflation and growth. Figure 4.19 shows two lines. The M line reflects the quantity theory of money, according to which the rate of monetary expansion is equal to the sum of the rates of price inflation and output growth (if the velocity of money is constant), so that the M line has a slope of -1. This means that, for a given rate of monetary expansion, inflation and growth are inversely related, without there being any presumption that inflation causes growth or the other way round. Monetary expansion, in its turn, depends on various factors; let us focus here on the government budget deficit. An increase in the deficit increases the rate of monetary expansion to the extent that the deficit is financed by printing money rather than by issuing bonds, so that the M line shifts up

Fig 4.19
Simultaneous determination of inflation and economic growth

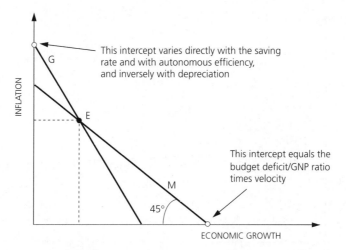

This intercept varies directly with the saving rate and with autonomous efficiency, and inversely with depreciation

This intercept equals the budget deficit/GNP ratio times velocity

and to the right. An increase in velocity, by reducing the amount of money that is necessary to sustain a given level of nominal income by the quantity theory, also shifts the M line up and to the right.

The G line reflects the relationship between economic growth and inflation through efficiency. The G line slopes down because, as we have argued, increased inflation reduces efficiency and thereby also growth, and we assume it to be steeper than the M line.[56] An increase in the saving rate or in variables other than inflation that increase efficiency shifts the G line upwards and to the right.

Alternatively, we can have a downward-sloping G schedule without viewing inflation as a production distortion if we view it as a potential consumption distortion instead. Suppose increased inflation reduces the real rate of interest, thereby weakening the incentive to save. Then the saving rate may decrease and drag down with it the rate of economic growth for given efficiency. Whether this is likely to occur in practice or not is a controversial issue, because the empirical evidence of a direct relationship between the saving rate and the real rate of interest is mixed. And it is not surprising that it is mixed, because saving is a major source of the financing of investment, and investment is inversely related to real interest rates through the opportunity cost of capital. This is a classic case of the so-called identification problem in econometrics: the problem is to identify a positive relationship between saving and real interest and a negative one between investment and real interest, even if saving and investment are closely related, and sometimes even hardly distinguishable, in the data.

Figure 4.20 illustrates the ambiguity involved. It shows the average saving rate from 1970 to 1995 on the vertical axis and the average inflation distortion over the same period on the horizontal axis. The regression line through the scatterplot is nearly flat. Yet, it hints that a slowdown in inflation from 50 to 5 per cent per year will increase the saving rate from 17 to almost 19 per cent, but the effect is not significant in a statistical sense.

Enough of this. Let us now experiment. First, an increase in the budget deficit shifts the M line up and to the right, so that inflation increases and economic growth decreases from E to F in Figure 4.21. The increase in the deficit reduces growth because it increases inflation.

Fig 4.20
Inflation and saving: Weak connection

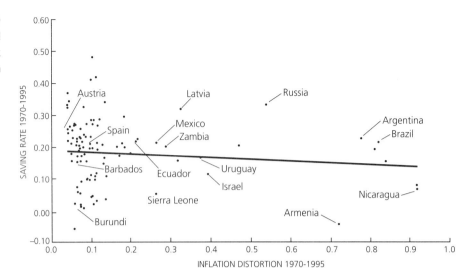

Fig 4.21
An increase in the government budget deficit or in velocity increases inflation and reduces economic growth

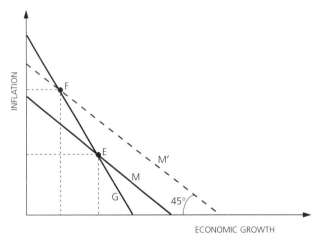

Second, an increase in velocity (i.e. a reduction in the demand for money) also shifts the M line up and to the right, so that inflation goes up and growth goes down from E to F in Figure 4.21, which covers this case as well. Why does velocity increase? One reason may be that inflation has increased, and inflation reflects the cost of holding money. When this cost increases, people and firms flee from money into real estate, foreign currency, indexed bonds, and what have you, in order to protect themselves against the inflation. This is an example of how inflation can increase of itself, and sometimes spin out of control.

Third, suppose there is an autonomous increase in efficiency, for example through trade liberalization, as in Case 1. Then the G line shifts upwards and to the right, so that the economy moves from E to F in Figure 4.22. Economic growth increases, as we saw in the preceding section, and inflation decreases, a new result. Now we see that increased efficiency through liberalization and other means is not only good for growth, but tends to reduce inflation as well. This is hardly surprising: liberalization boosts the supply side of the economy and should be expected to stem inflation accordingly.

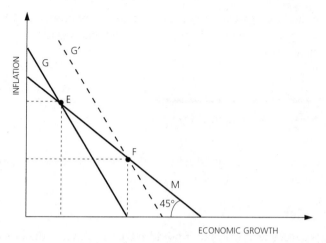

Fig 4.22
An increase in the saving rate or in autonomous efficiency or a decrease in depreciation increases economic growth and reduces inflation

Fourth, consider an increase in the saving rate. The G line shifts up and to the right (Figure 4.22 again), so that growth increases and inflation decreases. A decrease in depreciation has the same effect.

The above account may shed light on the following phenomenon. Several writers have found that their econometric cross-country growth equations could be improved by adding a dummy variable for Africa, without attempting to explain what is it about Africa that makes it so. Others have suggested that a weak private sector, an excessive reliance on natural resources, and geography (essentially heat and distance from navigable rivers and the sea) may have something to do with it, as we will discuss in subsequent sections, in addition to the various factors that tend to perpetuate poverty, as we discussed earlier in the chapter. Here we pause only to point out that, as a whole, the countries of Sub-Saharan Africa have, since independence, been characterized by high inflation and slow growth. In 1990–95, for example, average inflation and economic growth (of GDP per capita) were 47 and 1.4 per cent in Sub-Saharan Africa compared with 2.4 and 2.0 per cent in the high-income countries. In 1980–90, we see the same pattern: inflation and growth were 19 and 1.7 per cent in Africa and 4.8 and 3.2 per cent in the high-income countries.[57]

Why has Africa been so inflation-prone? One reason may be immature financial markets, which have biased the financing of fiscal deficits towards printing money (i.e. borrowing from the banking system) rather than issuing bonds (i.e. borrowing from the public), which is a less inflationary financing method. Financial immaturity and fragile banking may also, by reducing overall economic efficiency, have contributed directly to slow growth in Africa.[58] Further, Sub-Saharan African economies are more closed than the world economy at large: their openness index, as defined above, was −8.5 in 1994 on average compared with 0.2 for the world as a whole. This means that the average Sub-Saharan country's ratio of exports to GNP was about 8.5 percentage points less than its size would seem to warrant. Less openness means less economic growth and more inflation, other things being equal.

One last point about inflation. Conceivably, it is not necessarily inflation in itself, through its tendency to distort firms' choices between real and financial capital and households' choices between consumption and saving, that impedes economic efficiency and growth. Rather, or simultaneously, perhaps, it could be that inflation is a common denominator for imperfect institutions (e.g. fragile banks and financial markets), unsound policies (e.g. persistent government budget deficits), and other factors (e.g. political upheaval and ethnic strife) that together help undermine economic efficiency and growth.

Case 3: Privatization

Our next case is completely different, and yet the same, once more, so that we can go through it more quickly than the ones before.

Reallocation

Consider a place where output is produced in two ways, in the private sector and in the public sector, including state-owned enterprises. Private and public output are the same, but they differ in quality. Suppose private output is better and, therefore, commands a higher price than public output. The production frontier DEFG in Figure 4.23 shows the different combinations of public and private output that are consistent with full use of the country's given resources. If private output is taxed and public output is subsidized, then the relative price of the two is distorted in favour of the public sector, so that more public output is produced and less private output than would be the case without the taxes and subsidies. Production thus takes place at E, where the distorted price line touches the production frontier. Public output is shown by OH and private output by ON.

Suppose now that the taxes and subsidies are rescinded. The undistorted price ratio, which is 1, is shown by the steeper price line EA in Figure 4.23. In response to the policy change, resources are transferred from the public sector to the private sector—through privatization, for example—and production moves from E to F, where the new, undistorted price line just touches the production frontier. Total output increases by AB, that is, from OA to OB. The output gain is once again proportional to the square of the initial price distortion, which is shown by the angle between the two price lines in the figure.[59] This is the reallocation effect, to which we can add the

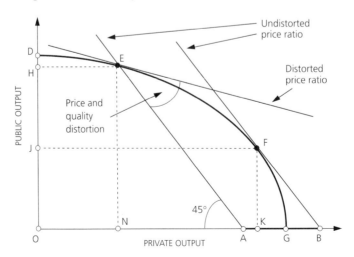

effect of reorganization, if the privatization improves efficiency in the private sector or the public sector or both, so that the production frontier shifts out.

Reorganization

Suppose productivity increases in the private sector. Then the production possibility frontier shifts outwards from DEFG to DLM as shown in Figure 4.24. Production moves from F to L. The total output gain is AC, that is, the reallocation gain AB plus the reorganization gain BC. The argument is analogous to the one behind Figure 4.14.

Numbers

How large are the efficiency gains from privatization? Table 4.5 suggests some hypothetical answers.

Let taxes and subsidies initially drive a wedge ranging from 100 to 400 per cent between the prices of private and public output. Further, let us assume the share of the private sector in total output following privatization to range from 50 to 90 per cent.[60] The table shows that the output gains are an increasing function of the magnitude of the initial distortion and of the size of the private sector at the end of the day, and range from 7 to 71 per cent of initial output. The calculation underlying the numbers in Table 4.5 is of necessity a highly tentative exercise, even more so than in Table 4.1, because the quality and price differential is unobservable. Table 4.5 is merely meant to serve as an illustration of the possibilities involved.

The empirical evidence on the links between private vs. public ownership and economic growth has hardly begun to be dug up. Figure 4.25 suggests that it may be worth digging. It shows GNP per capita in 1995 on the vertical axis and the average share of state-owned enterprises in employment from 1970 to 1995 on the horizontal axis. The regression line through the scatterplot has a significantly negative slope. When the share of state-owned enterprises in employment increases from 10 to 20 per cent, GNP per capita decreases from US$ 1,100 to US$ 800. This impression seems to receive some support from recent attempts to quantify the effects of privatization on economic growth.[61]

Fig 4.24
Privatization increases economic efficiency: The reorganization effect

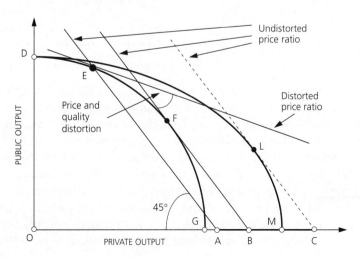

Table 4.5 **Static output gains: The proportional once-and-for-all increase in total output resulting from privatization (%)**

Panel A. Gains from reallocation

No gain from reorganization	Private-sector share = 0.5	Private-sector share = 0.7	Private-sector share = 0.9
100% differential	7	10	13
200% differential	13	18	25
300% differential	16	25	34
400% differential	19	29	40

Panel B. Gains from reallocation and reorganization

Productivity rises by 90% of differential	Private-sector share = 0.5	Private-sector share = 0.7	Private-sector share = 0.9
100% differential	18	27	37
200% differential	25	39	56
300% differential	28	45	66
400% differential	30	48	71

Source: Author's computations based on eqs. (12) and (15) in Appendix 4.3, with k = 0.0 in Panel A and k = 0.9 in Panel B. A 100 per cent differential means that q = 1 in eq. (1) in Appendix 4.3.

Fig 4.25 **More state enterprise goes along with less income**

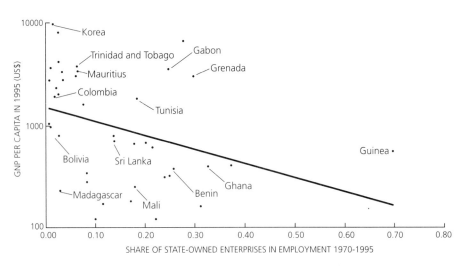

Private vs. public ownership of the means of production is one thing, and the size of the public sector is another. In general, it is not possible to state that small government is good for growth, neither in theory nor practice. There are cases, it is true, where the tax burden has become so heavy as to constitute a probable threat to overall economic efficiency and growth. Sweden seems to be a fairly clear case in point, even if it is impossible to point to unequivocal, irrefutable econometric evidence, let alone proof, in support of this commonly held, but controversial, view.[62] There are other places—Haiti is an extreme case!—where the provision of public services is clearly inadequate. The point is that it makes a great deal of difference what the government does with the tax revenue it raises. If it builds bunkers like Enver Hoxha, high taxes will stifle growth. This view is to some extent corroborated by studies reporting an inverse relationship between economic growth and government spending on things other than defence and education.[63] On the other hand, high taxes may well be good for growth, if the government spends its tax revenue wisely and well, for example on health and education, to which we now turn.[64]

Case 4: Education, health, and distribution

The case for a close connection between education and economic growth was clear already to Adam Smith and his followers, including John Stuart Mill and Alfred Marshall, as we saw in Chapter 2. Mill, for one, while believing that 'Laisser-faire . . . should be the general practice: every departure from it, unless required by some great good, is a certain evil',[65] favoured compulsory school attendance for children against parental opposition, and he lived to see the legislation of the Education Act of 1870, which established compulsory, government-financed elementary schools in England. To Mill, this was an obvious economic and social necessity.

What is the evidence?

Since the early 1990s, as we have already mentioned, numerous empirical studies have sought to identify the major determinants of economic growth based on an econometric scrutiny of the new international data banks that became available in the late 1980s. This literature is succinctly summarized by Robert Barro and Xavier Sala-i-Martin in their excellent book *Economic Growth* (1995).[66] While many variables have been found to affect growth significantly in a few studies, and the list is quite long, only a few variables have been confirmed, in study after study, to be economically and statistically significant and robust determinants of growth.[67] One study of the robustness of these empirical findings concluded that only initial income per head and the saving rate showed up consistently enough as significant determinants of growth to merit inclusion in this robust category.[68] However, some have warned that too stringent criteria for robustness may block our vision, and argued that more variables deserve to be regarded as robust determinants of growth.[69]

The problem here is this. Because economic efficiency is unobservable, it needs to be represented by its proximate determinants in empirical studies, and the potential determinants of efficiency are virtually countless. To complicate matters further, several of the determinants of efficiency are themselves unobservable—education is a case in point—and, moreover, tend to be closely interrelated, so that their effects on growth can be difficult to distinguish by econometric methods. For example, if inflation (Case 2) tends to be high in countries with restrictive foreign trade regimes (Case 1) and in countries with a preponderance of inefficient state-owned enterprises (Case 3), then the separate contributions of the three factors to economic growth can be difficult to identify, let alone disentangle, in practice. One can, therefore, never be quite sure whether the explanatory variables that are suggested as significant determinants of economic growth belong in the regression as explanations in their own right or represent some other excluded factors. This even applies to the saving rate, which, according to the theory of optimal saving, is an endogenous variable, which depends on many of the same factors as economic growth itself.[70] For this reason, some researchers prefer to leave the saving rate out of their growth regressions.[71] Others prefer to include the saving rate. When they do, they typically find that an increase in the saving (i.e. investment) rate from 20 to 30 per cent from one country or time to another increases the annual rate of economic growth per capita by 1 or 2 percentage points, other things being equal.

Among the explanatory variables most often included in empirical growth studies are various proxies for educational attainment, based on years of schooling, school enrolment rates, or government expenditure on education. Those are imperfect proxies, because they are meant to measure output by input: no account is taken of the quality of an education attained at school. The general impression conveyed by the empirical literature is that more years of secondary and higher education for males are good for growth, while economically and statistically significant effects on growth of primary education for either sex, of female education at any level, or of government spending on education cannot be established. The weakness of these results, however, probably says more about the poor quality of the proxies used for education in these studies than it does about the significance of the underlying relationship between education and economic growth.

All this notwithstanding, the idea that education must be good for growth and vice versa rhymes well with Figure 4.11, which we encountered earlier in the chapter in connection with poverty traps; Figure 4.11 indicates a direct association between GNP per capita and primary-school enrolment. The same message emerges more clearly in Figure 4.26, which shows a scatterplot of secondary-school enrolment rates for both sexes on the vertical axis and GNP per capita on the horizontal axis. The figure shows a clear tendency for more secondary-school attendance to go along with higher income per capita. Specifically, along the regression line shown an increase in the secondary-school enrolment rate from 40 to 80 per cent goes hand in hand with an increase in income per head from US$ 500 to US$ 7,000. One well-known study interpreted secondary-school enrolment as a proxy for the stock of human capital and concluded from a traditional growth-accounting exercise that labour, physical capital, and human capital contribute about one-third each to the rate of economic growth in a large sample of countries.[72]

Fig 4.26
Secondary-school enrolment varies directly with income

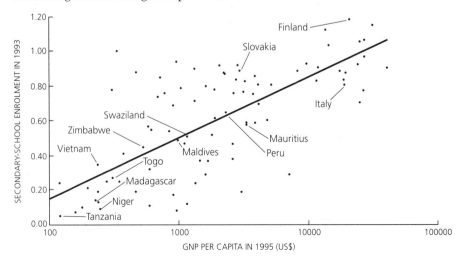

The human-capital interpretation of the relationship between education and economic growth calls for the consideration of other factors that seem likely to help increase or improve the stock of human capital, not least health. Taking life expectancy as a proxy for national health, several studies have reported a significant effect of longer lives on economic growth. Figure 4.27 makes a similar point. It shows that an increase in life expectancy at birth from 60 years (the 1995 figure for Bolivia, for example) to 80 years (the 1995 figure for Japan, a world record)[73] is associated with an increase in GNP per capita by a factor of 12, or from US$ 900 to US$ 10,700. Thus, good health and longevity are no doubt good for growth and vice versa.

At least one further aspect of human capital calls for our attention, that is, equality in the distribution of income and wealth. In Chapter 2, we heard Alfred Marshall say that 'human faculties are as important a means of production as any other kind of capital; and . . . any change in the distribution of wealth which gives more to the wage receivers and less to the capitalists is likely, other things being equal, to hasten the increase of material production'. In Marshall's opinion, 'well distributed' wealth was good for growth through human capital, among other things. Increased public and private commitment to education around the world has almost surely increased both equality and growth. In our times and earlier, gross inequality has tended to be associated with social and economic conflict, which seems likely to impede economic efficiency and growth.[74]

On the other hand, some observers seem to be under the impression that the rapid economic growth of the East Asian countries since 1965 was achieved at the expense of equality and that quick economic growth, more generally speaking, somehow constitutes an impediment to economic and social equality. Available statistics do not permit us to make comparisons between measures of inequality in East Asia at present and in the past. Even so, the available empirical evidence seems to show that the distribution of income or consumption in Hong Kong, Indonesia, the Philippines, Singapore, and Thailand is no less equitable than in, say, the United Kingdom and the United States.[75]

Table 4.6 shows the ratio of the income or consumption of the top quintile of the income distribution to those of the bottom quintile (the 20/20 ratio) in selected countries. This measure of inequality is available for more countries than the more

Fig 4.27
Longer lives go along with higher income

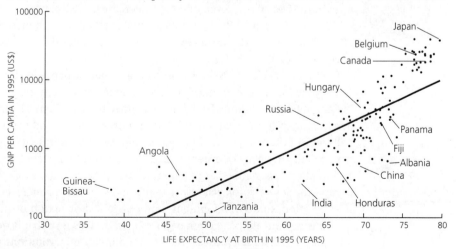

Table 4.6
The 20/20 ratio and
the Gini index of
inequality in
selected countries

	20/20 ratio	Gini index
Sweden	4.6	n/a
Indonesia	4.7	31.7
India	5.0	33.8
Germany	5.8	n/a
Denmark	7.1	n/a
Philippines	7.4	40.7
China	8.6	41.5
Hong Kong	8.7	n/a
United States	8.9	n/a
Thailand	9.4	46.2
Singapore	9.6	n/a
United Kingdom	9.6	n/a
Malaysia	11.7	48.4
Mexico	13.5	50.3
Russia	14.5	49.6
Kenya	18.3	57.5
Brazil	32.1	63.4

n/a = not available

Source: World Bank, World Development Indicators 1997, OUP,
Oxford, 1997, table 2.6. The indices are based on surveys
taken in the late 1980s or early 1990s.

comprehensive and more widely used Gini index, which, where available, is also shown in the table for comparison. The two measures of inequality are closely correlated, as the table shows.

Figures 4.28 and 4.29 show scatterplots of GNP per capita in 1995 on the vertical axes and the two inequality indices on the horizontal axes. Figure 4.28 suggests that income per head is virtually unrelated to inequality as measured by the Gini index. Figure 4.29 suggests a negative, but statistically and economically weak, relationship between income per head and inequality, indicating that an increase in the 20/20 ratio from 10 to 20 is accompanied by a decrease in GNP per capita from US$ 3,500 to US$ 2,500. But even so, the figure shows that most of the high-income countries have 20/20 ratios below 10, far below the extreme inequality observed, say, in Russia, Kenya, or Brazil.

The human-capital perspective on economic performance leads us at last in yet another direction. The economic damage wrought by the reigns of, for example, Pol Pot in Cambodia and Idi Amin in Uganda stemmed to some degree from their deliberate destruction of human capital: while Amin drove many good people into exile, and had some of them killed (including, for example, the president of Makarere University in Kampala), Pol Pot ordered mass executions of suspected middle-class people and intellectuals, defined at one point as people wearing glasses. The ultimate collapse of the Soviet Union was also no doubt aided by inefficiencies created by a severe misallocation, underdevelopment, and outright destruction of human capital before, during, and after the reign of Joseph Stalin. This is probably one of the reasons why political instability, measured by the number of revolutions per year and the

Fig 4.28
Income and inequality (Gini index)

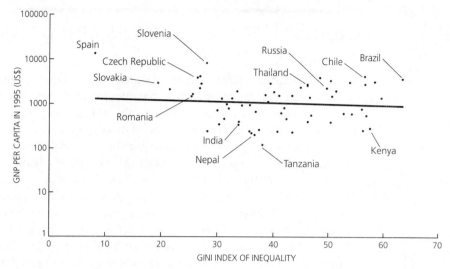

Fig 4.29
Income and inequality (20/20 ratio)

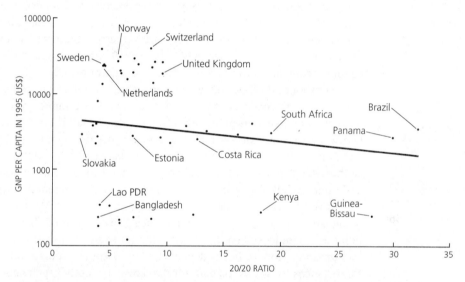

number of political assassinations per million inhabitants, has been reported in some studies to be detrimental to economic growth. Another interpretation of this result is that political instability is a threat to private property rights, and reduces the incentives to save and invest. A third possibility is that slow growth breeds political discontent, which may even result in revolution and bloodshed. In any case, this idea of a relationship between revolution and growth was accepted by economists all the way from Adam Smith to Arthur Lewis, who stressed the importance of political stability—and rainfall, which brings us to our fifth and last case.[76]

Case 5: Natural resources and geography

As you will recall from Chapter 1, Adam Smith suggested that a country's progress of wealth, which was his way of saying economic growth, depends on 'the nature of its soil, climate, and situation', among many other things.[77] Recently, Jeffrey Sachs and his associates and others have investigated this hypothesis by exploring the effects of geographical variables on economic growth across countries.[78] They have used variables such as natural resource abundance, the ratio of coastline distance to land area, and whether the country in question is tropical or landlocked. One measure that has proved useful is a country's distance from the equator. It turns out that these variables make a difference. They do not necessarily compete with the main determinants of growth that we have discussed thus far, because most of them remain significant when the geographical variables have been added. Rather, the main contribution of the geographical variables is to increase the explanatory power of the growth regressions. While the R^2 in regressions without geographical variables is typically in the vicinity of 0.5 or 0.6,[79] suggesting that the equations in question explain about 50 or 60 per cent of the observed cross-country variation in economic growth, the adjusted R^2 increases to 0.8 or 0.9, when geography is taken into account.[80] Adam Smith would probably have been impressed.

The upshot of this research is that geography matters. First, being situated in the tropics tends to reduce a country's annual rate of economic growth per capita by more than 1 percentage point, other things being equal. The main problem seems to be the sweltering heat. With few exceptions (among them Hong Kong, Mauritius, and Singapore), tropical countries are poor. Malaria, a debilitating disease, is concentrated in the tropics. One study reports that 'Iceland, Finland, Norway, Sweden, and Denmark all receive more than a 145 per cent increment in output per worker due to their location, relative to the median country of Mozambique.'[81] Second, being landlocked similarly tends to reduce growth by more than half a percentage point. Few landlocked countries are rich, but some are (Austria, Luxembourg, and Switzerland). Third, a heavy dependence on natural resources (oil, minerals, fish, forests, etc.) also seems to be harmful to growth, whether such dependence is measured by the share of the primary sector in the labour force, in total exports, or in GNP.[82] A typical result is that an increase in the share of primary exports in total exports by 25 percentage points reduces annual per capita growth by 1 percentage point, other things being equal.

This tendency is illustrated in Figure 4.30, which shows GNP per capita in 1995 on the vertical axis and the share of primary exports in total exports of merchandise in 1995 on the horizontal axis. The regression line through the scatterplot slopes down, and indicates that an increase in the primary export share from, say, 20 to 60 per cent is accompanied by a decrease in GNP per head from US$ 8,200 to US$ 2,400.

We can think of at least three possible reasons for the observed inverse relationship between natural resource abundance and economic performance or growth. First, natural resources have long had a tendency to be poorly managed. Overfishing and declining or even collapsing stocks of marine species around the world are one example of this.[83] The prevalence of inefficient state enterprises in primary indus-

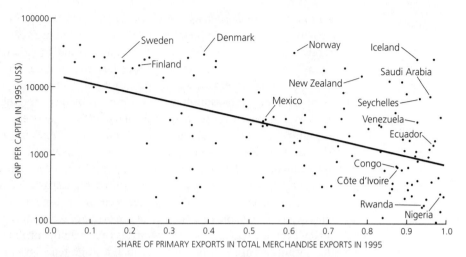

Fig 4.30
**More primary
exports go along
with less income**

tries and of government-run export marketing boards in parts of Africa and else-where is another case in point. Countries that are rich in natural resources tend to fall prey to excessive rent-seeking, whereby powerful special interests in and around the primary sector try to sway political decisions in their favour, which, sometimes even deliberately, may lead to the neglect of or discrimination against non-primary economic activity and exports.[84]

In second place, a natural resource boom tends to drive up the value of the do-mestic currency in real terms, thereby reducing the profitability of non-primary ex-ports, without a compensating real exchange-rate correction when the boom subsides. This is the so-called Dutch disease, which derives its name from the after-math of the natural gas discoveries by the Netherlands in the 1960s. The expansion of primary exports tends to discourage non-primary exports and even total exports and imports and hence also economic growth, if previously profitable non-primary products and services no longer can compete in world markets at the equilibrium (i.e. market-determined) real exchange rate after the boom. The Dutch disease is something of a misnomer, however. In the Netherlands, the share of exports in GDP increased from 43 per cent in 1970 to 53 per cent in 1995. The Netherlands are thus a wide-open economy, with an openness index of 19 in Figure 4.15. Norway discov-ered huge oil deposits in the North Sea in the 1970s, making it the second largest oil exporter in the world (after Saudi Arabia). Since then, Norway's export ratio has been stagnant, or worse: from 1970 to 1995, it fell from 42 per cent to 38 per cent.[85] Nor-way's oil exports have thus displaced non-oil exports krone for krone. Norway is only a moderately open economy: its openness index in Figure 4.15 is 4. Iceland is an even clearer case. With a little over a half of its export earnings from goods and services and about one-sixth of its GDP derived from fish, its export ratio has hovered around one-third since 1945, giving Iceland an openness index of −22, a value shared with Burkina Faso, Burundi, Niger, and Sierra Leone, all of which also rely heavily on pri-mary exports. Occasional references to pound sterling as a petrocurrency are an-other side of the same coin.

Third, there is a tendency for heavy reliance on natural-resource-based economic activity, including agriculture, fishing, forestry, and mining, to be associated across countries not only with low levels of saving and investment, but also with low levels of education. This can be seen by comparing Figure 4.26, which shows a direct relationship between secondary education and income, and Figure 4.30, which shows an inverse relationship between primary exports and income. Together, the two figures imply an inverse relationship between secondary education and primary exports. This suggests that an abundance of natural resources and a corresponding preponderance of primary production may inhibit growth by discouraging investment in human as well as physical capital. The primary sector may need—and also generate—less human capital than manufacturing and services. Agriculture in developing countries, in particular, does generally not make intensive use of highly qualified manpower and high technology that confer significant external benefits on other industries. For these reasons, some countries with a comparative advantage in primary production may experience less economic growth, other things being equal. In some cases, it is even conceivable that the size of the primary sector may give a better picture of the level of education across countries than school enrolment rates, which measure output by input. In other cases, such as high-tech agriculture or mining, natural resource abundance may help rather than hurt growth by benefiting education, among other things.

Before natural resources and geography entered into empirical growth studies, a dummy variable for Africa was frequently found to be a significant determinant of growth, as we mentioned earlier in this chapter. Being located in Africa was bad news from the point of view of growth, it was observed, but why was not well understood. One hypothesis was that Africa's problem is precisely that it is full of African countries, because poor neighbours do not buy enough of your exports. This was a straightforward application of Adam Smith's dictum that 'The wealth of a neighbouring nation . . . is certainly advantageous to trade', which we cited in Chapter 2. The inclusion of natural resources and geography in growth regressions tends to undermine the Africa dummy in many cases, which suggests that the dummy may have worked as a proxy for primary exports and related variables in earlier studies.

But even if natural resources and other geographical considerations may provide part of the reason for sluggish economic growth in Africa since independence, this does not diminish the importance of economic policy in promoting growth: on the contrary, it should make it even more urgent for African countries to grab every opportunity to promote economic growth and prosperity by stimulating saving, investment, and efficiency through policy reform.

Natural resources and their management matter for economic growth also from another angle. By neglecting their natural environment, some countries have managed to maintain their national incomes temporarily at higher levels than otherwise would have been attainable. In the former Soviet Union, for example, tremendous environmental and, ultimately, economic damage was inflicted by rampant pollution. Partly, the Soviet system of national income accounts was to blame. Expenditures on environmental clean-up were not counted as production, any more than maintenance of dilapidated housing and other infrastructure was counted as production. To build a new house was to produce, but to maintain an old one was not. Quantity was the key; quality didn't count. By thus diverting resources from environmental upkeep to current spending on other things, the flow of national income, or net material product, as it was called, appeared to be larger than it really was. By dumping the cost of cleaning up the environment on future generations (including the upkeep of leaky nuclear power plants all over the place), the current generation was able to extract larger incomes from the country's resources at the expense of its offspring. The near-disappearance of the Aral Sea is a related case. It used to be one of the largest inland seas in the world, 64,000 sq. km. in area. Excessive irrigation from the Aral Sea at the command of politically powerful cotton farmers in Uzbekistan gradually reduced the sea down to a third of its former size, blowing salt and disease across vast expanses of land. One of the largest seaports of the former Soviet Union now lies in the middle of a desert, more than 60 km. away from water.

Economic growth and environmental protection are complementary to one another. A clean environment does not preclude rapid growth. On the contrary, economic growth is necessary for countries to be able to afford a cleaner environment. This is why London, for example, despite all the exhaust from cars, is probably a cleaner city today than it was earlier, when horse-powered carriages were the main mode of transportation.

These examples underline the need for a new measure of national income which is consistent with sustainable management of natural resources. This is what so-called green national income accounting is all about. It involves an attempt to correct current measures of national income flows for changes in the stocks of natural resources. Some fast-growing countries owe part of their rapid growth to the run-down of their resources (or to the accumulation of external debt). In Thailand, for example, almost a half of the tropical forests were cleared in the 1980s. The same applies to the Philippines. Yet, one-quarter of the surface of both countries was still covered by forests in 1990. Haiti holds the world record in deforestation: its forests have virtually disappeared, a unique situation so far away from the asphalt of Singapore and the sands of Sahara. The annual rate of deforestation in Haiti in the 1980s was 5 per cent, compared with 3.5 per cent in Thailand and the Philippines, and 0.3 per cent in the world as a whole.[86]

The point of these examples is this. Economic growth, as it is measured by traditional methods in the national income accounts, isn't everything. Some countries may register artificially inflated economic growth over extended periods by running down their resources and by running up debts. But such growth is not sustainable. Green accounts can be useful not only by setting the economic record straight, but also by sending a timely warning signal to those nations which attempt, often unwittingly, to increase their incomes by squandering their resources, including the natural environment.

The natural environment, however, is not all that counts in environmental affairs. Several empirical studies of economic growth have found that variables reflecting the social and cultural environment also matter for growth. One study stresses the importance of language: speaking a world language, like English, is good for growth.[87] Other studies stress infrastructure and the quality of government institutions, including the absence of corruption, which is also good for growth.[88] Still others would conjecture that flexible labour market institutions of the kind that enabled the East Asian countries to combine rapid growth with low inflation and low unemployment all these years must also in themselves be good for growth. This list could be much longer, of course. You just name it: if it increases efficiency, it is good for growth.

Summary

This chapter has covered a lot of ground with a broad brush. We began with the question of convergence, and argued that there is no presumption in theory or practice that poor countries will automatically catch up with rich ones, even if (a) the club of rich countries seems to grow together and (b) poor countries tend to grow faster than rich ones when every determinant of economic growth other than initial income is held constant. The main point, however, is that economic growth depends on a multitude of factors, many of which are within human reach. Next we discussed some vicious circles which tend to entrap poor countries in continued poverty. If you are living from hand to mouth from day to day, it is easier said than done to sacrifice current consumption for increased saving to create conditions for more rapid growth of national income. It can be expensive to be poor. It is easier to become rich if you are rich already.

We then went on to discuss various ways in which economic policy can be used to foster economic growth. The discussion was organized around five cases: (1) liberalization of prices and trade; (2) stabilization; (3) privatization; (4) education; and (5) natural resources. The underlying problem in the first four of these cases and, in part, even the fifth and last results from—and can, therefore, be corrected by— human action. Free trade, stable prices, private enterprise, a well-educated and healthy labour force, and diversified exports free from the dominance of a few primary products are all conducive to increased economic efficiency and growth. Whether nations grow faster or slower than their neighbours is, therefore, in large measure, but not wholly, a matter of choice, which will be our main theme in the last chapter.

Questions for review

1. Do poor countries generally grow more or less rapidly than affluent ones? Does economic growth theory suggest an answer to this question? Does the answer depend on whether growth is exogenous or endogenous? What is the empirical evidence?

2. The prime minister asks you to draw up a list of policy measures designed to stimulate economic growth. Does it matter much whether the country in question is Jamaica, Japan, or Jordan? If so, how? What information about the country in question do you request before you offer your advice?

3. Suppose international capital flows are severely restricted by law in an attempt to stabilize exchange rates. Would you expect such legislation to affect economic growth? Where? How?

4. Suppose the government decides to lower taxes. What other information do you need in order to be able to determine whether the tax cut is likely to stimulate economic growth or not?

5. 'An increased deficit in the government budget may raise national income in the short run, but it may also retard economic growth in the long run.' Evaluate this statement.

6. 'Natural resource abundance generally tends to increase national income per capita in the resource-rich country, but it may also retard its economic growth.' Does this statement involve a contradiction? Discuss.

Notes

1. George Bernard Shaw, *John Bull's Other Island*, Act 4, 1907.

2. Alfred Marshall, *Principles of Economics,* 8th edn. (Macmillan, London, 1920), 91.

3. The purchasing-power-parity-adjusted GNP per capita in Bangladesh in 1995 was IUS$ 1,380, in Bolivia IUS$ 2,540, and in Burundi IUS$ 630. The unadjusted figures are US$ 240, US$ 800, and US$ 160. See World Bank, *World Development Report 1997* (Oxford University Press, Oxford, 1997), table 1.

4. See Donella H. Meadows, Dennis L. Meadows, Jørgen Randers, and William W. Behrens III, *The Limits to Growth, A Report for the Club of Rome's Project on the Predicament of Mankind*, New American Library, New York, 1972.

5. Robert Solow, also from MIT, wrote a scathing review of the Club-of-Rome report, his main point being that prices and people adjust: when oil seems uncomfortably close to depletion, its price will rise, so that it will be used more sparingly. See Robert M. Solow, 'Is the End of the World at Hand?', *Challenge* (Mar.–Apr. 1973), 39–50.

6. See Marian Radetzki, *Tjugo år efter oljekrisen* (*Twenty Years After the Oil Crisis*) (SNS Förlag, Stockholm, 1995).

7. See Gunnar Myrdal, *Asian Drama: An Inquiry into the Poverty of Nations* (Pantheon, New York, 1968). (Notice the subtitle.)

8. See Assar Lindbeck, *The Swedish Experiment* (SNS Förlag, Stockholm, 1997). See also Thorvaldur Gylfason, Torben M. Andersen, Seppo Honkapohja, Arne J. Isachsen, and John Williamson, *The Swedish Model under Stress: A View from the Stands* (SNS Förlag, Stockholm, 1997).

9. This view was not shared by empirically oriented development economists, however, including Simon Kuznets and Hollis Chenery, as we discussed in Ch. 2, for they were always keenly interested in the patterns of development in different countries and regions.

10. A long history, however, offers no guarantee for good macroeconomic data. The former Soviet Union is itself a case in point. Soviet data were conspicuous by their unreliability and inavailability. The Soviet Union and several of its satellites did not provide information to the main international economic organizations such as the World Bank and the IMF.

11. This group, stationed at the University of Pennsylvania, was led by Irving B. Kravis, Alan W. Heston, and Robert Summers, who made their large, new data set, the so-called Penn World Tables, available on the Internet. See http://www.nber.org/pwt56.html. See also Irving B. Kravis, A. W. Heston, and Robert Summers, 'Real GDP Per Capita for More than One Hundred Countries', *Economic Journal*, 88/2 (1978), 215–42, and Robert Summers and Alan W. Heston, 'The Penn World Table (Mark 5): An Expanded Set of International Comparisons: 1950–1988', *Quarterly Journal of Economics*, 106/2 (1991), 327–68.

12. See references in n. 11.

13. This group overlaps with, but is not identical to, the OECD membership. For example, Greece is not in the high-income group, even if it is a long-standing member of the OECD. For another example, Israel is a high-income country, but not a member of the OECD.

14. This was first pointed out by William J. Baumol, 'Productivity Growth, Convergence, and Welfare', *American Economic Review*, 76/5 (1986), 1072–85, where he reports a strong negative relationship between the growth of income per capita from 1870 to 1979 and the level of income per capita in 1870. See also Steve Dowrick and Duc-Tho Nguyen, 'OECD Comparative Growth, 1950–85: Catch-Up and Convergence', *American Economic Review*, 79/5 (1989), 1010–30, and Robert J. Barro and Xavier Sala-i-Martin, 'Convergence across States and Regions', *Brookings Papers on Economic Activity*, 1 (1991), 107–82, and 'Convergence', *Journal of Political Economy*, 100/2 (1992), 223–51.

15. See Robert J. Barro and Xavier Sala-i-Martin, *Economic Growth*, ch. 11 (McGraw-Hill, New York, 1995).

16. That is, $Y_{1992} = Y_{1970} (1+g)^{22}$, where Y is income and g is the average growth rate.

17. See J. Bradford De Long, 'Productivity Growth, Convergence, and Welfare: Comment', *American Economic Review*, 78/5 (1988), 1138–54.

18. This argument was initially used in an attempt to interpret apparent convergence among industrial countries from 1870 to 1979. The argument appears less convincing when applied to much shorter periods, such as 1970–92. See the reference in n. 17.

19. See eq. (16) in Appendix 2.2.

20. See e.g. Barro and Sala-i-Martin, *Economic Growth*, ch. 12, table 12.3. See also Robert J. Barro, *Determinants of Economic Growth: A Cross-Country Empirical Study* (MIT Press, Cambridge, Mass., and London, 1997), ch. 1.

21. Robert J. Barro, *Determinants of Economic Growth*, 47.

22. See Alan S. Blinder, *Hard Heads, Soft Hearts: Tough-minded Economics for a Just Society* (Addison-Wesley, Reading, Mass., 1987), ch. 5.

23. The theory of optimal saving and growth conveys the same message: our formulae for the optimal saving rate in Appendix 3.3 (eqs. (17)–(19)) show no sign of a systematic relationship between the saving rate and the level of national income.

24. In what remains of this chapter, GNP is measured by the World Bank's Atlas method, which is designed to reduce the bias created by over- or undervalued domestic currencies. This measure of GNP shows a larger variation in incomes per capita across countries than the purchasing-power-parity-adjusted measure, but smaller than the standard measure, which is based on current exchange rates, over- or undervalued as the currencies in question may be in many cases.

25. On the merits of measuring economic performance by current GNP rather than by average economic growth since, say, 1960 or 1970, see Robert E. Hall and Charles I. Jones, 'Levels of Economic Activity across Countries', *American Economic Review*, 87/2 (1997), 173–7, and 'The Productivity of Nations', NBER Working Paper 5812 (1996).

26. See Appendix 3.2. It should be noted that, in general, the regression line through the scatterplot in Figure 4.8 is not exactly the same in the two cases, because it matters whether the variable on the vertical axis is being regressed against the variable on the horizontal axis or vice versa. In this particular case, however, the difference is small.

27. Such a strategy was recommended by Ronald I. McKinnon, *Money and Capital in Economic Development*, Brookings Institution, Washington, DC, 1973.

28. See World Bank, *World Development Indicators* (Oxford University Press, Oxford, 1997), table 2.1.

29. See e.g. eq. (16) in Appendix 2.2.

30. See Appendix 3.2. This case, of course, is also subject to the qualification described in n. 26.

31. This is essentially the story told by Kevin M. Murphy, Andrei Shleifer, and Robert W. Vishny, 'Industrialization and the Big Push', *Journal of Political Economy*, 97/5 (1989), 1003–26. The Big Push concept was introduced by P. N. Rosenstein-Rodan, 'Problems of Industrialization in Eastern and Southeastern Europe', *Economic Journal*, 53 (1943), 202–11. See also Paul Krugman, *Development, Geography, and Economic Theory* (MIT Press, Cambridge, Mass., 1995), ch. 1.

32. W. Arthur Lewis, *Some Aspects of Economic Development* (Ghana Publishing Corporation,

Accra and Tema, 1968), p. ix. Towards the end of this chapter it will be argued that economic growth is available also to countries *without* natural resources, such as Singapore.

33. That is, when the amount OH = CE of traditional output is converted into units of modern output by dividing by the price ratio between the two, P_M/P_T, which is the slope of the line EA, the outcome is CA. See Appendix 4.1.

34. This is shown in Appendix 4.1.

35. That is, FK/JK = P_M/P_T, so that P_TFK = P_MJK, which means that the price times quantity of traditional output imported is equal to the price times quantity of modern output exported.

36. This type of efficiency gain is sometimes referred to as an increase in X-efficiency. See Harvey Leibenstein, 'Allocative Efficiency vs. X-Efficiency', *American Economic Review*, 56/3 (1966), 392–415.

37. The total output gain would be larger if the initial position were assumed to be inside the production possibility frontier, for this would add a third source of increased efficiency. By assuming full employment, we bypass this potentially important source of temporary growth. We return to the relationship between unemployment and economic growth in Ch. 5.

38. See Ulrich Koester, 'The Experience with Liberalization Policies: The Case of the Agricultural Sector', *European Economic Review*, 35 (1991), 562–70.

39. See Appendix 4.1.

40. For comparison, the mean tariff rate in a narrow sense in 1990–3 was, for example, 84% in Bangladesh, 56% in India, 51% in Pakistan, 36% in China, 35% in Kenya, 34% in Nigeria, 30% in Tunisia, and 24% in Morocco compared with 6% in the USA and 7% in the European Union. These figures refer to nominal rates of protection. Effective rates of protection, which are more relevant for the discussion in the text, are typically much higher. See World Bank *Atlas* 1997.

41. See Paulo Cecchini, *The European Challenge 1992* (Gower, Aldershot, 1988). See also Richard Baldwin, 'The Growth Effects of 1992', *Economic Policy*, 9/2 (1989), 247–81.

42. See eq. (5) in Appendix 4.1.

43. The rate of growth of output can be negative, if the growth generated by the interaction between saving and efficiency is not enough to meet depreciation. See eq. (6) in Appendix 2.3.

44. This index is reported and used in Thorvaldur Gylfason, 'Exports, Inflation, and Growth', *World Development*, 27 (1999). The regression equation for 159 countries in 1994 is X/Y = 86.3 − 5.7 ln(N), where X/Y is the export ratio and N is population (in thousands). The t-statistics are 11.0 and 6.4, respectively, and R^2 = 0.21.

45. See Jeffrey D. Sachs and Andrew M. Warner, 'Economic Reform and the Process of Global Integration', *Brookings Papers on Economic Activity* 1 (1995), 1–118, and 'Natural Resource Abundance and Economic Growth', *Quarterly Journal of Economics* (forthcoming).

46. See e.g. World Bank, *World Development Report 1987*; David Dollar, 'Outward-Oriented Developing Countries Really Do Grow More Rapidly: Evidence from 95 LDCs 1976–85', *Economic Development and Cultural Change*, 40/4 (1992), 523–44; Sebastian Edwards, 'Trade Orientation, Distortions and Growth in Developing Countries', *Journal of Development Economics*, 39/1 (1992), 31–57; William Easterly, 'How Much Do Distortions Affect Growth?', *Journal of Monetary Economics*, 32 (1993), 187–212; Jong-Wha Lee, 'International Trade, Distortions, and Long-Run Economic Growth', IMF *Staff Papers*, 40/2 (1993), 299–328; and Sebastian Edwards, 'Openness, Productivity and Growth: What do we Really Know?', *Economic Journal*, 108/1 (1998), 383–98.

47. See Arnold C. Harberger, 'Taxation, Resource Allocation, and Welfare', in *The Role of Direct and Indirect Taxes in the Federal Revenue System* (National Bureau of Economic Research and Brookings Institution, Princeton University Press, Princeton, 1964). Harberger's welfare triangles led him to conclude that the efficiency loss from taxing labour income rather than levying a lump-sum tax amounts to about 2.5% of the revenue raised. Much larger efficiency losses are reported in Martin Feldstein, 'Tax

Avoidance and the Deadweight Loss of the Income Tax', NBER Working Paper 5055, March 1995.

48. See Appendix 4.2.

49. This should become clear if you turn Figure 4.17 upside down, i.e. by 180°, and then compare it with Figure 4.12.

50. This is shown in Appendix 4.2.

51. The costs of inflation are discussed in Stanley Fischer, *Indexing, Inflation, and Economic Policy* (MIT Press, Cambridge, Mass., 1986), chs. 1–2.

52. These ratios correspond to the following values of the exponent of capital in the production function (9) in Appendix 4.2: 0.9, 0.8, 0.67, and 0.5. See eq. (12) in Appendix 4.2. The last column, with a financial/real capital ratio of 1, is included for comparison with the stylized model presented in the appendix; the lower ratios shown in the first two columns are more realistic.

53. These figures are based on the implicit GDP deflator. See *World Development Indicators*, table 4.20. The number of countries for which this information is reported is 130.

54. One study suggests an even lower threshold, i.e. that inflation rates above 8% per annum impede economic growth, whereas inflation rates below 8% have no effect on growth, or may even stimulate growth. See Michael Sarel, 'Nonlinear Effects of Inflation on Economic Growth', IMF *Staff Papers* 43/1 (1996), 199–215.

55. The sample includes some countries for which the data on inflation do not extend all the way back to 1970, in which case the average inflation distortion spans a correspondingly shorter period.

56. The reasons for this assumption are given in Appendix 4.2.

57. See *World Development Indicators*, tables 4.1 and 4.20.

58. For evidence on financial markets, see Robert G. King and Ross Levine, 'Finance and Growth: Schumpeter Might Be Right', *Quarterly Journal of Economics*, 108/3 (1993), 717–37. For a detailed study of the African Growth record, see William Easterly and Ross Levine, 'Africa's Growth Tragedy: Politics and Ethnic Divisions', *Quarterly Journal of Economics*, 112/4 (1997), 1203–50.

59. See Appendix 4.3.

60. For comparison, the average share of state-owned enterprises in economic activity in 8 industrial countries and 40 developing countries in 1988 was 6% and 11%, respectively. See World Bank, *Bureaucrats in Business: The Economics and Politics of Government Ownership* (Oxford University Press, Oxford, 1995) table A1.

61. See *World Development Indicators*, and Thorvaldur Gylfason, Tryggvi Thor Herbertsson, and Gylfi Zoega, 'Ownership and Growth', CEPR Discussion Paper 1900, June 1998.

62. See e.g. Magnus Henrekson, Lars Jonung, and Joakim Stymne, 'Economic Growth and the Swedish Model', ch. 9 in Nicholas Crafts and Gianni Toniolo, *Economic Growth in Europe since 1945*, Centre for Economic Policy Research and Cambridge University Press, London and Cambridge, 1996. See also the references in n. 8.

63. See Robert J. Barro, *The Determinants of Economic Growth* (MIT Press, Cambridge, Mass., 1997). Barro's measure of productive government spending is questionable, however, because it leaves out government spending on health, justice, and public works and institutions, which many people view as socially useful—including, e.g. Adam Smith, *The Wealth of Nations* (Liberty Classics, Indianapolis, 1976), ii. bk. v.

64. See Appendix 4.4.

65. John Stuart Mill, *Principles of Political Economy*, ed. by W. J. Asley (Longmans, Green, 1909), 950.

66. Robert J. Barro and Xavier Sala-i-Martin, *Economic Growth* (McGraw-Hill, New York, 1995). See also Angel de la Fuente, 'The Empirics of Growth and Convergence: A Selective Review', *Journal of Economic Dynamics and Control*, 21 (1997), 23–73, and Jonathan Temple, 'The New Growth Evidence', *Journal of Economic Literature* (forthcoming).

67. There is, for instance, not a word about inflation as a possible determinant of growth in Barro and Sala-i-Martin's *Economic Growth*, a book of more than 500 pages, nor in

Philippe Aghion and Peter Howitt, *Endogenous Growth Theory* (MIT Press, Cambridge, Mass., and London, 1998). But see Barro, *Determinants of Economic Growth*, where a whole chapter is devoted to inflation and growth.

68. See Ross Levine and David Renelt, 'A Sensitivity Analysis of Cross-Country Growth Regressions', *American Economic Review*, 82/4 (1992), 942–63.

69. See Xavier Sala-i-Martin, 'I Just Ran Two Million Regressions', *American Economic Review*, 87/2 (1997), 178–83.

70. See eqs. (13), (18), and (19) in Appendix 3.3.

71. See e.g. Robert Barro, *Determinants of Economic Growth*, table 1.1.

72. See N. Gregory Mankiw, David Romer, and David N. Weil, 'A Contribution to the Empirics of Economic Growth', *Quarterly Journal of Economics*, 107/2 (1992), 407–37.

73. Hong Kong, Iceland, and Sweden shared the second place in the life-expectancy league in 1995, with 79 years.

74. See e.g. Dani Rodrik, 'Where Did All the Growth Go? External Shocks, Social Conflicts and Growth Collapses', CEPR Discussion Paper 1789, Jan. 1998.

75. See Joseph E. Stiglitz, 'Some Lessons from the East Asian Miracle', The World Bank, *Research Observer*, 11/2 (1996), 151–77. See also Torsten Persson and Guido Tabellini, 'Is Inequality Harmful for Growth?', *American Economic Review*, 84/3 (1994), 600–21; Alberto Alesina and Roberto Perotti, 'The Political Economy of Growth: A Critical Survey of the Recent Literature', *World Bank Economic Review*, 8/3 (1994), 351–71; and Roland Bénabou, 'Inequality and Growth', NBER *Macroeconomics Annual* (1996), 11–74.

76. See W. Arthur Lewis, *The Theory of Economic Growth* (Allen & Unwin, London, 1955).

77. Adam Smith, *Wealth of Nations*, i. 111–12.

78. See Asian Development Bank, *Emerging Asia: Changes and Challenges* (Manilla, 1997). See also Robert E. Hall and Charles I. Jones, 'The Productivity of Nations', NBER Working Paper 5812, Nov. 1996.

79. See e.g. Robert Barro and Xavier Sala-i-Martin, *Economic Growth*, table 12.3, or Robert Barro, *Determinants of Economic Growth*, table 1.1.

80. See Asian Development Bank, *Emerging Asia*, tables A2–A5.

81. Robert E. Hall and Charles I. Jones, 'The Productivity of Nations', 30.

82. See Jeffrey D. Sachs and Andrew M. Warner, 'Natural Resource Abundance and Economic Growth', *Quarterly Journal of Economics* (forthcoming) and Thorvaldur Gylfason, Tryggvi Thor Herbertsson, and Gylfi Zoega, 'A Mixed Blessing: Natural Resources and Economic Growth', *Macroeconomic Dynamics*, 3 (1999).

83. See Rögnvaldur Hannesson, *Fisheries Mismanagement: The Case of the North Atlantic Cod* (Fishing News Books, Oxford, 1996).

84. See Philip R. Lane and Aaron Tornell, 'Power, Growth, and the Voracity Effect', *Journal of Economic Growth* (1996), 213–41.

85. For comparison, as world trade has grown much more rapidly than world output over the past 25 years or so, the unweighted average share of exports in GDP in the world economy at large has increased by a half since 1970, or from 14% in 1970 to 21% in 1994.

86. See *World Development Report 1997*, table 10.

87. See Robert E. Hall and Charles I. Jones, 'The Productivity of Nations'.

88. See e.g., David A. Aschauer, 'Does Public Capital Crowd Out Private Capital?', *Journal of Monetary Economics*, 24/3 (1989), 171–88; Asian Development Bank, *Emerging Asia*; and Paolo Mauro, 'The Effects of Corruption on Growth, Investment, and Government Expenditure', International Monetary Fund Working Paper 96/98, 1996.

5

Reforms and Growth

Those who want and intend
To wake and comprehend
Will muster a thousand means.[1]

EINAR BENEDIKTSSON

There is practically no limit to what you can accomplish in politics as long as you don't care who gets the credit.[2]

HARRY S. TRUMAN

We have now reached the mountain top, so to speak, where we can look at the landscape from above, and where all seems so easy—almost too easy. We can now see that Adam Smith and those who later stood on his shoulders, like Mill and Marshall, seem to have got it right: lasting economic growth is available to all those who bother to save and judiciously invest enough of their national income and who use their resources as efficiently as possible through free trade, low inflation, private enterprise, good education, and export diversification away from excessive dependence on natural resources, among other things. Some countries still have severe economic difficulties, it is true, in part because external circumstances, like location, prevent them from growing rapidly, but even they can do much to improve their situation. Why is it, then, that so many countries have failed to grow fast? World output per capita grew by $1\frac{1}{2}$ per cent per year from 1965 to 1990 and by only $\frac{3}{4}$ per cent per year from 1985 to 1995? Why not more?

One obvious explanation has to do with knowledge. Too many just did not know what it takes to grow. As we saw in Chapter 1, even some of the best and the brightest among economists, let alone politicians and the public, believed that the Soviet Union would, as Khrushchev predicted, 'bury' the mixed market economies by 1970, or by 2000 or some such date. Such mentality was not a good compass for growth-friendly policies, not in Europe and certainly not in Africa where, from the 1960s onwards, many of the newly independent states took their cue from the Soviet Union, at least in economic affairs. In Sub-Saharan Africa, total GNP per capita grew by 0.2 per cent per year from 1965 to 1990 and fell by 1 per cent per year from 1985 to 1995.[3]

The collapse of communism in 1989–91 dealt a fatal blow to such beliefs. It removed blinders[4] and it opened eyes and windows and doors around the world. In all this, it almost surely helped that the collapse coincided with the beginning of the endogenous-growth revolution. Theory and experience have paved the way: it is by now widely acknowledged among economists that market-friendly economic and institutional reforms are generally good for growth. More and more political leaders from different parts of the political spectrum have also become more receptive to the same message. For this is not a question of right and left. This is, rather, a question of what economic theory and empirical evidence can teach us about the sources of economic growth. This does not, however, mean the end of political choice. Growth-friendly reforms do not dictate the political agenda in its entirety. No, they leave important issues open for political judgement. Reforms are not the prerogative of a particular part of the political spectrum.[5]

Another obvious explanation of economic failures has to do with politics. We reviewed several examples in Chapter 1; here, one more should suffice. Figure 5.1 shows the development of national income per capita in Uganda since 1970. The Pearl of Africa, as the country used to be called, imploded under the crushing weight of Idi Amin's extremely brutal mismanagement and crippling ethnic conflict from 1971 onwards: income per head declined by more than a third in just eight years. Few natural calamities have created such national havoc. The economic collapse of Uganda was not arrested until Amin was overthrown in 1979. However, the country did not begin to recover until 1986, when Yoweri Museveni came to power, pledging peace, progress, and, little by little, political democracy. The correlation between economic performance and politics can sometimes be that close, and not only in Africa. Such correlations do not have to be contemporaneous, however, for some waves are long in the economic life of nations. In many cases, economic stagnation or even collapse is a consequence of economic policies, attitudes, and institutions whose roots lie deep in the economic, political, and social fabric and extend back a long way. We shall have a little more to say about politics later in the chapter.

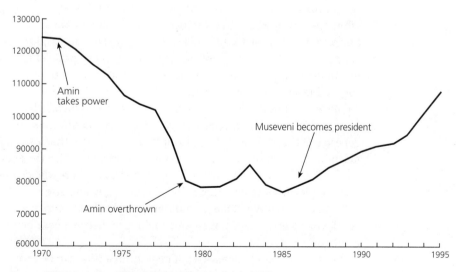

Fig 5.1
Uganda: Real per capita GDP, 1970–1995, Uganda shillings (1990 prices)

Source: IMF, *International Financial Statistics*, Yearbook 1997.

Unemployment and growth

But first this. In Chapter 4, we reviewed some reasons why poor countries so often remain poor. Poor countries generally have less scope for saving than rich ones, more mouths to feed, more worries, and so on, all of which tends to constrain their capacity for growth. Now the time has come to address perhaps the greatest inefficiency of all: unemployment.[6] Is unemployment an impediment to economic growth?

It may surprise you, but the answer is not self-evident. Clearly, increased unemployment generally causes inefficiency and economic waste by reducing a nation's output below its productive potential, sometimes far below, as has been the case in Europe since the early 1980s, and much longer in many other parts of the world. Output lost through lack of work is like loss of sleep: it cannot be recovered. But does this type of inefficiency impede growth?

Recall how we defined efficiency: it is the amount of output produced per unit of capital (or, where relevant, per unit of all inputs combined). To recapitulate, trade liberalization is good for growth because it increases output at full employment and a given stock of capital. Stabilization is good for growth because it increases the amount of output produced by a given stock of total, i.e. real and financial, capital at full employment (and may also stimulate saving). Privatization is good for growth because it increases the quantity and quality of the output that can be squeezed out of given inputs at full employment. Education is good for growth—well, you know how to finish the sentence. The reduction or eradication of unemployment, however, is different from the five cases of increased growth through increased efficiency discussed in Chapter 4 in that the very existence of unemployment violates our assumption of full employment, an assumption maintained throughout Chapter 4, unless otherwise indicated.

There are two possibilities. On the one hand, when output decreases because of increased unemployment, the amount of output per unit of capital also decreases if the capital stock remains unchanged, or if it decreases less than employment, which is often the case. In such circumstances, increased unemployment is generally inimical to economic growth. But this is not to say that full employment is necessarily good for growth, not at all. Full employment was the pride of the Soviet Union and its satellites in Central and Eastern Europe. And how did they do it? By force. It was simply illegal to be unemployed. The unemployed were regularly denounced as 'hooligans' in *Pravda* and other local news media. This meant that millions upon millions of workers were trapped in gigantic, grossly inefficient state enterprises, thus deprived of the mobility between employers and places that is the hallmark of an efficient labour market in a mixed economy. Moreover, when the State is the sole employer, firms do not compete for workers, nor do workers who do not get along with their employer move elsewhere, for they have nowhere else to go. In a market economy, on the other hand, labour mobility is typically accompanied by temporary unemployment as workers move about, looking for better jobs or better wages. But that is the cost of efficiency.

On the other hand, increased joblessness for a time can be an inevitable, even desirable, consequence of necessary reallocation and reorganization in order to increase economic efficiency. This is part of what Joseph Schumpeter meant by 'creative destruction'.[7] For example, the transformation of economic activity in the former Soviet Union in recent years was bound to shift workers from the collapsing state sector to the rapidly expanding private sector. In Russia, this occurred with remarkably little fuss. In 1993, one in five Russian workers found a new job.[8] In 1995, the registered unemployment rate was $3\frac{1}{2}$ per cent of the labour force and the open unemployment rate was about 8 per cent (and 9 per cent in 1996), which is not much in view of the massive contraction of recorded Russian output since communism collapsed. In Russia, therefore, the fairly modest increase in unemployment in the 1990s is a sign of increased efficiency and of a well-functioning, flexible labour market. Is Russia's sheer size responsible for the resilience of its labour market?—a huge area, almost twice as large as the United States, also without language barriers. Hardly. A similar resilience has been observed, for example, in the Baltic countries, (Estonia, Latvia, and Lithuania), where unemployment hovered between 5 and 9 per cent in 1994–6, despite massive restructuring.

Take another case: Ireland. Earlier, in Chapter 4, we mentioned Ireland's impressive growth performance over the past decade or so (per capita growth of more than 5 per cent per year in 1985–95 and even more growth in 1996 and 1997). The growth of Irish output per head, a European record, has been accompanied by one of Europe's highest rates of unemployment in this period, or one-sixth of the labour force on average.[9] The massive, persistent unemployment has clearly involved considerable inefficiency and waste, but it can also be viewed as a natural consequence of the radical transformation of the Irish economy that has taken place, away from agriculture via industry to trade and services. The share of agriculture in Ireland's labour force fell from 37 per cent in 1960 to 14 per cent in 1990, which means that almost a quarter of the labour force left the land in a period of 30 years. The share of agriculture in GDP fell from 30 per cent in 1949 to 8 per cent in 1994. The share of exports of goods and services in Irish GDP rose from 48 per cent in 1980 to 75 per cent in 1995, the highest such figure in Europe.[10] Such shifts in economic structure call for flexibility in work and pay and footloose labour. However, the economic transformation of Ireland does not explain the country's unemployment problem in full because, after all, Ireland shares with the rest of the European Union many of the labour market rigidities that have helped make lack of work so persistent and problematic in Europe since the early 1980s.

Consider this. European labour markets are, with few exceptions, relatively rigid. The wages of most workers are set, directly or indirectly, through collective bargaining between labour unions and employers' associations. Work and pay are tightly regulated. Real wages in the European Union have risen by more than 60 per cent on average since 1970, and unemployment has more than quadrupled, from $2\frac{1}{2}$ per cent of the labour force in 1970 to 11 per cent in 1996. European labour unions have succeeded in raising real wages, yes, but at the expense of jobs. In the United States, on the other hand, labour markets are generally flexible and wages are negotiated firm by firm. Real wages have increased by about 15 per cent since 1970 and unemployment has fluctuated between 5 and 10 per cent, without a tendency to increase over time. Today, unemployment in America is no higher than it was before the first oil crisis in the early 1970s. The American way of work and pay thus seems more conducive to job creation than the European one—at the cost of a considerably less even distribution of income in the United States than in many European countries (recall Table 4.6).

In the 1950s and 1960s, on the other hand, approximately the same labour market institutions on both sides of the Atlantic produced the opposite outcome, that is, less unemployment in Europe than in the United States. In those years, rapid economic growth helped to prevent the rigidity of European labour markets from becoming a binding constraint. When growth began to falter after the first oil shock in the 1970s, however, the rigidity became binding. Take firing restrictions, for example. They did not deter the hiring of new workers in the 1960s because employers had reason to expect economic growth to continue and thus to be able to expand their workforce. By the 1980s, however, this had changed. Economic growth had slowed down. This meant that legal restrictions on firing deterred hiring and unemployment began to rise. Less economic growth gave rise to more unemployment.[11]

It would thus neither be wise nor fair to attribute unemployment in Europe to labour union activity alone. There are more reasons why joblessness persists and wages do not adjust to clear the labour market, including the reluctance of employers to reduce wages to market-clearing levels for fear of demoralizing the labour force and thus reducing its efficiency (this is the so-called efficiency–wage hypothesis),[12] in addition to various welfare-state-policy stipulations and tax wedges that tend to compress the wage structure and thus price some low-skilled workers out of their jobs.

A comparison of Europe and East Asia conveys a similar impression. Take Singapore. Since the 1960s, the Singaporeans have succeeded in creating conditions for exceptionally rapid economic growth combined with low inflation and little or no unemployment—$2\frac{1}{2}$ per cent of the labour force in 1995. Flexible labour markets have almost surely contributed to this outcome. By design, the labour market in Singapore is essentially free. Wages are set by supply and demand without much interference from the authorities, labour unions, or employers' associations. This liberal arrangement has probably increased income differentials in the city state, true, but still not beyond those observed in, for example, the United States and the United Kingdom, as we saw in Table 4.6. Labour relations are generally peaceful.

Like the people of Singapore, several other East Asian nations, including Japan, Korea, Taiwan, and Thailand—and Malaysia, too, to some extent—long ago resolved to decentralize their labour markets by making each firm rather than each industry or even the economy as a whole the chief forum for wage decisions. The aim was to reduce the risk of excessive wage claims that are frequently put forward by large labour unions with many members from different backgrounds, some of whom work in well-run, efficient enterprises able to pay good wages, while others do not. In this way, it was thought, wage claims would accord more closely with productivity developments because workers would have a personal stake in the success of the firms that gave them work. The idea was that the advantages of efficiency through non-intervention by the State are no smaller, and no less tangible, in labour markets than in other markets:

> In East Asia, more than elsewhere, governments resisted the temptation to intervene in the labour market to counter outcomes unpalatable in the short run or to particular groups . . . A relatively high level of efficiency in the allocation of labour was achieved by allowing wages and employment to be determined largely by the interaction of those

supplying and those demanding labour services, rather than by government legislation, public sector leadership, or union pressure.[13]

The efficiency thus attained seems likely to have contributed significantly to East Asia's rapid economic growth over the past 30 years. However, the sudden exposure to a serious economic shock, such as the one of 1997–8, when currency and equity values collapsed across the region, is a useful, if unpleasant, reminder that efficiency and flexibility are not the sole desirable attributes of labour market arrangements. There is also a basic human need for a fair system of social security, including unemployment insurance in some form, designed to fend off the worst social and economic ramifications of the shock and of others that may follow in the future.

The upshot of this discussion is this: there is no simple, all-encompassing relationship between unemployment and economic growth. In some cases, such as that of the European Union since the early 1980s, persistent lack of work reflects deep-seated inefficiency through lack of flexibility in labour markets, and thus leads to economic waste and social misery, both of which are inimical to growth. In other cases, such as Ireland and Russia, for example, or Chile in the 1970s and early 1980s, increased unemployment is to some extent a natural consequence of necessary structural change: increased joblessness in the short run is then a price you pay for more growth and more and better jobs in the future. Widespread urban unemployment in parts of Africa and Latin America is most often a mixture of both phenomena. And then there is the tendency for a slowdown in economic growth to increase unemployment. The connection between jobs and growth needs to be assessed case by case.

Some obstacles to reforms and growth

The complex interaction between unemployment and economic growth helps explain why growth-friendly reforms often fail to be implemented, and thus also why many countries fail to grow as fast as they could. It is not always easy, in a democracy, to convince enough people in the political arena that the future gain from reforms outweighs the present pain—for example, that more unemployment for a while may be worth having if it indirectly helps generate more rapid economic growth over the long haul. Would it be easier with less democracy? No, hardly. Empirical evidence seems to indicate that democracy actually is good for growth, at least up to a point,[14] and conversely. Liberal democracy usually produces better political leadership and better governance than other forms of government, and thus increases the probability that growth-enhancing policies will be implemented, other things being equal.

The fear of unemployment in the wake of economic reforms is only part of the problem. For good practical reasons, many people have an instinctive fear of change, especially sudden change. Such fears stack the cards in favour of those who advocate the *status quo* in economic affairs, and hence generally against growth, almost independently of the initial conditions. For example, parents and grandparents may resist change, even if this seems likely to leave less for their children and grandchildren. Why, they may wonder, should the older generation make painful

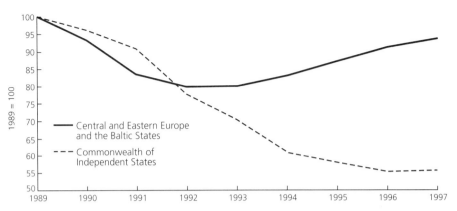

Fig 5.2
Central and Eastern Europe and the former Soviet Union: The path of output, 1989–1997

Note: 1996 estimate and 1997 projection.
Source: European Bank for Reconstruction and Development, Transition Report 1997, table 7.1.

sacrifices for the younger one?—which, even in a slow-growing economy, will eventually become better off than their parents anyway.

The experience of the countries of Central and Eastern Europe in the 1990s illustrates the point. Without exception, the economic and institutional reforms—liberalization, stabilization, privatization, and so on—were initially accompanied by a substantial decrease in recorded output, followed by recovery (Figure 5.2). The pattern is the same everywhere: the path of output looks like a sickle blade as shown in Figure 4.13.[15] Unemployment, forbidden by law under communism, suddenly emerged, and jumped to double-digit rates in several countries in the region (Poland, for example), while in others, with more flexible labour markets, it remained remarkably low, as discussed earlier. The reformers were typically young, well-educated people, acting principally on behalf of their young constituents, and partly against the will and wishes of many members of the older generation, who would have preferred less rapid, less radical reforms (and who revealed their preference by voting for the old or born-again communist parties and related groups).

Such intergenerational conflict of interest is only the beginning of the story, however. There is also the conflict between those who stand to gain from reforms and those who lose. This is one reason why free trade has taken so long to take hold. After more than 50 years of continuous negotiations under the General Agreement on Tariffs and Trade (GATT) and now under the auspices of the World Trade Organization, even the United States and the European Union still levy tariffs of 6 to 7 per cent on average on their imports from abroad, despite the significant macroeconomic gains to be had from the abolition of these tariffs. The Common Agricultural Policy (CAP) of the European Union is another example: despite the enormous cost it imposes on consumers and taxpayers in Europe through unnecessarily high food prices and taxes,[16] it has proved extremely resistant to reform.[17] The problem is that, in practice, the benefits of economic reforms are almost always unevenly distributed. Some gain, while others lose, at least in the short run, and those who gain do not, in general, compensate those who lose, even if there is, in principle, ample scope for such compensation.

This isn't all. Among the potential losers, each usually stands to lose quite a lot from reforms compared with the gains expected by each player on the winning team—say, consumers and taxpayers in the case of the CAP. This is because the losses are typically confined to relatively few, while the benefits accrue to many.[18] Therefore, it pays special interest groups to organize themselves well in order to be able to exert as much pressure as possible on political authorities. This helps explain why farmers' organizations are typically strong, while consumers' organizations are weak, even if farmers are few and consumers are many. One of the prime purposes of growth-friendly economic and institutional reforms, therefore, is generally to uproot, or at least reduce, economic privileges. This aspect of the reform process is bound to engender resistance. Conflict resolution is one of the chief purposes of politics, including, in particular, the intrinsic conflict of interest between the few and the many and between those who favour policy reforms intended to increase economic growth and those who don't, because they do not believe that they themselves will benefit from the reforms in the short run. In the long run, however, a rising tide lifts all boats.

And there is more. Some argue that most politicians, in democracies and elsewhere, are out not to promote the public interest, but their own: this is the chief tenet of the theory of public choice.[19] The main idea is that politicians should be viewed like consumers, businessmen, and other economic agents: they seek to maximize their profit or power or whatever else it may be that makes them tick, even if this means advocating and implementing policies that go against the public interest they have pledged to serve. Harry Truman would probably not have been impressed, but, to the extent that politicians actually behave in this way, this is likely to stack the cards even further against reforms and rapid growth by increasing the probability of all manner of collusion of vested interests at public expense.

In conclusion

In spite of these obstacles, much progress has been made in economic policy around the world in the 1990s, perhaps more progress than in any previous decade, ever. Growth-friendly reforms have perhaps never before been so widely embraced among ordinary people and politicians across the political spectrum. Yet, many find the progress made disappointingly slow, because there is so much at stake.

'Progress must be slow,' said Alfred Marshall. True, he added,

> . . . progress may be hastened by thought and work . . . and by the appropriate education of the faculties of either sex; but however hastened it must be gradual and relatively slow. It must be slow relative to man's growing command over technique and the forces of nature; a command which is making ever growing calls for courage and caution, for resource and steadfastness, for penetrating insight and breadth of view. And it must be very much too slow to keep pace with the rapid inflow of proposals for the prompt reorganization of society on a new basis . . . Thus progress itself increases the urgency of the warning that in the economic world, *Natura non facit saltum*.[20]

Perhaps the main reason for the slow progress made on the reform front in many countries over the years has to do with imperfect information: most people simply do not know about the macroeconomic consequences of poor policies and imperfect institutions—such as, for example, protectionism in general and the Common Agricultural Policy of the European Union in particular. If they did, the conditions for overcoming the remaining obstacles against more rapid reforms and growth would improve.

But there are no guarantees. As George Bernard Shaw said, 'Reformers have the idea that change can be achieved by brute sanity.' But sanity is not enough. You must also 'want and intend to wake and comprehend'—and even that may not be enough to remove remaining hindrances and make your country grow. But at least you know that to grow or not to grow is in large measure a matter of choice.

Questions for review

1. 'Liberalization and decentralization of European labour markets would reduce unemployment in Europe at the cost of increased wage dispersion without any effect on economic growth over time.' Do you agree? Explain why or why not.
2. 'High unemployment is always and everywhere a sign of economic inefficiency, which inhibits economic growth in the long run.' True or false? Why?
3. Take a country of your choice and outline the main economic and institutional reforms that you think would improve the country's growth performance in the long run. In your view, what are the main obstacles to the implementation of the growth-promoting reforms that you advocate?

Notes

1. Einar Benediktsson, 'Íslandsljóð' ('Poems for Iceland'), in his *Sögur og kvæði (Stories and Poems)* (Reykjavik, 1987). Author's translation from Icelandic.

2. Attributed by oral tradition, printed source unknown.

3. The corresponding annual growth figures for East Asia and the Pacific were 5.3% in 1965–90 and 7.2% in 1985–95. See World Bank, *World Development Report*, 1992 and 1997, table 1.

4. Recall the quotation from Ragnar Frisch in ch. 1.

5. See Thorvaldur Gylfason, Torben M. Andersen, Seppo Honkapohja, Arne J. Isachsen, and John Williamson, *The Swedish Model under Stress: A View From the Stands* (Centre for Business and Policy Studies, Stockholm, 1997), ch. 7.

6. For good, readable accounts of unemployment, see e.g. Richard Layard, *How to Beat Unemployment* (Oxford University Press, Oxford, 1986); Assar Lindbeck, *Unemployment and Macroeconomics* (MIT Press, Cambridge, Mass. 1993); and Marian Radetzki, *Klarspråk om arbetslöshet (Plain Speaking about Unemployment)* (SNS Förlag, Stockholm, 1996).

7. See Joseph Schumpeter, *Capitalism, Socialism and Democracy*, 3rd edn. (Harper & Row, New York, 1950), ch. 7. A modern version of the story is offered in Philippe Aghion and Peter Howitt, 'Growth and Unemployment', *Review of Economic Studies*, 61 (1994), 477–94. See also Philippe Aghion and Peter Howitt, *Endogenous Growth Theory* (MIT Press, Cambridge, Mass., and London, 1998).

8. See Richard Layard and Andrea Richter, 'Labor Market Adjustment—The Russian Way', in Anders Åslund (ed.), *Russian Economic Reform at Risk* (St Martin's Press, New York, 1995).

9. In Europe, only Spain had (marginally) more unemployment than Ireland from 1985 to 1995. Spain's GNP per capita also grew quite fast during this period, or by 2½% per year on average.

10. Belgium and Estonia tied for second place in the European export league in 1995, with an export share of 74%.

11. See Christopher A. Pissarides, *Equilibrium Unemployment Theory* (Blackwell, Oxford, 1990).

12. See e.g. Carl Shapiro and Joseph E. Stiglitz, 'Equilibrium Unemployment as a Worker Discipline Device', *American Economic Review,* 74/3 (1984), 433–44.

13. World Bank, *The East Asian Miracle: Economic Growth and Public Policy* (Oxford University Press, Oxford, 1993), 266.

14. See Robert J. Barro, *Determinants of Economic Growth: A Cross-Country Empirical Study* (MIT Press, Cambridge, Mass. and London, 1997), ch. 3. The qualifier 'up to a point' refers to Barros' finding that 'too much' democracy may tend to impede growth by increasing the possibilities of special interest groups to sway political decisions in their favour at public expense. See also Alberto Alesina and Roberto Perotti, 'The Political Economy of Growth: A Critical Survey of the Recent Literature', *World Bank Economic Review*, 8/3 (1994), 351–71.

15. Bulgaria's relapse in 1996–7 and that of Albania (and, barely, Romania) in 1997 are the only aberrations from an otherwise uniform pattern. See Olivier Blanchard, *The Economics of Post-Communist Transition* (Clarendon Press, Oxford, 1997).

16. According to the OECD, the cost of agricultural protection in OECD countries in 1996 amounted to US$ 297 bn., which was more than the GNP of Switzerland in 1996. Of this amount, the European Union accounted for US$ 120 bn, which was only a little less than Norway's GNP in 1996. See OECD, *Agricultural Policies in OECD Countries*, i: *Monitoring and Evaluation*, and ii: *Measurement of Support and Background Information* (OECD, Paris, 1997).

17. See D. Gale Johnson, *Less than Meets the Eye: The Modest Impact of CAP Reform*, Rochester Paper 5 (Centre for Policy Studies, London, 1995). See also Anne O. Krueger, *Political Economy of Policy Reform in Developing Countries* (MIT Press, Cambridge, Mass. 1994); John

Williamson (ed.), *The Political Economy of Policy Reform* (Institute for International Economics, Washington, DC, 1994); and Avinash Dixit, *The Making of Economic Policy: A Transactions-Cost Politics Perspective* (MIT Press, Cambridge, Mass. 1996).

18. See Mancur Olson, *The Logic of Collective Action* (Harvard University Press, Cambridge, Mass., 1965).

19. See James M. Buchanan and Gordon Tullock, *The Calculus of Consent* (University of Michigan Press, Ann Arbor, Mich., 1962).

20. 'Nature does not make jumps.' Alfred Marshall, *Principles of Economics*, 8th edn. (Macmillan, London, 1920), 207.

Appendices

Appendix 2.1.
The Harrod–Domar Model

The Harrod–Domar model rests on two simple assumptions about economic behaviour. First, household saving (S) is taken to be proportional to output (Y), so that

$$S = sY \tag{1}$$

where s is the saving rate, a number like 0.2, for example, which is close to the 1995 world average. Second, the stock of capital (K) is also taken to be proportional to output:

$$K = vY \tag{2}$$

where v is the capital/output ratio, a number like 1, 2, 3, or 4, depending on the state of development of the country in question. Rich countries typically have more capital than poor countries relative to output. Capital is difficult to measure accurately except as the sum of previous investments discounted by the assumed rate of depreciation (assumed, because depreciation of capital, like capital itself, cannot easily be measured directly).

To these two assumptions about the behaviour of households and firms is then added the definition of gross investment (I) as the sum of net investment (i.e. the change in the capital stock ΔK, where Δ denotes change) and replacement investment δK, where the depreciation rate δ is the proportion of the capital stock that wears out every year by assumption:

$$I = \Delta K + \delta K \tag{3}$$

The unobservable depreciation rate δ can be a number like, say, 0.04 or 0.10, or even a much larger number in countries where capital loses its worth or wastes away rapidly.

At last, we write down the condition that saving must equal investment for the national economy to be in equilibrium:

$$S = I \tag{4}$$

Notice now that for a given capital/output ratio (v), equation (2) can be rewritten as $\Delta K = v\Delta Y$. Using this, substituting equations (1) and (3) into equation (4), and manipulating the result, we get the following expression for the proportional increase in output—the rate of economic growth:

$$\frac{\Delta Y}{Y} = \frac{s}{v} - \delta \tag{5}$$

This is the Harrod–Domar equation for growth. For example, if the saving rate (s) is 0.21, the capital/output ratio (v) is 3, and the depreciation rate (δ) is 0.04, not unreasonable assumptions in many cases, then the corresponding rate of growth of output ($\Delta Y/Y$) is 0.03 or 3 per cent. If the saving rate rises from 0.21, the world average in 1995, to 0.36, as in Thailand in 1995,[1] then the growth rate would increase from 3 per cent per year to 8 per cent, other things being equal. If the capital/output ratio decreases from 3 to 2.1 (and s = 0.21 again), then growth rises from 3 to 6 per cent a year. An increase in the depreciation rate, however, reduces growth point for point. We see that reasonable variations in the parameters of the model yield rates of growth within a plausible range.

But this cannot be the end of the story since population growth has not yet been taken into consideration, as discussed in Appendix 2.2.

Appendix 2.2. The Solow Model: Exogenous Growth

Let output (Y) be made by labour (L) and capital (K) through a Cobb–Douglas production function with constant returns to scale:

$$Y = L^a K^{1-a} \tag{1}$$

where a lies between 0 and 1. As we will see towards the end of this appendix, the coefficients a and 1 − a can be shown to represent the shares of labour and capital in output, which makes the values a = 2/3 and 1 − a = 1/3 plausible for our purposes. Taking logarithms on both sides of the equation and differentiating all the variables with respect to time, we can express the production function in terms of growth rates as follows:

$$g = an + (1 - a)\frac{\Delta K}{K} \tag{2}$$

where g = ΔY/Y is the rate of growth of output, n = ΔL/L is the rate of growth of the labour force, and ΔK/K is the rate of growth of the capital stock. Now, if the capital/output ratio, K/Y, is in fact constant in the long run, as reported by Simon Kuznets[2] and corroborated by Angus Maddison,[3] so that ΔK/K = g, then output per capita must also be constant, because equation (2) means that g = n. Therefore, long-run growth is exogenous.

The result that g = n means that the growth of output per capita is zero. To explain the observed growth in output per head and in the average standard of life, Solow invoked technological progress, adding a technological shift parameter (A) to the production function in equation (1) as follows:

$$Y = AL^a K^{1-a} \tag{3}$$

It is convenient to assume technology to grow at a given rate aq and to be embodied in labour, so that $A = Be^{aqt}$, where B is a constant representing the initial state of technology. The idea is that, with more and better education, labour becomes more productive over time. Equation (3) can now be rewritten thus:

$$Y = B(e^{qt}L)^a K^{1-a} \tag{4}$$

where labour input is now expressed in units of efficiency, $e^{qt}L$. The rate of technological progress aq is less than the rate of growth of labour productivity q, because the quality of capital is unchanged by assumption. Hereafter, however, we will use the terms technological progress and labour productivity growth interchangeably, because all technical progress will be assumed to be in the form of increased labour productivity.

It follows from equation (4) that the rate of growth of output is

$$g = a(n + q) + (1 - a)\frac{\Delta K}{K} \tag{5}$$

As before, if $\Delta K/K = g$, then output per efficiency unit of labour is constant and

$$g = n + q \tag{6}$$

Therefore, long-run growth is still exogenous. The long-run growth of output per capita is no longer zero, however, because now we have $g - n = q > 0$. Saving makes no difference for growth in the long run, nor does efficiency, except insofar as they affect the rate of technological progress.

Equation (6) means that the Harrod–Domar model has become overidentified: we cannot have *both* $g = n + q$ *and* $g = s/v - \delta$, as in equation (5) in Appendix 2.1, unless one of the five exogenous right-hand-side variables (s, v, δ, n, or q) is made endogenous. Solow resolved the inconsistency by solving the Harrod–Domar equation for the capital/output ratio:

$$v = \frac{s}{g + \delta} = \frac{s}{n + q + \delta} \tag{7}$$

How certain can we be that the capital/output ratio can be treated as an endogenous constant as in equation (7)?—when we know that the stock of capital can be measured only indirectly, and probably inaccurately, as the sum of all previous investments net of depreciation. Look at it this way. Gross investment (I) is defined as the sum of net investment (ΔK) and replacement investment (δK)—recall equation (3) in Appendix 2.1. This allows us to write

$$\frac{I}{Y} = \frac{K}{Y}\left(\frac{\Delta K}{K} + \delta\right) \tag{8}$$

Because saving equals investment (S = I) in the long run (and in a closed economy also in the short run), I/Y equals s (the saving rate) and equation (8) can be solved for the capital/output ratio as follows:

$$\frac{K}{Y} = \frac{s}{\frac{\Delta K}{K} + \delta} \tag{9}$$

As long as the saving rate, the depreciation rate, and the rate of growth of the capital stock are constant, the capital/output ratio must also be constant. For given s and δ, a constant rate of growth of the capital stock must be equal to the rate of growth of output, for that is the only way for the capital/output ratio to stay put. But what if, say, the saving rate increases over a long period?—as it did, for example, in the East Asia and Pacific region over the past generation, to reach 38 per cent of GDP on average in 1995 compared with 28 per cent in 1980. Meanwhile, the capital/output ratio must show an upward trend, other things being equal.

There is a story behind Solow's derivation of his crucial equation (7). We saw from equation (9) that if the rate of growth of the capital stock ($\Delta K/K$) is constant, then it must be equal to the rate of growth of output (g). Therefore, the Harrod–Domar equation (5) in Appendix 2.1 can also be used to describe the rate of growth of the capital stock:

$$\frac{\Delta K}{K} = s\frac{Y}{K} - \delta \tag{10}$$

Substituting this expression for $\Delta K/K$ into equation (5) in Appendix 2.2, we get

$$g = a(n + q) + (1 - a)\left(s\frac{Y}{K} - \delta\right) \tag{11}$$

This equation tells us that an increase in the saving rate (s) must increase the rate of growth of output (g) so long as the capital/output ratio remains unchanged.

Dynamics

But will the capital/output ratio stay put? Solow showed that it will not. Consider first the capital/labour ratio, where labour is expressed in units of steadily increasing efficiency as in equation (4), in order to take technical progress into account: $k' = K/(Le^{qt})$. The rate of change of this ratio over time is equal to the rate of change of K in the numerator, which from equation (10) is equal to $sY/K - \delta$, minus the rate of change of Le^{qt} in the denominator:

$$\frac{\Delta k'}{k'} = \frac{\Delta K}{K} - n - q = s\frac{Y}{K} - \delta - n - q \tag{12}$$

If we denote output per efficiency unit of labour by $y' = Y/(Le^{qt})$, then, by dividing through the production function in equation (4) by Le^{qt}, we can rewrite it as $y' = B(k')^{1-a}$. Hence, $Y/K = y/k = y'/k' = B(k')^{-a}$. Therefore,

$$\frac{\Delta k'}{k'} = sB(k')^{-a} - \delta - n - q \tag{13}$$

This equation plays a pivotal role in Solow's model. It implies an inverse relationship between the level of the ratio of capital to labour in efficiency units (k') and its rate of change $(\Delta k'/k')$, other things being equal. If k' is small initially, so that the right-hand side of equation (13) is positive, then k' is on the rise. However, the increase in k' will reduce $\Delta k'/k'$, thus making k' rise more slowly, until k' stops rising. If, on the other hand, k' is large initially, so that the right-hand side of equation (13) is negative, then k' is decreasing. The decrease in k' will increase $\Delta k'/k'$ and thus make k' fall more slowly, until k' stops falling. Therefore, independently of its initial position, k' gravitates automatically towards an equilibrium where $\Delta k'/k' = 0$. When this long-run equilibrium has been reached, equation (13) can be solved for the long-run equilibrium value of k':

$$k' = \left(\frac{sB}{n + q + \delta}\right)^{\frac{1}{a}} \tag{14}$$

and for the corresponding long-run equilibrium values of capital per worker $(k = k'e^{qt} = k'(A/B)^{1/a})$ and output per head $(y = Ak^{1-a})$:

$$k = \left(\frac{sA}{n + q + \delta}\right)^{\frac{1}{a}} \tag{15}$$

$$y = A^{\frac{1}{a}}\left(\frac{s}{n + q + \delta}\right)^{\frac{1-a}{a}} \tag{16}$$

Because the long-run equilibrium levels of k and y are endogenously determined by equations (15) and (16), their ratio (k/y) is also endogenous. Specifically, the capital/output ratio can be found by dividing equation (16) into equation (15). This gives

$$\frac{k}{y} = \frac{s}{n + q + \delta} \tag{17}$$

Solow resolved the overidentification problem in the Harrod–Domar model by making the capital/output ratio endogenous.

Taking logarithms on both sides of equation (16) and differentiating all the terms with respect to time, we see that if $A = Be^{aqt}$, the growth rate of output per head must be the same as the rate of technological progress: $g - n = q$, as before. This result is confirmed by the long-run constancy of the ratio $k' = K/(e^{qt}L)$ in equation (14), at least as long as s, B, n, q, and δ are all constant. Even so, equation (16) shows that an increase in the saving rate increases the level of output per capita in the long run. This means that increased saving increases economic growth at least as long as it takes output per head to reach its new long-run equilibrium value. The same applies to an improvement in technology and a reduction of population growth or depreciation. We shall return to these equations and their implications in Appendix 3.2.

Distribution of income

The long-run equilibrium of the Solow model is also consistent with a constant distribution of national income between labour and capital. Maximization of profit requires labour and capital to be employed to the point where they earn the equivalent of their marginal product. Thus, setting the real wage (w) and the real interest rate (r) equal to the marginal products of labour and capital obtained from the production function (3) gives

$$w = a\frac{Y}{L} \tag{18}$$

$$r + \delta = (1 - a)\frac{Y}{K} \tag{19}$$

By equation (18), the real wage increases over time at the same rate as output per head, while by equation (19), the real interest rate is constant, because the capital/output ratio and the depreciation rate are constant. The depreciation rate appears in equation (19) because output (Y) is gross output (GNP). The shares of labour and capital in output are given by the constant coefficients of the production function, which means that the distribution of income between the two factors of production is constant:

$$\frac{wL}{Y} + \frac{(r + \delta)K}{Y} = a + (1 - a) = 1 \tag{20}$$

Appendix 2.3.
Endogenous Growth

Let output be produced by labour L and capital K as before:

$$Y = AL^aK^{1-a} \tag{1}$$

where A represents accumulated technological know-how, which is now tied to capital per worker by

$$A = E\left(\frac{K}{L}\right)^a \tag{2}$$

where E is a constant. This is what is meant by 'learning by doing': by using capital, workers learn how to use it more productively. The assumption that the elasticity of technology with respect to the capital/labour ratio in equation (2) is equal to the elasticity of output with respect to labour in equation (1), both labelled a, is made for simplicity, because substituting equation (2) into equation (1) gives

$$Y = EK \tag{3}$$

where E reflects efficiency. Output thus depends solely on the capital stock and the efficiency with which it is used in production. Output depends, in other words, on the quantity and quality of capital.

By taking logarithms on both sides of equation (2) and differentiating with respect to time, we get the following expression for the rate of technological progress, which we denote aq as before:

$$aq = a\left(\frac{\Delta K}{K} - n\right) \tag{4}$$

Because E is a constant, we have $\Delta Y = E\Delta K$, which means that output and capital must grow at the same rate ($g = \Delta Y/Y = \Delta K/K$). Therefore, equation (4) can be re-expressed as

$$q = g - n \tag{5}$$

just as in the Solow model (see equation (6) in Appendix 2.2).

Suppose now, as before, that saving is proportional to output ($S = sY$) and is equal to gross investment ($I = \Delta K + \delta K$), i.e. $sY = \Delta K + \delta K$. Combining this with $\Delta Y = E\Delta K$ by eliminating ΔK and solving for $\Delta Y/Y$, we get

$$g = sE - \delta \tag{6}$$

Thus the Harrod–Domar model from Appendix 2.1 has been restored, with two modifications. First, instead of the capital/output ratio (v) we now have its inverse, E, emerging from a story about how technology depends on capital per worker through learning by doing. Second, unlike in the Harrod–Domar model, the condition that the growth of per capita output equals the rate of technological progress neither involves an inconsistency (because now we derive, rather than just assume, the proportionality of capital to output), nor does this condition make economic growth exogenous, precisely because technological progress is now itself endogenous. This is the essence of endogenous growth.

Appendix 3.1. More on Endogenous Growth

We saw in Appendix 2.3 how learning by doing turns technological advance into an endogenous variable, thus freeing economic growth to respond, as in the Harrod–Domar model, to changes in saving, efficiency, and depreciation, even in the long run. We saw there that the rate of growth remains equal to population growth plus the rate of technological progress. Even so, precisely because technical progress is endogenous, growth also is endogenous.

The structure of our benchmark model of endogenous growth is simple. The model consists of just two equations, the Harrod–Domar equation and an equation showing how technological progress, q, mirrors economic growth per capita:

$$g = sE - \delta \tag{1}$$

$$q = g - n \tag{2}$$

These equations provide the basis for Figures 3.1 to 3.4. The G lines in the figures are horizontal: they show that growth, by equation (1), depends solely on the saving rate, efficiency, and depreciation, without regard to technological change. If we want to focus on growth of output per head rather than on growth of output, we can subtract population growth (n) from both sides of equation (1). The 45° lines labelled T in the figures show the equality between technological progress and output growth per capita by equation (2).

Research and development

Learning by doing is not the only reason why technological progress and hence growth can be viewed as endogenous. Research and development (R&D) is another.[4] Suppose for a moment that there is no capital. Accordingly, output is made by labour alone. Consider, for instance, the following linear production function:

$$Y = A(1 - b)L \tag{3}$$

Here A reflects technology as before and b represents the fraction of the labour force that is engaged in the production of R&D. This means that the rest of the labour force, $(1 - b)L$, is available to produce other than R&D. Suppose also that knowledge accumulates, i.e. is produced, according to this production function:

$$\Delta A = BbLA \tag{4}$$

where B is a constant. This tells us that new knowledge flows from two sources: (i) the number of workers (bL) producing knowledge in the R&D sector and (ii) existing knowledge (A). By equation (4), knowledge grows at the rate BbL per year, which means that $A = Ce^{BbLt}$, where C is a constant. By equation (3), if b is fixed, output must grow at a rate that equals the rate of accumulation of knowledge plus the rate of population growth:

$$g = BbL + n \tag{5}$$

Equivalently, growth of output per capita, $g - n$, equals BbL.

Economic growth is endogenous in this R&D model, but in a special way. It can be increased by devoting more labour to the production of knowledge in the R&D sector (for example, through tax-financed government subsidy of research), but growth nevertheless remains immune to changes in the saving rate and in the depreciation of capital. Also, growth varies directly with the size of the population in this model, because the larger the population, the more workers there will be in the R&D industry. These results continue to hold when capital is included to the model. Then our production function (3) can be replaced by

$$Y = [A(1 - b)L]^a K^{1-a} \tag{6}$$

Therefore, if output grows at the same rate as the capital stock, we see that both output and capital must grow at the rate given in equation (5).

Education

Consider once again the Cobb–Douglas production function

$$Y = AL^a K^{1-a} \tag{7}$$

where A reflects technology as before. Let us now assume that the state of technology depends on the stock of human capital per person (c) as follows:

$$A = c^a \tag{8}$$

The production function (7) can then be rewritten as follows:

$$Y = (cL)^a K^{1-a} \tag{9}$$

where cL is the stock of human capital—i.e. the amount of human capital per person times the number of persons. Moreover, let us assume that c evolves over time according to

$$\frac{\Delta c}{c} = 1 - h \tag{10}$$

where h is the proportion of hours of work devoted to current production and $1 - h$ is the remainder, which is allotted to education by assumption.[5] The more time is spent at school, the less time remains available for work—current production falls, whereas the rate of growth of human capital per person increases. The structure of this model is exactly the same as that of the Solow model (see equations (3) and (4) in Appendix 2.2). Therefore, the rate of growth of output must be

$$g = n + 1 - h \tag{11}$$

just as in equation (6) in Appendix 2.2, so long as $1 - h = q$. This makes growth endogenous in this model because the resources, including time, devoted to education are themselves endogenous. More education (i.e. a decrease in h) means more rapid growth. We revisit this case in Appendix 4.4.

The level of income per head

To find the levels of capital per worker and output per head, as we did in the Solow model in Appendix 2.2, we now turn to the theory of the firm, which tells us that corporate profits reach a maximum when capital is employed up to, but not beyond, the point where its marginal product is equal to the gross real rate of interest $(r + \delta)$:

$$\frac{dY}{dK} = (1 - a)\frac{Y}{K} = (1 - a)E = r + \delta \tag{12}$$

This equation is the same as equation (19) in Appendix 2.2, except there we did not replace Y/K by E.

In a closed economy or a large open economy, the interest rate (r) can be viewed as an endogenous variable, which can be influenced by domestic monetary, financial, and fiscal policy, and E as an exogenous variable: then, we see that $r = (1 − a)E − \delta$ by equation (12).[6] If, for example, the share of capital in national income $1 − a = 1/3$, $E = 0.3$, and $\delta = 0.04$, then $r = 0.06$. In a small open economy, on the other hand, it may be reasonable to view the domestic rate of interest rate as an exogenous variable, which follows the world interest rate set in international financial markets and is, therefore, immune to changes in domestic policies. In this case, the roles of r and E are reversed. Now E is the endogenous variable: $E = (r + \delta)/(1 − a)$. Therefore, if $r = 0.06$, $\delta = 0.04$, and $1 − a = 1/3$ as above, then $E = 0.3$, which entails a capital/output ratio of 3.3.

Let us stick to the closed-economy or large-open-economy version of the model, and thus view the domestic interest rate as an endogenous variable. Then efficiency can be viewed as exogenous. And since our main interest is in output per head rather than in output itself, let us reformulate equation (12) in per capita terms. If the production function is rewritten as $y = Ak^{1−a}$, where $y = Y/L$ and $k = K/L$ as before, then equation (12) becomes

$$\frac{dy}{dk} = (1 − a)Ak^{−a} = r + \delta \tag{13}$$

Solving this equation for k and substituting the result into the production function $y = Ak^{1−a}$, we obtain the following expressions for capital per worker and output per capita:

$$k = \left[\frac{(1 − a)A}{r + \delta}\right]^{\frac{1}{a}} \tag{14}$$

$$y = A^{\frac{1}{a}}\left(\frac{1 − a}{r + \delta}\right)^{\frac{1 − a}{a}} \tag{15}$$

The capital/output ratio is found by dividing equation (15) into equation (14). This gives

$$\frac{k}{y} = \frac{1 − a}{r + \delta} \tag{16}$$

Endogenous vs. exogenous growth

Equation (15) shows that the long-run steady-state level of output per head varies directly with technology, including efficiency, and the share of capital in output (A and $1 − a$), and inversely with the rates of real interest depreciation (r and δ). These are the same results as the ones we derived from the Solow model in Appendix 2.2, with two modifications. First, while an increase in the share of capital increases output per head in the endogenous-growth model, an increase in the saving rate increases output per head in the Solow model. Second, while an increase in the real rate of interest reduces output per head in the endogenous-growth model, an increase in the sum of the rates of population growth and technological progress reduces output per head in the Solow model.

There is more here than meets the eye. We saw in Appendix 2.2, equations (12)–(15), that the saving rate can be expressed as

$$s = \frac{I}{Y} = \left(\frac{\Delta K + \delta K}{K}\right)\frac{K}{Y} = (g + \delta)\frac{K}{Y} \tag{17}$$

Because $K/Y = k/y$, we can substitute equation (16) into equation (17) to get

$$s = (1 − a)\left(\frac{g + \delta}{r + \delta}\right) \tag{18}$$

Dividing through this equation by $g + \delta$ and replacing g by $n + q$, which always holds, whether technological change and economic growth are endogenous or exogenous, we obtain

$$\frac{s}{n + q + \delta} = \frac{1 − a}{r + \delta} \tag{19}$$

There is only one free parameter in this equation, the real interest rate, r, for all the others are either exogenous (s, n, δ, and a) or already determined (q). Suppose r adjusts to satisfy equation (19). Then efficiency must follow by equation (12). If so, efficiency is no longer free to adjust: a key feature of endogenous growth has then been lost. Substituting equation (19) into equations (14), (15), and (16), we are, in fact, back in the Solow model:

$$k = \left(\frac{sA}{n + q + \delta}\right)^{\frac{1}{a}} \tag{20}$$

$$y = A^{\frac{1}{a}}\left(\frac{s}{n + q + \delta}\right)^{\frac{1-a}{a}} \tag{21}$$

$$\frac{k}{y} = \frac{s}{n + q + \delta} \tag{22}$$

which are identical to equations (15), (16), and (17) in Appendix 2.2.

The two models do not coincide, however, if some additional mechanism (e.g. increasing returns to scale)[7] is brought into the endogenous-growth story in order to 'free' the real interest rate and thereby also efficiency and output per head, so that they can differ in the long run from those that follow from the Solow model.

Let us look more closely at the capital/output ratio in equations (16) and (22). In the endogenous-growth model, as in the Harrod–Domar-model and in the Solow model, the capital/output ratio is constant, that is, shows no trend, provided that its underlying determinants—here, the real interest rate, depreciation, and the share of capital in output by equation (16) and, equivalently, the saving rate, population growth, productivity growth, and depreciation by equation (22)—are all constant. As there is no *a priori* reason or empirical evidence to believe that any of these determinants of the capital/output ratio move up or down along trend over long periods, either model accordingly predicts that the capital/output ratio will remain constant over time.

Notice also the implication of equations (15) and (21) for economic growth. If there were no growth in A, there would be no growth in y either (Y would grow at the same rate as L, the labour force). But we have assumed that $A = E(K/L)^a$ through learning by doing (this is, after all, the key to endogenous growth), so that A grows at the rate aq. This, in turn, means that technology advances at the rate $a(g - n)$, so that $q = g - n$. The result that q follows $g - n$ means that g is free to react endogenously to increased saving and so on, even if $g = q + n$ by equations (15) and (21). From equations (14) and (15), and equations (20) and (21), we see that both capital per worker and output per head grow at the rate q, so that the capital/output ratio must be constant, as confirmed by equations (16) and (22).

Endogenous growth accounting

Now consider two countries, 1 and 2, each of which grows in keeping with the Harrod–Domar formula, $g = sE - \delta$. Then the difference between their growth rates is

$$g_1 - g_2 = s_1 E_1 - \delta_1 - s_2 E_2 + \delta_2 \tag{23}$$

where g_1 is the growth rate of country 1 and so on. Adding and subtracting $s_2 E_1$ from the right-hand side of equation (23) we get

$$g_1 - g_2 = (s_1 - s_2)E_1 + s_2(E_1 - E_2) - \delta_1 + \delta_2 \tag{24}$$

If we denote $g_1 - g_2$ by Δg and so on, we have

$$\Delta g = E_1 \Delta s + s_2 \Delta E - \Delta \delta \tag{25}$$

which is the formula employed in the text. The formula can be applied to comparisons of economic growth at different times as well as in different places.

Appendix 3.2. More on Exogenous Growth

As we saw in Appendix 2.2, an increase in the propensity to save cannot have any effect on economic growth in the long run in the neoclassical model, simply because long-run growth is exogenous in that model. However, we also saw that an increase in the saving rate increases economic growth for a time, that is, as long as it takes the capital/output ratio to move to its new long-run steady-state equilibrium level.

The capital/output ratio

Let us now consider this adjustment mechanism in more detail. It is worth repeating equation (11) from Appendix 2.2:

$$g = a(n + q) + (1 - a)\left(s\frac{Y}{K} - \delta\right)$$
(1)

This equation tells us that an increase in the saving rate increases growth, other things being equal. Differentiating g with respect to s, if you prefer, we get $dg/ds = (1 - a)Y/K > 0$. But the capital/output ratio will not stay put, because an increase in the saving rate increases the capital stock more than it increases output, so that K/Y increases. Why? Increased saving increases the capital stock, which in turn increases output, but—this is a key point—output increases less than capital because of diminishing returns to capital. For example, if the share of capital in output $(1 - a)$ is one-third, then a 15 per cent increase in capital will increase output by 5 per cent, other things being equal. This is why the capital/output ratio will increase, thus offsetting the initially stimulating effect of increased saving on growth.

How far will the capital/output ratio increase? Solow showed that it will increase all the way up to the level

$$\frac{K}{Y} = \frac{s}{n + q + \delta}$$
(2)

which restores the term sY/K to its original level, $n + q + \delta$, thereby nullifying the growth stimulus from increased saving in the long run.[8]

But even if the saving rate has no effect on economic growth in the long run, it does affect output per capita in the long run, as shown by equation (16) in Appendix 2.2 (and also in equation (21) in Appendix 3.2), which we repeat here once again:

$$y = A^{\frac{1}{a}}\left(\frac{s}{n + q + \delta}\right)^{\frac{1-a}{a}}$$
(3)

This equation states that a high saving rate is associated with a high level of output per head. An increase in the saving rate must increase output per head and, thereby, also its rate of growth in the medium term, that is, as long as it takes output per capita to reach its new long-run equilibrium level.

Equations (1)–(3) tell a similar story about technology, including economic efficiency. An increase in the rate of technological progress, q, increases growth immediately through the first term on the right-hand side of equation (1). At the same time, it reduces the long-run capital/output ratio by equation (2), thus gradually stimulating growth further through the second term on the right-hand side of equation (1). In the end, output growth will increase by the amount of the increase in the rate of technological progress, which started the process. Notice also from equation (3) that a once-and-for-all increase in the level of technology (A), like an increase in the saving rate, lifts the level of output per head in the long run and, thereby, increases also its rate of growth until a new long-run equilibrium is reached. In this case, however, as in the case of saving, the rate of economic growth in the long run is not affected by a static, once-and-for-all improvement in technology or efficiency. To have a lasting effect on the rate of economic growth in the long run, a change in technology or efficiency must be dynamic: it must involve a permanent increase in the pace of technological progress.

Equation (3) also shows that the long-run level of output per capita is inversely related to population growth, technical progress, and depreciation. The reason is this: the more rapidly the labour force grows in quantity and quality, the latter through productivity gains, and the more rapidly the capital stock depreciates, the more of society's saving it takes to maintain the ratio of capital to labour (in efficiency units) intact, thereby leaving correspondingly less available for increasing the capital stock to keep up with population growth, technological progress, and depreciation. But remember also that $A = Be^{aqt}$. This means that any initial dip in output per head due to an increase in q in the denominator of the right-hand side of equation (3) will soon be offset by the positive effect of q on A in the same equation.

How strong are the effects?

Equation (3) can be used to quantify the sensitivity of output per capita to its determinants. Suppose that the shares of labour and capital in national income are $a = 2/3$ and $1 - a = 1/3$. Equation (3) then takes the following form:

$$y = \sqrt{\frac{sA^3}{n + q + \delta}} \tag{4}$$

From this equation we infer that

- A doubling of the saving rate (say, from 0.1 to 0.2) increases output per head by 50 per cent in the long run (because, by taking logarithms and differentiating, we find that $d \ln(y)/d \ln(s) = 0.5$).
- A doubling of efficiency has an even stronger effect: it increases output per head by 150 per cent in the long run (because $d \ln(y)/d \ln(A) = 1.5$).
- If $q = 0.01$ and $\delta = 0.03$, then a doubling of population growth from 1 to 2 per cent per year reduces output per head in the long run by 10 per cent (as $d \ln(y)/d n = -0.5/(n+q+\delta) = -0.5/(0.01+0.01+0.03) = -10$, evaluated at the initial value of n).
- A doubling of depreciation from 3 to 6 per cent per year reduces output per head in the long run by 10 per cent (because $d \ln(y)/d \delta = -0.5/(n+q+\delta) = -0.5/(0.01+0.01+0.03) = -10$, again evaluated at the initial value of δ).

Equation (4) can further be used to assess the extent to which the Solow model can explain observed differences in output per capita. The ratio of a rich country's income per head, y_R, to that of a poor country, y_P, is

$$\frac{y_R}{y_P} = \sqrt{\left(\frac{A_R}{A_P}\right)^3 \left(\frac{s_R}{s_P}\right) \left(\frac{n_P + q_P + \delta_P}{n_R + q_R + \delta_R}\right)} \tag{5}$$

Suppose that the rich country (a) is twice as efficient as the poor country ($A_R/A_P = 2$); (b) saves twice as much of its income ($s_R/s_P = 2$); and (c) has 50 per cent less population growth plus technological progress plus depreciation $[(n_P+q_P+\delta_P)/(n_R+q_R+\delta_R) = 2]$. Then the rich country's output per head in the long run will be almost six times that of the poor country. If the differences between the two countries' efficiency, saving rates, etc., are threefold rather than twofold, then the corresponding income difference is almost 16-fold, and so on.

Appendix 3.3. Optimal Saving and Growth

The rule for optimal growth described in the text can be derived as follows. Consider an individual who needs to decide how to divide the present value of his total earnings (Y^*) between consumption today (C_1) and consumption tomorrow (C_2) in order to maximize his utility over time, i.e. both today and tomorrow. Suppose the following logarithmic utility function

$$U = \ln(C_1) + \frac{\ln(C_2)}{1 + \rho} \tag{1}$$

where ρ is the discount rate, which reflects the shape of the indifference map associated with the utility function. Utility needs to be maximized subject to the constraint that the present discounted value of consumption today and consumption tomorrow equals that of total earnings (Y^*):

$$C_1 + \frac{C_2}{1 + r} = Y^* \tag{2}$$

where r is the real interest rate, which, like the discount rate, is measured in per cent per year. Solving equation (2) for C_2 and substituting the result into equation (1) gives

$$U = \ln(C_1) + \left(\frac{1}{1 + \rho}\right) \ln[(1 + r)(Y^* - C_1)] \tag{3}$$

The maximization of U with respect to C_1 requires

$$\frac{dU}{dC_1} = \frac{1}{C_1} - \left(\frac{1}{1 + \rho}\right)\left(\frac{1}{Y^* - C_1}\right) = 0 \tag{4}$$

which gives the following solution for the optimal amount of C_1:

$$C_1 = \left(\frac{1 + \rho}{2 + \rho}\right) Y^* \tag{5}$$

Plugging equation (5) into equation (2), we find the corresponding optimal amount of C_2:

$$C_2 = \left(\frac{1 + r}{2 + \rho}\right) Y^* \tag{6}$$

We see that C_1 and C_2 are both proportional to Y^*.

Dividing equation (6) by equation (5), we find the optimal ratio of C_2 to C_1: [9]

$$\frac{C_2}{C_1} = \frac{1 + r}{1 + \rho} \approx 1 + r - \rho \tag{7}$$

The optimal rate of growth of consumption per capita, $g - n = C_2/C_1 - 1$, is thus equal to the real rate of interest adjusted for impatience, $r - \rho$, or: [10]

$$g = r - \rho + n \tag{8}$$

This is the optimal growth equation depicted by the G lines in Figures 3.19–3.27. Because an increases in the real interest rate increases optimal growth point for point, the G lines form 45° angles with the horizontal axes in the figures.

Exogenous growth

The model behind Figures 3.19–3.23 consists of two equations, equation (8) above for optimal growth (the G line) and the Solow equation g = n + q (the S line). Solving these two equations together for the optimal growth rate and the real interest rate gives

$$g = n + q \tag{9}$$

$$r = q + \rho \tag{10}$$

From this pair of reduced-form equations we can immediately see that (a) an increase in population growth increases the optimal rate of economic growth, but not the real interest rate; (b) increased technological progress increases both optimal growth and the real interest rate; and (c) increased impatience—i.e. an increase in ρ, which reflects a reduction in the willingness to save—increases the real interest rate, but not the optimal rate of economic growth.

Endogenous growth

The model behind Figures 3.24–3.27 also consists of two equations, equation (8) above for optimal growth as before (the G line) and equation (12) from Appendix 3.1, r = (1 − a)E − δ, for the real interest rate (the R line). The reduced-form solution to these two equations is

$$g = (1 - a)E - \delta - \rho + n \tag{11}$$

$$r = (1 - a)E - \delta \tag{12}$$

These equations show that (a) an increase in efficiency increases both optimal economic growth and the real interest rate; (b) an increase in depreciation reduces both optimal growth and the interest rate; (c) increased impatience—i.e. an increase in ρ, with less willingness to save—now reduces the optimal rate of growth, but leaves the real interest rate unchanged; and (d) an increase in population growth increases optimal economic growth, but not the real interest rate.

Optimal saving and the golden rule

In either case, the optimal saving rate—i.e. the saving rate that is consistent with the chosen consumption path that produces optimal economic growth—can be found by referring back to equation (18) in Appendix 3.1, which we repeat here:

$$s = (1 - a)\left(\frac{g + \delta}{r + \delta}\right) \tag{13}$$

Notice that if the discount rate (ρ) happens to equal the population growth rate (n), so that economic growth equals the real rate of interest by equation (8), then equation (13) boils down to s = 1 − a, which is known as the golden rule of capital accumulation.[11]

By the golden rule, the typical consumer maximizes his consumption over time by saving his capital income (because 1 − a is the share of capital in national income) and consumes the rest, i.e. his labour income. Let us see why. We view the typical consumer also as an investor, for example in his capacity as a co-owner or stockholder in a firm. The golden rule dictates that the consumer, as an investor, should accumulate capital as long as the accumulation increases consumption—that is, as long as it adds more to output than it does to investment. This is because output equals consumption plus investment by definition. When the critical point is reached where the build-up of capital adds as much to investment as to output, consumption is at a maximum and no further capital should be accumulated. If it is, consumption will fall, because further accumulation beyond the critical point increases investment more than it does output.

How do we locate this critical point? It is where consumption per capita $[c = (1 - s)y]$ is at a maximum, i.e. where

$$c = (1 - s)y = (1 - s)A^{\frac{1}{a}}\left(\frac{s}{n + q + \delta}\right)^{\frac{1-a}{a}} \tag{14}$$

where the long-run equilibrium level of output per capita from equation (3) in Appendix 3.2 has been substituted for y, is at a maximum. Differentiating c with respect to s in equation (14) yields

$$\frac{dc}{ds} = (1 - s)A^{\frac{1}{a}}\left(\frac{s}{n + q + \delta}\right)^{\frac{1-a}{a}}\left(\frac{1-a}{a}\right)\left(\frac{1}{s}\right) - A^{\frac{1}{a}}\left(\frac{s}{n + q + \delta}\right)^{\frac{1-a}{a}} = 0 \tag{15}$$

Dividing through this equation by the second term on the right-hand side leaves us with

$$\left(\frac{1-s}{s}\right)\left(\frac{1-a}{a}\right) = 1 \tag{16}$$

which means that

$$s = 1 - a \tag{17}$$

Hence the golden rule.

When we add impatience to the above story, the plot thickens a bit. By substituting the reduced-form solutions for g and r in equations (9)–(12) into the right-hand side of equation (13), we can express the optimal saving rate in terms of exogenous parameters only. In the case of exogenous growth, this gives

$$s = (1 - a)\left(\frac{n + q + \delta}{q + \rho + \delta}\right) \tag{18}$$

With endogenous growth, we get

$$s = (1 - a)\left(\frac{(1 - a)E - \rho + n}{(1 - a)E}\right) = 1 - a - \frac{\rho - n}{E} \tag{19}$$

The optimal saving rate is endogenously determined in either case. Notice, in particular, the inverse relationship between impatience (ρ) and the saving rate in equations (18) and (19): in both cases, less patience leads to less saving, as it should. These formulae are slightly more complex than the golden rule, but when $\rho = n$, we have $s = 1 - a$ as in equation (13) and the golden rule is restored.

Numbers

In its simplest form, where $s = 1 - a = 1/3$, the golden rule prescribes a saving rate which exceeds those observed in the world with only a few exceptions, as is discussed in the text. However, when economic growth is, say, 3 per cent per year, the real interest rate is 6 per cent, and depreciation is 4 per cent, then equation (13) yields an optimal saving rate of 23 per cent, the weighted world average in 1995.

Appendix 4.1.
Liberalization, Efficiency, and Growth

Consider a country with two sectors, a traditional sector and a modern sector. Let the production possibility frontier be described by

$$T = a - \left(\frac{1}{2b}\right)M^2 \tag{1}$$

where T is traditional output, M is modern output, and a and b are positive parameters. The quadratic form of the equation ensures a concave production frontier like the one shown in Figure 4.12 in the text.

The ratio of the world market prices of modern and traditional output is $p^* = P_M^*/P_T^*$. The world price line through points E and A in Figure 4.12 has the slope $-p^* = -CE/CA$, so that CA $= CE/p^* = CE(P_T^*/P_M^*)$. CA reflects the amount of traditional output CE measured in units of modern output, i.e. the nominal value of traditional output P_T^*CE deflated by the price of modern output P_M^*.

The domestic, distorted ratio of the prices of modern and traditional output is $p = P_M/P_T$. Suppose restrictions on trade—say, a tariff on imports competing with traditional output—drive the domestic price ratio artificially low, because $P_T = (1+t)P_T^*$, where t is the tariff rate, and that modern output commands the same price at home and abroad, so that $P_M = P_M^*$. The slope of the domestic price line touching the production frontier at point E in the figure can now be expressed as $-p = -p^*/(1+t)$. The absolute value of the difference between the two slopes is

$$p^* - p = p^* - \frac{p^*}{1+t} = \left(\frac{t}{1+t}\right)p^* \tag{2}$$

The domestic and foreign price ratios are, therefore, related by

$$p = (1-c)p^* \tag{3}$$

where $c = t/(1+t)$, which lies between 0 and 1, is a measure of the domestic price distortion. If $c = 0$, because $t = 0$, there is no distortion and $p = p^*$. As t approaches infinity and c approaches 1, the distortion becomes infinitely large. In Figure 4.12, c is reflected by the angle between lines showing the domestic, distorted price ratio and the world price ratio.

Profit maximization by domestic producers requires that

$$\frac{dT}{dM} = -\left(\frac{1}{b}\right)M = -p \tag{4}$$

Therefore, the supply of modern output is described by

$$M = bp \tag{5}$$

Modern output is directly proportional to its relative price.

The reallocation effect

Now suppose the trade restrictions are lifted, so that world market price ratio (p^*) becomes relevant to domestic producers. It is no longer profitable for them to produce at point E in the figure. Accordingly, resources are transferred from the traditional sector to the modern sector. Production moves from E to F in the figure. The resulting increase in total output (i.e. GNP) is shown by the bold segment AB on the horizontal axis.

Let us now work out the relationship between the output gain from liberalization and the initial relative price distortion. Total output, measured in units of modern output at world market prices, is given by

$$Y = M + \left(\frac{1}{p^*}\right)T \tag{6}$$

The increase in output from the pre-trade equilibrium point E in the figure to the free-trade equilibrium point F is

$$\Delta Y = Y_F - Y_E \tag{7}$$

This amount corresponds to AB on the horizontal axis.

We now have to assess the two terms on the right-hand side of equation (7). Equations (1), (5), and (6) permit us to write total output at the new equilibrium F and at the old equilibrium E as follows:

$$Y_F = bp^* + \left(\frac{1}{p^*}\right)\left[a - \left(\frac{1}{2b}\right)b^2 p^{*2}\right] \tag{8}$$

$$Y_E = bp + \left(\frac{1}{p^*}\right)\left[a - \left(\frac{1}{2b}\right)b^2 p^2\right] \tag{9}$$

Subtracting equation (9) from equation (8) yields the increase in total output from E to F:

$$\Delta Y = Y_F - Y_E = b(p^* - p) + \left(\frac{1}{p^*}\right)\left[\left(\frac{b}{2}\right)(p^2 - p^{*2})\right] \tag{10}$$

Substituting $p = (1 - c)p^*$ from equation (3) into equation (10), using $M = bp^*$ at point F from equation (5), simplifying, and dividing through the result by Y_E, we get at last[12]

$$\frac{Y_F - Y_E}{Y_E} = \frac{1}{2}\left(\frac{M_F}{Y_E}\right)c^2 \tag{11}$$

The percentage increase in total output from E to F in Figure 4.12 is thus proportional to the square of the original price distortion c.

This result can be interpreted as follows. First, the larger the original trade distortion, the greater will be the gain from removing it. Second, the larger the share of the modern sector after liberalization, i.e. the more ambitious the liberalization effort, the greater will be the output gain at the end of the day.

Because liberalization increases total economic output at full employment, it increases efficiency by definition, and thereby also economic growth.

The reorganization effect

Let the liberalization also trigger an increase in productivity in the previously protected traditional sector. Equation (1) then needs to be respecified as follows

$$T = h\left[a - \left(\frac{1}{2b}\right)M^2\right] \tag{12}$$

where h is a positive parameter that reflects productivity in the traditional sector. Let h increase by

$$\frac{\Delta h}{h} = kc \tag{13}$$

in response to the liberalization undertaken to eliminate the distortion c, and k is a positive constant. The larger the initial price distortion c, the larger is the induced proportional productivity increase in the traditional sector. The production frontier shifts upwards from DEFG to JHG in Figure 4.14.

At point H in the figure, we now have the new tangency condition

$$\frac{dT}{dM} = -\left(\frac{h}{b}\right)M = -p^* \tag{14}$$

so that the relationship between the supply of modern output and its relative price is

$$M = \frac{bp^*}{h} \tag{15}$$

Therefore, the increase in productivity in the traditional sector by Δh reduces modern output according to

$$\Delta M = -\left(\frac{bp^*}{h^2}\right)\Delta h = -M\frac{\Delta h}{h} = -Mkc \tag{16}$$

The corresponding change in traditional output is found by a second-order Taylor expansion of equation (12): [13]

$$\Delta T = \frac{\partial T}{\partial M}\Delta M - \frac{1}{2}\frac{\partial^2 T}{\partial M^2}(\Delta M)^2 = -\left(\frac{h}{b}M\right)(-Mkc) - \frac{1}{2}\left(-\frac{h}{b}\right)(Mkc)^2 \tag{17}$$

The increase in total output resulting from these changes is found by combining equations (6), (16), and (17):

$$\Delta Y = \Delta M + \left(\frac{1}{p^*}\right)\Delta T = -Mkc + \left(\frac{1}{p^*}\right)\left[-\left(\frac{h}{b}M\right)(-Mkc) - \frac{1}{2}\left(-\frac{h}{b}\right)(Mkc)^2\right] \tag{18}$$

which, because M = bp*/h by equation (15), simplifies to

$$\Delta Y = \frac{1}{2}Mk^2c^2 \tag{19}$$

This is the output gain from reorganization, i.e. the change in output from F to H in Figure 4.14, which is shown by the segment BC on the horizontal axis in the figure. Adding this to the output gain from reallocation from equation (11), which is shown by the segment AB, we obtain

$$\Delta Y = \frac{1}{2}M(1 + k^2)c^2 \tag{20}$$

Here we have the total output gain from liberalization through reallocation and reorganization—that is, AC = AB + BC.[14] By dividing through equation (20) by initial output, we obtain

$$\frac{\Delta Y}{Y} = \frac{1}{2}\left(\frac{M}{Y}\right)(1 + k^2)c^2 \tag{21}$$

As the reallocation gain from liberalization is proportional to the square of the original price distortion by equation (11), so the combined reallocation and reorganization gain from liberalization is proportional to the square of the same original price distortion, except now the proportionality factor is a slightly more complicated expression. If there is no reorganization effect, i.e. if k = 0, then equation (21) simplifies to equation (11).

Appendix 4.2.
Stabilization, Efficiency, and Growth

Imagine now an economy where two different kinds of capital are used in production, real capital (K) and financial capital (M), i.e. money (in real terms). Let us abstract from other factors of production, or hold them fixed. Output (Y) is produced by K and M:

$$Y = \sqrt{KM} \tag{1}$$

The equation of an isoquant corresponding to the production function (1) is

$$K = \frac{Y^2}{M} \tag{2}$$

For given output, the substitutability between K and M can be approximated by a second-order Taylor expansion:

$$\Delta K = -\frac{Y^2}{M^2}\Delta M - \frac{1}{2}(-2)\left(\frac{Y^2}{M^3}\right)(\Delta M)^2 = -\frac{Y^2}{M^2}\Delta M + \left(\frac{Y^2}{M^3}\right)(\Delta M)^2 \tag{3}$$

Linearizing the production function (1) by writing

$$\Delta Y = \frac{1}{2}\sqrt{\frac{M}{K}}\Delta K + \frac{1}{2}\sqrt{\frac{K}{M}}\Delta M \tag{4}$$

and substituting equation (3) into equation (4) and simplifying, we obtain

$$\frac{\Delta Y}{Y} = \frac{1}{2}\left(\frac{\Delta M}{M}\right)^2 \tag{5}$$

Now refer to Figure 4.17 in the text. At the original equilibrium point E, where the inflation rate is equal to π, the slope of the price line EH is $-(1 + \pi)$. At E, the slope of the isoquant tangential to the price line must, therefore, also be $-(1 + \pi)$:

$$\frac{dK}{dM} = -\frac{Y^2}{M^2} = -(1 + \pi) \tag{6}$$

Hence, the income velocity of money ($v = Y/M$) is an increasing function of inflation: $v = \sqrt{1 + \pi}$. Linearizing equation (6) and using the fact that $\Delta\pi = -\pi$, when inflation is brought down to zero, we obtain

$$\frac{2Y^2}{M^2}\left(\frac{\Delta M}{M}\right) = -\Delta \pi = \pi \tag{7}$$

Solving equation (7) for $\Delta M/M$ and substituting the result into equation (5) gives

$$\frac{\Delta Y}{Y} = \frac{1}{8}\left(\frac{\pi}{1 + \pi}\right)^2 \tag{8}$$

Hence, the output gain from economic stabilization is proportional to the square of the original inflation distortion.[15] Now you are probably wondering where the number 8 came from. It is like this. If equation (1) is replaced by a more general Cobb–Douglas function

$$Y = K^a M^{1 - a} \tag{9}$$

where a is between 0 and 1, then, by repeating the steps from equations (2) to (7), it can be shown that the proportional output gain from stabilization is

$$\frac{\Delta Y}{Y} = \frac{1}{2}a(1 - a)\left(\frac{\pi}{1 + \pi}\right)^2 \tag{10}$$

which is identical to equation (8), when a = 0.5 as in equation (1). This formula places an upper bound on the damage that inflation can do by distorting production. In the worst possible case of hyperinflation, where the inflation distortion tends to 1, the cost of inflation, which is the mirror image of the gains from stabilization, can be at most 12.5 per cent (i.e. 1/8). But this is not to say that inflation cannot cause greater damage to output through other channels.

The slope of the isoquant at point E in Figure 4.17 is

$$\frac{dK}{dM} = -\frac{dY/dM}{dY/dK} = -\frac{(1 - a)Y/M}{aY/K} = -\left(\frac{1 - a}{a}\right)\frac{K}{M} = -(1 + \pi) \tag{11}$$

Therefore, the optimal ratio of financial to real capital is inversely related to inflation as follows:

$$\frac{M}{K} = \left(\frac{1 - a}{a}\right)\left(\frac{1}{1 + \pi}\right) \tag{12}$$

There is another, simpler way to capture the link between inflation and growth within this framework. The production function (1) can be rewritten as $Y = \sqrt{KM} = EK$ where $E = \sqrt{M/K}$. The inverse relationship between M/K and π in equation (12) means that increased inflation hurts efficiency and thereby also economic growth. Whether it is 'always and everywhere a monetary phenomenon' (in Milton Friedman's words) or not, there can be no doubt that inflation can have real effects.

Money, inflation, and growth

Consider now the case where the quantity theory of money holds, so that Mv = PY, where M is money (now in nominal terms), v is velocity, P is the price level, and Y is real GNP. Then, if velocity is constant, we can write

$$g = m - \pi \tag{13}$$

where g is the rate of growth of GNP, m is the rate of monetary expansion, and π is the rate of inflation. If the government's budget deficit is financed by printing money, so that $\Delta M/P = G - T$, where G and T are real government expenditures and taxes, then $m = \Delta M/M = [(G - T)/Y](PY/M) = zv$, where z is the budget deficit relative to GNP. Thus, equation (13) can be rewritten as

$$g = vz - \pi \tag{14}$$

Next, suppose growth is endogenous and that efficiency varies inversely with inflation, so that $E = a - b\pi$, for example, through the mechanism laid out in equations (1)–(10), and a and b are positive parameters.[16] Then

$$g = sE - \delta = s(a - b\pi) - \delta \tag{15}$$

Equations (14) and (15) are illustrated by the M schedule and the G schedule in Figure 4.19. Both schedules slope down: we see from equation (14) that the M schedule has the slope -1 and from equation (15) that the G schedule has the slope $-1/sb$. Solving the two equations (14) and (15) together gives the equilibrium rates of inflation and growth:

$$\pi = \frac{vz - sa + \delta}{1 - sb} \tag{16}$$

$$g = \frac{sa - \delta - vzsb}{1 - sb} \tag{17}$$

We assume that $sb < 1$, so that the G schedule is steeper than the M schedule in Figure 4.19 and the denominator in equations (16) and (17) is positive.

The following results can be read directly from equations (16) and (17):

- An increase in the budget deficit (z), in velocity (v), or in depreciation(δ) increases inflation and reduces growth;
- An increase in the autonomous component of efficiency (i.e. in that part (a) which is independent of inflation) reduces inflation and increases growth; and
- An increase in the saving rate reduces inflation and increases growth.

The last conclusion is not as obvious from the equations as the first two, but it becomes clear if you divide through the right-hand side of equation (17) by s: then the only term involving s in the numerator of the equation is $-\delta/s$ and the only term involving s in the denominator is $1/s$, so that a higher saving rate means more growth, even if the relationship is non-linear in this case. From equation (14) we then see that a higher saving rate, by increasing growth, must reduce inflation, because v and z are fixed in this experiment.

A similar story can be told about the simultaneous determination of inflation and growth by assuming the saving rate rather than efficiency to vary inversely with the inflation rate: $s = a - b\pi$, where, again, a and b are positive parameters. Then equation (15) becomes

$$g = (a - b\pi)E - \delta \tag{18}$$

and s can be replaced by E in equations (16) and (17). The only difference this change makes for the three conclusions listed above is that the qualifier 'the autonomous component of' now applies to the saving rate rather than to efficiency.

Appendix 4.3.
Privatization, Efficiency, and Growth

Consider a country with two sectors, a private sector and a public sector. Private and public output are one and the same good, but they differ in quality.[17] Specifically, private output is superior to and, therefore, commands a higher price than public output:

$$P_{priv} = (1 + q)P_{pub} \tag{1}$$

where q is a positive parameter reflecting the quality and price differential. This differential may stem from subsidies (at rate s) to public production and taxes (at rate t) on private production. If so, consumers and producers are willing to buy and sell both private and public output as long as their prices net of taxes and subsidies are the same:

$$(1 - t)P_{priv} = (1 + s)P_{pub} \tag{2}$$

Equations (1) and (2) imply that

$$1 + q = \frac{1 + s}{1 - t} \tag{3}$$

If total output is expressed in terms of public output, then

$$Y = \left(\frac{1-t}{1+s}\right)Y_{priv} + Y_{pub} = \left(\frac{1}{1+q}\right)Y_{priv} + Y_{pub} \tag{4}$$

where $1/(1+q)$ reflects the price ratio between private and public output net of taxes and subsidies. Without taxes and subsidies, we have $q = 0$ and the price ratio is 1.

Suppose now that the production frontier in Figure 4.23 is described by

$$Y_{pub} = a - \left(\frac{1}{2b}\right)Y_{priv}^2 \tag{5}$$

where a and b are positive parameters. The quadratic form of the equation ensures that the production frontier is concave as shown in the figure.

Profit maximization requires that production take place at point E, where the distorted price line is tangential to the production frontier:

$$\frac{dY_{pub}}{dY_{priv}} = -\left(\frac{1}{b}\right)Y_{priv} = -\left(\frac{1}{1+q}\right) \tag{6}$$

so that, at E, we have

$$Y_{priv} = \frac{b}{1+q} \qquad (7)$$

This amount is shown by the distance ON in Figure 4.23. Private output is thus inversely related to the quality and price differential q. Full privatization brings q down to zero, so that Y_{priv} increases from $b/(1 + q)$ to b by equation (7).

The reallocation effect

But our main interest is in total output. At E, total output is the sum of private output from equation (7) and public output from equation (5), that is, OA = ON + OH = ON + NA in the figure:

$$Y_E = \frac{b}{1+q} + a - \frac{1}{2b}\left(\frac{b}{1+q}\right)^2 \qquad (8)$$

After full privatization, when the economy has reached equilibrium at point F in the figure and q has dropped to zero, total output is OB = OK + OJ = OK + KB:

$$Y_F = b + a - \frac{1}{2b}b^2 \qquad (9)$$

Subtracting equation (8) from equation (9) and simplifying we obtain

$$\Delta Y = Y_F - Y_E = \frac{b}{2}\left(\frac{q}{1+q}\right)^2 \qquad (10)$$

where $q/(1 + q)$ is a measure of the quality and price distortion. Once again, the output gain is proportional to the square of the initial price distortion. As before, this distortion is measured by the difference between the slopes of the two price lines, or the angle between them, in Figure 4.23:

$$\frac{q}{1+q} = 1 - \frac{1}{1+q} \qquad (11)$$

By dividing through equation (10) by total pre-privatization output (Y_E) we can express the proportional increase in total output as

$$\frac{Y_F - Y_E}{Y_E} = \frac{1}{2}\left(\frac{Y_{priv}}{Y_E}\right)\left(\frac{q}{1+q}\right)^2 \qquad (12)$$

where Y_{priv}/Y_E is the ratio of private output after privatization to total output before privatization.[18]

The change in output thus varies directly with (a) the scale of the privatization (the larger the chunk of public production that is transferred to the private sector, the larger will be the resulting increase in output) and (b) the magnitude of the initial quality and price distortion q (the larger the distortion, the larger will be the gain from removing it).

The reorganization effect

Suppose now that privatization triggers an increase in productivity in the private sector, so that the production frontier shifts to the right as shown in Figure 4.24 in the text. We can describe this shift by an increase in the coefficient b in equation (5) according to

$$\frac{\Delta b}{b} = kq \qquad (13)$$

where k is a positive constant. The outward shift of the production frontier is thus proportional to the initial quality and price differential. This means that we now have to respecify the equation describing the production frontier as follows:

$$Y_{pub} = a - \left(\frac{1}{2b(1+kq)}\right)Y_{priv}^2 \qquad (14)$$

By repeating the steps we took in equations (6)–(9), it can be shown that the total output gain from privatization is[19]

$$\frac{Y_F - Y_E}{Y_E} = \frac{1}{2}\left(\frac{Y_{priv}}{Y_E}\right)\left[\left(\frac{q}{1+q}\right)^2 + kq\right]\left(\frac{1}{1+kq}\right) \tag{15}$$

The total output gain is still a function of the square of the initial distortion. Without the reorganization effect, we have k = 0 and equation (15) simplifies to equation (12).

Appendix 4.4. Education, Taxes, and Growth

Suppose output is made by human and physical capital as follows:

$$Y = \sqrt{HK} \tag{1}$$

where H is human capital, which is created by and directly proportional to government expenditure on education. To make the example as transparent as possible, let us assume the factor of proportionality connecting human capital to government spending G to be 1, so that H = G, which is financed by a tax on physical capital:

$$G = tK \tag{2}$$

Therefore,

$$Y = \sqrt{t}K \tag{3}$$

where the efficiency parameter in the aggregate production function (3), i.e. the level of output per unit of capital, equals the square root of the tax rate. It follows that the rate of economic growth is

$$g = s\sqrt{t} - \delta \tag{4}$$

Here we have a case where higher taxes are good for growth, other things being equal.

Notes

1. You may remember from Ch. 1 that Thailand's investment rate in 1995 was 43%. In an open economy like that of Thailand, an excess of investment over saving means that imports exceed exports, i.e. that there is a deficit in the current account of the balance of payments. It was this persistent deficit and the associated, but ultimately unsustainable, short-term borrowing from abroad that caused the Thai currency, the baht, to collapse in 1997.

2. See Simon Kuznets, 'Modern Economic Growth: Findings and Reflections', *American Economic Review*, 63 (1973): 247–58. See also Simon Kuznets, *Modern Economic Growth*, Yale University Press, New Haven, 1966, and *Economic Growth of Nations: Total Output and Production Structure*, Harvard University Press, Cambridge, Mass., 1971.

3. Angus Maddison, *Phases of Capitalist Development*, OUP, Oxford, 1982.

4. See Paul M. Romer, 'Endogenous Technical Change', *Journal of Political Economy*, 98 (1990): Pt. 2, S71–S102.

5. This formulation is due to Robert E. Lucas, Jr., 'On the Mechanics of Economic Development', *Journal of Monetary Economics*, 22 (1988): 3–42.

6. In this case, for instance, monetary expansion, by increasing inflation, will reduce efficiency and hence also the real interest rate. The relationship between inflation and growth is discussed in Ch. 4.

7. See Paul M. Romer, 'Increasing Returns and Long-run Growth', *Journal of Political Economy*, 94 (1986): 1002–37.

8. You encountered eq. (2) twice already in Appendix 2.2, first as eq. (7) and then as eq. (17).

9. The approximation in eq. (7) holds for small values of r and ρ.

10. This result is a variation on the so-called Ramsey rule, named after Frank P. Ramsey, 'A Mathematical Theory of Saving', *Economic Journal*, 38 (1928): 543–59. A more general derivation of the Ramsey rule by dynamic optimization methods is provided e.g. by Robert J. Barro and Xavier Sala-i-Martin, *Economic Growth*: ch. 2, McGraw-Hill, New York, 1995, and David Romer, *Advanced Macroeconomics*: ch. 2, McGraw-Hill, New York, 1996.

11. The golden rule was discovered by Edmund Phelps. See e.g. his *Golden Rules of Economic Growth*, W.W. Norton, New York, 1966.

12. Notice that equation (11) shows M_F/Y_E, i.e. modern output at F divided by initial GNP at E, on the right-hand side. If we replace M_F/Y_E by M_F/Y_F, i.e. modern output at F divided by final GNP at F, then the left-hand side of the equation changes accordingly to $(Y_F - Y_E)/Y_F = g/(1 + g)$, where $g = (Y_F - Y_E)/Y_E$.

13. The Taylor expansion is used in order to capture the curvature of the production frontier in eq. (12).

14. For a general statement of these results and for examples of other functional forms, see Thorvaldur Gylfason, *The Macroeconomics of European Agriculture*, Princeton Studies in International Finance, 78, May 1995.

15. For a general statement of this result and an application to a production function with a constant elasticity of substitution, see Thorvaldur Gylfason, 'Output Gains from Economic Stabilization', *Journal of Development Economics*, 56, (1998): 81–96.

16. The coefficient a is not to be confused with its unrelated namesake in eqs. (9)–(12).

17. See Olivier Blanchard, *The Economics of Post-Communist Transition*, Clarendon Press, Oxford, 1997.

18. If we replace Y_{priv}/Y_E by Y_{priv}/Y_F, i.e. private output at F divided by total output at F, then the left-hand side of eq. (12) changes accordingly to $(Y_F - Y_E)/Y_F = g/(1 + g)$, where $g = (Y_F - Y_E)/Y_E$.

19. The derivation is presented in detail in Thorvaldur Gylfason, 'Privatization, Efficiency, and Economic Growth', CEPR Discussion Paper 1844, March 1998.

References

Aghion, Philippe, and Peter Howitt, 'Growth and Unemployment', *Review of Economic Studies* 61 (1994).

—— *Endogenous Growth Theory*, MIT Press, Cambridge, Mass. and London, 1998.

Alesina, Alberto, and Roberto Perotti, 'The Political Economy of Growth: A Critical Survey of the Recent Literature', *World Bank Economic Review* 8 (1994).

Arrow, Kenneth J., 'The Economic Implications of Learning by Doing', *Review of Economic Studies* 29 (1962).

Aschauer, David A., 'Does Public Capital Crowd Out Private Capital?', *Journal of Monetary Economics* 24 (1989).

Asian Development Bank, *Emerging Asia: Changes and Challenges*, Manila, 1997.

Baldwin, Richard, 'The Growth Effects of 1992', *Economic Policy* 9 (1989).

Barro, Robert J., 'Inflation and Economic Growth', Bank of England *Quarterly Bulletin*, May 1995.

—— *The Determinants of Economic Growth*, MIT Press, Cambridge, Mass., 1997.

—— and Xavier Sala-i-Martin, 'Convergence across States and Regions', *Brookings Papers on Economic Activity* 1 (1991).

—— 'Convergence', *Journal of Political Economy* 100 (1992).

—— *Economic Growth*, McGraw-Hill, New York, 1995.

Baumol, William J., 'Productivity Growth, Convergence, and Welfare', *American Economic Review* 76 (1986).

Bénabou, Roland, 'Inequality and Growth', NBER *Macroeconomics Annual* (1996).

Benediktsson, Einar, 'Íslandsljóð' ('Poems for Iceland'), in his *Sögur og kvæði (Stories and Poems)*, Reykjavík, 1897.

Blanchard, Olivier, *The Economics of Post-Communist Transition,*, Clarendon Press, Oxford, 1997.

Blaug, Mark, *Economic Theory in Retrospect*, Irwin, Homewood, Ill., 1962.

Blinder, Alan S., *Hard Heads, Soft Hearts: Tough-minded Economics for a Just Society*, Addison-Wesley, Reading, Mass., 1987.

Branson, William H., *Macroeconomic Theory and Policy*, 3rd edn., Harper & Row, New York, 1989.

Bruno, Michael, and William Easterly, 'Inflation Crises and Long-Run Growth', *Journal of Monetary Economics* 41 (1998).

Buchanan, James M., and Gordon Tullock, *The Calculus of Consent*, University of Michigan Press, Ann Arbor, Mich., 1962.

Cecchini, Paulo, *The European Challenge 1992*, Gower, Aldershot, 1988.

Chenery, Hollis B., and Moshe Syrquin, *Patterns of Development, 1950–1970*, OUP, London, 1975.

—— Sherman Robinson, and Moshe Syrquin, *Industrialization and Growth, A Comparative Study*, OUP, New York, and World Bank, Washington DC, 1986.

De Gregorio, Julio, 'The Effects of Inflation on Economic Growth: Lessons from Latin America', *European Economic Review* 36 (1992).

De Long, J. Bradford, 'Productivity Growth, Convergence, and Welfare: Comment', *American Economic Review* 78 (1988).

Denison, Edward F., *Trends in American Economic Growth, 1929–82*, Brookings Institution, Washington, DC, 1982.

Dixit, Avinash, *The Making of Economic Policy: A Transactions-Cost Politics Perspective*, MIT Press, Cambridge, Mass., 1996.

Dollar, David, 'Outward-Oriented Developing Countries really do Grow more Rapidly: Evidence from 95 LDCs 1976–85', *Economic Development and Cultural Change* 40 (1992).

Domar, Evsey D., 'Capital Expansion, Rate of Growth, and Employment', *Econometrica* 14 (1946).

Dougherty, Christopher, *A Comparison of Productivity and Economic Growth in the G-7 Countries*, Ph. D. diss., Harvard University, 1991.

Dowrick, Steve, and Duc-Tho Nguyen, 'OECD Comparative Growth, 1950–85: Catch-Up and Convergence', *American Economic Review* 79 (1989).

Easterly, William, 'How Much Do Distortions Affect Growth?', *Journal of Monetary Economics* 32 (1993).

—— and Ross Levine, 'Africa's Growth Tragedy: Politics and Ethnic Divisions', *Quarterly Journal of Economics* 112 (1997).

Edwards, Sebastian, 'Trade Orientation, Distortions and Growth in Developing Countries', *Journal of Development Economics* 39 (1992).

—— 'Openness, Productivity and Growth: What do we Really Know?', *Economic Journal* 108 (1998).

Elias, Victor J., *Sources of Growth: A Study of Seven Latin American Economies,* ICS Press, San Francisco, 1990.

Feldstein, Martin, 'Tax Avoidance and the Deadweight Loss of the Income Tax', NBER Working Paper 5055 (1995).

Fischer, Stanley, *Indexing, Inflation, and Economic Policy*, MIT Press, Cambridge, Mass. 1986.

—— 'Growth, Macroeconomics, and Development', NBER *Macroeconomics Annual* (1991).

—— 'The Role of Macroeconomic Factors in Growth', *Journal of Monetary Economics* 32 (1993).

Fisher, Irving, *The Rate of Interest*, Macmillan, New York, 1907.

—— *The Theory of Interest*, Macmillan, New York, 1930.

Frisch, Ragnar, 'Foreword' to Leif Johansen, *Norge og fellesmarkedet (Norway and the Common Market)*, Oslo, 1961.

Fuente, Angel de la, 'The Empirics of Growth and Convergence: A Selective Review', *Journal of Economic Dynamics and Control* 21 (1997).

Goodstein, David L., and Judith R. Goodstein, *Feynman's Lost Lecture: The Motion of the Planets Around the Sun*, Vintage, California Institute of Technology, 1997.

Grossman, Gene M., and Elhanan Helpman, *Innovation and Growth in the Global Economy*, MIT Press, Cambridge, Mass., and London, 1991.

—— 'Endogenous Innovation in the Theory of Growth', *Journal of Economic Perspectives* 8 (1994).

Gylfason, Thorvaldur, 'Inflation, Growth, and External Debt: A View of the Landscape', *World Economy* 14 (1991).

—— 'Optimal Saving, Interest Rates, and Economic Growth', *Scandinavian Journal of Economics* 95 (1993).

Gylfason, Thorvaldur, *The Macroeconomics of European Agriculture,* Princeton Studies in International Finance, 78 (1995).

—— 'Output Gains from Economic Stabilization', *Journal of Development Economics* 56 (1998).

—— 'Privatization, Efficiency, and Economic Growth', CEPR Discussion Paper 1844 (1998).

—— 'Exports, Inflation, and Growth', *World Development* 27 (1999).

—— Torben M. Andersen, Seppo Honkapohja, Arne J. Isachsen, and John Williamson, *The Swedish Model under Stress: A View from the Stands*, SNS, Förlag, Stockholm, 1997.

—— and Tryggvi Thor Herbertsson, 'Does Inflation Matter for Growth?', CEPR Discussion Paper 1503 (1996).

—— , —— and Gylfi Zoega, 'A Mixed Blessing: Natural Resources and Economic Growth', *Macroeconomic Dynamics* 3 (1999).

—— , —— , —— 'Ownership and Growth', CEPR Discussion Paper 1900, (1998).

Hall, Robert E., and Charles I. Jones, 'The Productivity of Nations', NBER Working Paper 5812 (1996).

—— 'Levels of Economic Activity Across Countries', *American Economic Review* 87 (1997).

Hammer, Armand, *Hammer: Witness to History*, Simon & Schuster, New York, 1987.

Hannesson, Rögnvaldur, *Fisheries Mismanagement: The Case of the North Atlantic Cod*, Fishing News Books, Oxford, 1996.

Harberger, Arnold C., 'Taxation, Resource Allocation, and Welfare', in *The Role of Direct and Indirect Taxes in the Federal Revenue System*, National Bureau of Economic Research and Brookings Institution, Princeton University Press, Princeton, 1964.

Harrod, Roy, *Towards a Dynamic Economics*, Macmillan, London, 1948.

Hayek, Friedrich von, *The Road to Serfdom*, Chicago University Press, Chicago, 1944.

Henrekson, Magnus, Lars Jonung, and Joakim Stymne, 'Economic Growth and the Swedish Model', ch. 9 in Nicholas Crafts and Gianni Toniolo, *Economic Growth in Europe Since 1945*, Centre for Economic Policy Research and Cambridge University Press, London and Cambridge, 1996.

Hume, David, *Writings on Economics*, ed. by Eugene Rotwein, University of Wisconsin Press, Madison, 1955.

Johnson, D. Gale, *Less Than Meets the Eye: The Modest Impact of CAP Reform*, Rochester Paper 5, Centre for Policy Studies, London, 1995.

Kaldor, Nicholas, 'Alternative Theories of Distribution', *Review of Economic Studies* 23 (1955–6).

—— 'Capital Accumulation and Economic Growth', in Friedrich A. Lutz and Douglas C. Hague (eds), *The Theory of Capital*, St Martin's Press, New York, 1961.

Keynes, John Maynard, 'Economic Possibilities for Our Grandchildren', in his *Essays in Persuasion,*, W. W. Norton & Co., New York, 1963.

—— *Treatise on Money*, London and New York, 1930.

King, Robert G., and Ross Levine, 'Finance and Growth: Schumpeter Might be Right', *Quarterly Journal of Economics* 108 (1993).

Koester, Ulrich, 'The Experience with Liberalization Policies: The Case of the Agricultural Sector', *European Economic Review* 35 (1991).

Kravis, Irving B., A. W. Heston, and Robert Summers, 'Real GDP Per Capita for More than One Hundred Countries', *Economic Journal* 88 (1978).

Krueger, Anne O., *Political Economy of Policy Reform in Developing Countries*, MIT Press, Cambridge, Mass., 1994.

Krugman, Paul, 'The Myth of Asia's Miracle', *Foreign Affairs,* Nov.–Dec. 1994.

—— *Development, Geography, and Economic Theory*, MIT Press, Cambridge, Mass., and London, 1995.

Kuznets, Simon, *Modern Economic Growth*, Yale University Press, New Haven, 1966.

—— *Economic Growth of Nations: Total Output and Production Structure*, Harvard University Press, Cambridge, Mass., 1971.

Kuznets, Simon, 'Modern Economic Growth: Findings and Reflections', *American Economic Review* 63 (1973).

Lane, Philip R., and Aaron Tornell, 'Power, Growth, and the Voracity Effect', *Journal of Economic Growth* 1 (1996).

Layard, Richard, *How to Beat Unemployment*, OUP, Oxford, 1986.

—— and Andrea Richter, 'Labor Market Adjustment—The Russian Way', in Anders Åslund (ed.), *Russian Economic Reform at Risk*, St Martin's Press, New York, 1995.

Lee, Jong-Wha, 'International Trade, Distortions, and Long-Run Economic Growth', IMF *Staff Papers* 40 (1993).

Leibenstein, Harvey, 'Allocative Efficiency vs. X-Efficiency', *American Economic Review* 56 (1966).

Levine, Ross, and David Renelt, 'A Sensitivity Analysis of Cross-Country Growth Regressions', *American Economic Review* 82 (1992).

Lewis, W. Arthur, *The Theory of Economic Growth*, Allen & Unwin, London, 1955.

—— *Some Aspects of Economic Development*, Ghana Publishing Corporation, Accra and Tema, 1968.

—— 'The State of Development Theory', *American Economic Review* 74 (1984).

Lindbeck, Assar, *Unemployment and Macroeconomics*, MIT Press, Cambridge, Mass., 1993.

—— *The Swedish Experiment*, SNS Förlag, Stockholm, 1997.

Lucas, Robert E. Jr., 'Expectations and the Neutrality of Money', *Journal of Economic Theory* 4 (1972).

—— 'Econometric Policy Evaluation: A Critique', *Carnegie-Rochester Conference Series on Public Policy* 1 (1976).

—— 'On the Mechanics of Economic Development', *Journal of Monetary Economics* 22 (1988).

McKinnon, Ronald, I., *Money and Capital in Economic Development*, Brookings Institution, Washington DC, 1973.

Maddison, Angus, *Phases of Capitalist Development*, OUP, Oxford, 1982.

Malthus, Thomas, *Essay on Population*, 5th edn., London, 1817.

Mankiw, N. Gregory, David Romer, and David N. Weil, 'A Contribution to The Empirics of Economic Growth', *Quarterly Journal of Economics* 107 (1992).

Marshall, Alfred, *Principles of Economics*, 8th edn., Macmillan, London, 1920.

Mauro, Paolo, 'The Effects of Corruption on Growth, Investment, and Government Expenditure', International Monetary Fund Working Paper 96/98 (1996).

Meadows, Donnella H., Dennis L. Meadows, Jørgen Randers, and William W. Behrens III, *The Limits to Growth, A Report for the Club of Rome's Project on the Predicament of Mankind*, New American Library, New York, 1972.

Mill, John Stuart, *Principles of Political Economy*, ed. by W. J. Asley, Longmans, Green, 1909.

Murphy, Kevin M., Andrei Shleifer, and Robert W. Vishny, 'Industrialization and the Big Push', *Journal of Political Economy* 97 (1989).

Myrdal, Gunnar, *Asian Drama: An Inquiry into the Poverty of Nations*, Pantheon, New York, 1968.

OECD, *Agricultural Policies in OECD Countries,* i: *Monitoring and Evaluation*, and ii: *Measurement of Support and Background Information*, OECD, Paris, 1997.

Olson, Mancur, *The Logic of Collective Action*, Harvard University Press, Cambridge, Mass., 1965.

Perkins, Dwight, 'Completing China's Move to the Market', *Journal of Economic Perspectives* 8 (1994).

Persson, Torsten, and Guido Tabellini, 'Is Inequality Harmful for Growth?', *American Economic Review* 84 (1994).

Phelps, Edmund, *Golden Rules of Economic Growth*, W. W. Norton & Co., New York, 1966.

Pissarides, Christopher A., *Equilibrium Unemployment Theory*, Blackwell, Oxford, 1990.

Radetzki, Marian, *Tjugo år efter oljekrisen (Twenty Years after the Oil Crisis)*, SNS Förlag, Stockholm, 1995.

—— *Klarspråk om arbetslöshet (Plain Speaking about Unemployment)*, SNS Förlag, Stockholm, 1996.

Ramsey, Frank P., 'A Mathematical Theory of Saving', *Economic Journal* 38 (1928).

Rock, David, *Argentina 1516–1987*, University of California Press, Berkeley, Calif., 1987.

Rodrik, Dani, 'Where Did all the Growth Go? External Shocks, Social Conflicts and Growth Collapses', CEPR Discussion Paper 1789 (1998).

Romer, David, *Advanced Macroeconomics*, McGraw-Hill, New York, 1996.

Romer, Paul M., 'Increasing Returns and Long-run Growth', *Journal of Political Economy* 94 (1986).

—— 'Endogenous Technical Change', *Journal of Political Economy* 98 (1990), Part 2.

—— 'The Origins of Endogenous Growth', *Journal of Economic Perspectives* (1994).

Ronnås, Per, and Örjan Sjöberg, 'Economic Reform in Vietnam: Dismantling the Centrally Planned Economy', *Journal of Communist Studies* 7 / 1 (1991).

Rosenstein-Rodan, P.N., 'Problems of Industrialization in Eastern and Southeastern Europe', *Economic Journal* 53 (1943).

Rostow, W. W., *Theories of Economic Growth from David Hume to the Present*, OUP, Oxford and New York, 1990.

Roubini, Nouriel, and Xavier Sala-i-Martin, 'Financial Repression and Economic Growth', *Journal of Development Economics* 39 (1992).

Sachs, Jeffrey D., and Andrew M. Warner, 'Economic Reform and the Process of Global Integration', *Brookings Papers on Economic Activity* 1 (1995).

—— 'Natural Resource Abundance and Economic Growth', *Quarterly Journal of Economics* (forthcoming).

Sala-i-Martin, Xavier, 'I Just Ran Two Million Regressions', *American Economic Review* 87 (1997).

Samuelson, Paul, *Economics,* 8th edn., McGraw-Hill, New York, 1970.

Sarel, Michael, 'Nonlinear Effects of Inflation on Economic Growth', IMF *Staff Papers* 43 (1996).

Schumpeter, Joseph, *The Theory of Economic Development*, 3rd edn., Harvard University Press, Cambridge, Mass., 1949.

—— *Capitalism, Socialism and Democracy,* 3rd edn., Harper & Row, New York, 1950.

Scott, Maurice Fitzgerald, *A New View of Economic Growth*, Clarendon Press, Oxford, 1989.

Shapiro, Carl, and Joseph E. Stiglitz, 'Equilibrium Unemployment as a Worker Discipline Device', *American Economic Review* 74 (1984).

Shaw, George Bernard, *John Bull's Other Island*, 1907.

Smith, Adam, *An Inquiry into the Nature and Causes of the Wealth of Nations*, Liberty Classics, Indianapolis, 1976.

Solow, Robert, 'A Contribution to the Theory of Economic Growth', *Quarterly Journal of Economics* 70 (1956).

—— 'Technichal Change and the Aggregate Production Function', *Review of Economics and Statistics* 39 (1957).

—— *Growth Theory: An Exposition*, OUP, Oxford, 1970.

—— 'Is the End of the World at Hand?', *Challenge*, March–April 1973.

Stiglitz, Joseph E., 'Some Lessons from the East Asian Miracle', World Bank *Research Observer* 11 (1996).

Summers, Robert, and Alan W. Heston, 'The Penn World Table (Mark 5): An Expanded Set of International Comparisons: 1950–1988', *Quarterly Journal of Economics* 106 (1991).

Temple, Jonathan, 'The New Growth Evidence', *Journal of Economic Literature* (forthcoming).

Williamson, John (ed.), *The Political Economy of Policy Reform*, Institute for International Economics, Washington, DC, 1994.

Winiecki, Jan, 'Are Soviet-Type Economies Entering an Era of Long-Term Decline?', *Soviet Studies* 38/3 (1986).

—— 'Soviet-Type Economies: Considerations for the Future', *Soviet Studies* 38/4 (1986).

World Bank, *Atlas* 1997.

—— *Bureaucrats in Business: The Economics and Politics of Government Ownership*, OUP, Oxford, 1995.

—— *The East Asian Miracle: Economic Growth and Public Policy*, OUP, Oxford, 1993.

—— *World Development Indicators 1997*, OUP, Oxford, 1997.

—— *World Development Report 1987*, OUP, Oxford, 1987.

—— *World Development Report 1992*, OUP, Oxford, 1992.

—— *World Development Report 1997*, OUP, Oxford, 1997.

Young, Alwyn, 'The Tyranny of Numbers: Confronting the Statistical Realities of the East Asian Growth Experience', *Quarterly Journal of Economics* 110 (1995).

Cast of Characters

Amin, Idi (1924/5–). Ugandan soldier and dictator (1971–9). He was born in Koboko of Muslim parents. After receiving a rudimentary education, he joined the army, rising from the ranks to become a colonel in 1964. An athlete, he was for nearly 10 years the heavyweight boxing champion of the army. As a friend of President Milton Obote, who had led Uganda to independence in 1962, Amin was made commander-in-chief of the army and air force in 1968. In 1971, he staged a *coup d'état* against Obote and established a military dictatorship. Under Amin's tyrannical rule, Uganda's economy collapsed and up to 300,000 Ugandans were killed, some say many more. In 1979, he was overthrown by an invasion force from Tanzania supported by Ugandan rebels. He found refuge in Saudi Arabia.

Armstrong, Neil A. (1930–). American astronaut, born in Wapakoneta, Ohio. He studied at Purdue University, and then became a fighter pilot in Korea, where he flew 78 combat missions, and was shot down once. In 1962, he became the first civilian to enter the astronaut training programme and commanded Gemini 8 in 1966, but a rocket-thruster malfunction forced him to make an emergency splashdown in the Pacific Ocean. In 1969, with Buzz Aldrin and Michael Collins, he set out in Apollo 11 on a successful Moon-landing expedition. On 20 July 1969 Armstrong and Aldrin became, in that order, the first persons to set foot on the Moon. Armstrong later taught aerospace engineering at Cincinnati University (1971–9). He published *First on the Moon* in 1970.

Aung San Suu Kyi, Daw (1945–). Burmese political leader, born in Yangon, Myanmar (formerly Rangoon, Burma), the daughter of the assassinated General U Aung San, who was hailed as the father of Burmese independence. She studied in India and at Oxford, where she earned a BA degree in philosophy, politics, and economics, and became committed to the cause of democracy in her country. When social unrest forced dictator General Ne Win to resign in 1988, and the military took power, Aung San Suu Kyi co-founded the National League for Democracy (NLD), but was arrested shortly thereafter along with many other NLD members. The NLD won a landslide victory in the ensuing parliamentary elections by winning 82 per cent of the seats, but the government refused to allow the elected parliament to convene. Aung Sun

Richard Feynman
Paul Romer

Einar Benediktsson

Isaac Newton
Thomas Malthus
David Ricardo
John Stuart Mill
Charles Darwin
Alfred Marshall
John Maynard Keynes
Roy Harrod

Harry Truman
Neil Armstrong
Robert Lucas

Irving Fisher
Joseph Schumpeter
Paul Samuelson
Robert Solow
Evsey Domar
Robert Barro
Paul Krugman
Jeffrey Sachs

Simon Kuznets
Hollis Chenery

Ernest Hemingway

Arthur Lewis

Juan Perón
Carlos Menem

Suu Kyi was to remain under house arrest, which drew world-wide attention. Awarded the Nobel Peace Prize in 1991, she was released in July 1995. Even so, her freedom to travel remains restricted. Her writings are collected in *Freedom from Fear and Other Writings* (1991). She has continued to speak out against the Burmese government.

Barro, Robert J. (1944–). American economist, educated at the California Institute of Technology (Caltech) and Harvard. He taught at Chicago and Rochester before joining the faculty of Harvard in 1987, a place where, he says, he 'sometimes feel[s] like the resident right-winger in a liberal establishment'. He regards Milton Friedman's macroeconomics as 'far too Keynesian'. In addition to numerous and widely cited articles in scientific journals and academic books, Barro has published an undergraduate text, *Macroeconomics* (5th edn., 1998), and a collection of short essays, *Getting It Right* (1996), based on his writings in the *Wall Street Journal* and other popular financial media. Listen to this, for example: 'Another adverse feature of representative democracy is the strong political power of interest groups, such as agriculture, environmental lobbies, defense contractors, and the handicapped' (*Getting It Right*, p. 2).

Benediktsson, Einar (1864–1940). Icelandic poet and entrepreneur. He studied law at the University of Copenhagen and became his country's first practising lawyer and real-estate agent, before becoming a county magistrate. He established and edited Iceland's first daily newspaper, where he, in 1896, advocated public works as a remedy for unemployment, among other things. A fervent nationalist and a man of the

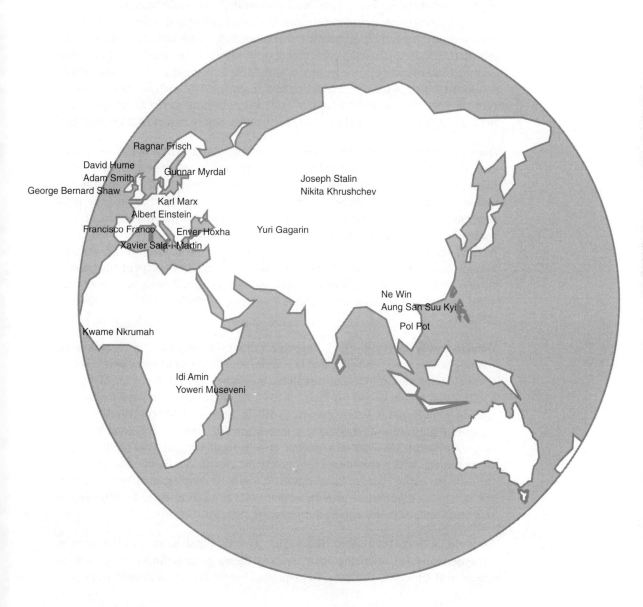

world, he became convinced that only a flood of foreign investment could bring prosperity to Iceland. He spent many years touring Europe trying (unsuccessfully) to raise enough capital for his ambitious industrial schemes to exploit Iceland's rich natural resources, especially its hydropower and fisheries. He published five volumes of poetry, which remains widely revered in Iceland, including these lines:

> *Through deeds invent*
> *Will's monument,*
> *For will is all it takes.*[1]

Chenery, Hollis B. (1918–1994). American economist, born in Richmond, Virginia, and educated at Arizona, Virginia, and Harvard, where he got his Ph.D. in 1950. A key figure in development economics, he demonstrated that self-sustaining economic growth depends on industrialization and declining agricultural export and initiated cross-sectional analysis of economic growth long before the advent of endogenous-growth theory. He advised the governments of Pakistan, Japan, and South Korea, the Central Banks of Israel and Sicily, and the United Nations, among others. He taught at Stanford 1952–61, worked in the State Department 1961–5, and then taught at Harvard 1965–70. Then he moved to the World Bank, where he served as vice-president in charge of development policy from 1972 to 1982, before moving back to Harvard.

Darwin, Charles R. (1809–1882). English scientist, who laid the foundation of modern evolutionary theory with his concept of the development of all forms of life through natural selection. He left medical school and completed his education at Cambridge, planning to become a clergyman. In 1831 he sailed aboard the HMS *Beagle* as an unpaid naturalist on a scientific expedition around the world, and returned in 1836, having travelled extensively throughout the South Pacific. By 1846 he had published several works on his geological and zoological discoveries, and had become one of the leading scientists of his day. From 1842 he spent his time at Downe, Kent, working in his garden and breeding pigeons and fowls, and here he devoted himself to his major work, *On the Origin of Species by Means of Natural Selection* (1859).

Domar, Evsey D. (1914–1997). American economist. Born in Lodz, Russia (now Poland), he was raised and educated in Harbin, Manchuria, but moved permanently to the United States in 1936 and completed his studies there at the UCLA, Michigan, and Harvard, where he got his Ph.D. in 1947. He taught at several universities, including Johns Hopkins, before moving to MIT in 1958. He made contributions in at least three main areas of economics: economic growth, comparative economics, and economic history. His work on economic growth began with his 1944 model on government debt, which considered how economic growth can lighten the burden of the debt. His major claim to fame, however, was in developing, parallel to Roy Harrod, a dynamic-equilibrium growth model (1946) as a way of extending the Keynesian demand-determined equilibrium into the long run.

Einstein, Albert (1879–1955). The world's greatest physicist in his time, born in Ulm, Germany. An undistinguished student there, he later flourished at a high school near Zurich, Switzerland. He requested Swiss citizenship in 1901 and took a post with the Swiss patent office (1902–5). By the time he received his Ph.D. (1905), he had achieved world fame for his publications on Brownian motion, his photo-electric theory that light and other radiation can behave as both waves and particles, and for his revolutionary special theory of relativity, which related matter and energy in the most famous of all equations, $e = mc^2$. He developed his general theory of relativity (1915), which displaced Newtonian mechanics as the cornerstone of physics and introduced the concept of space-time. In 1921, two years after a prediction of his general theory of relativity was verified, he received the Nobel Prize, specifically for his ideas on photons and the photoelectric effect. He taught at several European institutions (1909–33), but after Hitler came to power in 1933, Einstein, a Jewish pacifist, emigrated to the United States and accepted a post at the newly created Institute for Advanced Studies at Princeton. He became an American citizen in 1940, and remained in Princeton after his retirement in 1945. Fear of Nazi expansion caused him to sign a letter to President Franklin Roosevelt in 1939 urging the United States to develop an atomic bomb. Einstein himself took no part in the bomb's construction and spent the remainder of his life promoting peace and humanitarian causes. He continued his unfulfilled search for a unified theory to combine quantum mechanics and relativity into one all-encompassing equation. A shy and gentle man, he was an accomplished violinist, and he made the world smirk when he once made an error while helping a young student with her maths homework.

Feynman, Richard P. (1918–88). American physicist, one of the greatest of all scientists in this century, second only to Einstein, whom he met only once—and Einstein asked him: 'Young man, where are they serving tea?' Feynman was born in Far Rockaway on the outskirts of New York, studied at MIT and Princeton, and then went to Los Alamos in 1943 to work on the Manhatten Project (to help build the bomb). He taught at Cornell 1946–51 and went from there, via Brazil, to Caltech, where he taught until he died in 1988. His publications included his celebrated *Lectures on Physics* (3 vols., 1963–5), which revolutionized the way physics is taught to undergraduates, and the best-seller, *'Surely You're Joking, Mr Feynman!'* (1985), followed by *'What Do You Care What Other People Think?'* (1988). He got the Nobel Prize in 1965 for his work on quantum electrodynamics. He was an accomplished draftsman, story-teller, and bongo-player; his music is available on a compact disc.

Fisher, Irving (1867–1947). American economist, one of the greatest—and most colourful—of economists of all time. He was by all accounts a brilliant teacher as well as an elegant and exceptionally prolific writer (his bibliography contains some 2,000 titles) and, moreover, a tireless crusader and reformer. Born in Saugerties, New York, Fisher was educated at Yale and remained there until his retirement in 1935. In connection with his 1891 dissertation, he constructed a machine equipped with pumps, wheels, levers, and pipes in order to illustrate his price theory. At the same time, he published poetry. He made several major contributions to mathematical economics; the theory of value and price (he invented the indifference curve and the isoquant); capital theory, which brought the Austrian intertemporal theories into the English-speaking world (the distinction between stocks and flows is mostly due to him); monetary theory, through his resurrection of the quantity theory of money; and statistics, especially index-number theory. His invention of a visible index file system brought him considerable financial success, but he suffered heavy financial losses in the crash of 1929, which, however, did not much reduce his optimism about American economic prospects and stock prices in particular; Yale had to buy his house and rent it to him to save him from eviction. In later years he also became known for his promotion of nutritional cures for diseases, world peace, and prohibition. Fisher was president of the American Economic Association in 1918 and the first president of the Econometric Society, which he co-founded (1930). After his death, Joseph Schumpeter and eighteen of his Harvard colleagues wrote of Fisher: 'No American has contributed more to the advancement of his chosen subject.'

Franco, Francisco (1892–1975). Spanish general and caudillo (authoritarian leader), who governed Spain from 1939 to 1975. Franco was born in El Ferrol, Spain. He became a national hero for his role in suppressing revolts in Morocco, and was appointed army chief of staff in 1935. In early 1936 the leftist government of the Spanish republic exiled Franco to an obscure command in the Canary Islands. Soon thereafter he joined other right-wing officers in a revolt against the republic. Franco emerged as the Nationalist leader, and his forces won the civil war in 1939. Franco kept Spain out of the Second World War, but after the war ended in 1945 he was ostracized by the United Nations as a Fascist leader. As the Cold War intensified, foreign opposition to Franco waned, and his regime became somewhat more liberal. Franco balanced various groups against one another, retaining for himself a position as arbiter above the affairs of day-to-day politics. In 1969 he designated Prince Juan Carlos, grandson of Spain's former king, Alfonso XIII, as his official successor. Within two years of Franco's death, almost every vestige of his dictatorship had disappeared.

Frisch, Ragnar (1895–1973). Norwegian economist. A goldsmith by trade like his father and grandfather, he took up economics, apparently because that was the quickest route to a university education. He then went on to France, Germany, Britain, the United States, and Italy to pursue further studies in economics and mathematics. He was, with Irving Fisher, a co-founder of the Econometric Society (1930). Aware of his talents, the Norwegian parliament established a personal professorship for him in 1931 at the University of Oslo, a post he held until his retirement in 1965. In 1969, he shared, with Jan Tinbergen, the first Nobel Prize in economics for his pioneering contribution to the statistical, theoretical, and mathematical advancement of social science. 'Frisch was a genius, useless for political or more routine assignments,' said his Swedish colleague, Erik Lundberg, who knew Frisch well. Frisch himself probably couldn't have disagreed more about the second part of this assessment, for he took himself seriously as an economic adviser. He fought hard against Norway's accession to the European Economic Community before the referendum in 1972, with fervently nationalistic arguments.

Gagarin, Yuri Alekseyevich (1934–68). Russian cosmonaut, born in Gagarin (formerly, Gzhatsk), Russia. He joined the Soviet air force in 1957, and in 1961 became the first man to travel in space, completing a circuit of the Earth in the Vostok spaceship satellite. A Hero of the Soviet Union, he shared the Galabert astronautical Prize with John Glenn in 1963. He was killed in a plane accident while training.

Harrod, Sir Roy F. (1900–78). English economist, born in London. He studied at Oxford and, apart from a short break for service in the Second World War, and again as adviser to the International Monetary Fund in the early 1950s, he remained there, at

Christ Church, throughout his career (1922–67). He wrote the official biography of Keynes (1951), and wrote also on philosophy and logic as well as economics. He made several discoveries more or less in parallel with others (the marginal revenue curve, the long-run envelope of short-run average cost curves, the theory of imperfect competition, the multiplier-accelerator model, and the IS-LM model). At last, another discovery brought him recognition: Harrod's 'Essay in Dynamic Theory' (1939). The idea, which marked the beginning of the modern theory of growth, had also been developed by Domar, but at least Harrod got his name on the model this time. In his 1948 book, *Towards a Dynamic Economics*, as well as in a series of essays, he developed this idea further, highlighting the instability problem of this model and launching the entire post-war research programme on economic growth. He was personal adviser to Winston Churchill during the Second World War.

Hemingway, Ernest M. (1899–1961). Novelist and short-story writer, born in Oak Park, Illinois. He worked as a reporter for *The Kansas City Star*, served with an ambulance unit in the First World War, was wounded in 1918 and decorated for heroism. His first important work was a collection of short stories, *In Our Time* (1925), and success came with his novel, *The Sun also Rises* (1926), inspired by his experience as one of the 'lost generation' of young expatriates in France and Spain after the First World War. Obsessed with war, big-game hunting, and bullfighting, his works include *A Farewell to Arms* (1929), *Death in the Afternoon* (1932), *For Whom the Bell Tolls* (1940), and *The Old Man and the Sea* (1952). When F. Scott Fitzgerald remarked to Hemingway that the rich 'are not as we are', Hemingway replied: 'No, they have more money.'

Hoxha, Enver (1908–85). Albanian prime minister (1944–54) and First Secretary (1954–85), Hero of the People (twice), Hero of Socialist Labour, and so on, born in Gjirokastër, Albania. A former teacher, educated in France, he founded and led the Albanian Communist Party (1941) in the struggle for national independence from Italy. In 1946 he deposed King Zog (who had fled in 1939), and became head of state. He gradually imposed almost complete isolation on his country, imprisoning, executing, and exiling thousands of his political opponents. He is survived by his unrepentant widow, Nexhmije, who served a prison sentence (for corruption and other offences) after the collapse of communism in Albania. She lives in one room in a former warehouse on the outskirts of Tirana, surrounded by memorabilia from her days of glory as First Lady, including her husband's collected works in some 20 or 30 volumes. Here is a sample: 'The so-called consumer society, so loudly advertised and praised to the skies by the bourgeoisie as the "society of the future", is nothing but a rotten, declining society, which is revealing more and more of the old permanent ulcers of capitalism which it tries to cover up. Such things will never occur with us' (1975).

Hume, David (1711–76). Philosopher, historian, economist, and essayist, together with his friend, Adam Smith, one of the most prominent figures in the 'Scottish Enlightenment'. He was born in Edinburgh, studied there, took up law, and in 1734 went to France, where he wrote his masterpiece, *A Treatise of Human Nature* (1739–40). His views became widely known only when he wrote two volumes of *Essays, Moral, Political, and Literary* (1741–2). He wrote the posthumously published *Dialogues Concerning Natural Religion* in the 1750s. His atheism thwarted his applications for professorships at Edinburgh and Glasgow, and he became a tutor, secretary, and keeper of the Advocates' Library in Edinburgh, where he lived from 1751 to 1763, except for two breaks in London, and published his popular *Political Discourses* (1752) and his path-breaking, six-volume *History of England* (1754–61). Other works include *An Enquiry Concerning Human Understanding* (1748) and *An Enquiry Concerning the Principles of Morals* (1751). In his various *Essays* (1758) on economics, Hume appears as an anti-Mercantilist free-trader and advocate of the quantity theory of money.

Keynes, John Maynard (1883–1946). English economist, journalist, and financier, born in Cambridge, England. He studied at Eton and Cambridge, where he later lectured in economics. He acquired fame for his second book, *The Economic Consequences of the Peace* (1919), where he warned against the huge reparation payments required of Germany after the First World War. The Great Depression inspired his two great works, *A Treatise on Money* (1930, 2 vols.) and *The General Theory of Employment, Interest and Money* (1936). In *A Short View of Russia, The End of Laissez-Faire* (1926), he wrote: 'Marxian Socialism must always remain a portent to the historians of opinion—how a doctrine so illogical and so dull can have exercised so powerful and enduring an influence on the minds of men, and, through them, the events of history.'

Khrushchev, Nikita Sergeyevich (1894–1971). Soviet statesman, first secretary of the Soviet Communist Party (1953–64), and prime minister (1958–64), born in Kalinovka, Ukraine, illiterate until age 25. Joining the Bolshevik Party in 1918, he fought in the Russian civil war, and rose rapidly in the Party organization. In 1939 he was made a full member of the Politburo and of the Presidium of the Supreme Soviet. In 1953, six months after the death of Stalin, he became first secretary of the Communist Party of the Soviet Union, and three years later, at the 20th Party Congress, denounced Stalinism. Among the events of his administration were the 1956 Poznan riots and the Hungarian uprising, and the failed attempt to install missiles in Cuba (1962). He was deposed in 1964, replaced by Brezhnev and Kosygin. To his son he said: 'My most important contribution to Soviet history is to have made it alive into retirement.'

Krugman, Paul R. (1953–). American economist, got his Ph.D. from MIT in 1977, and is now Ford International Professor of Economics there, having also taught at Yale and Stanford. He also spent an eye-opening year working at the White House (Council of Economic Advisers) in 1982–3, when Ronald Reagan was president. In 1991 he received his major professional gong, as he calls it himself, the John Bates Clark Medal. A brilliant and innovative economic theorist, he also writes eloquently and clearly for the public. Among his many books, there is an undergraduate textbook, co-authored by Maurice Obstfeld, *International Economics* (4th edn., 1997).

Kuznets, Simon (1901–85). Economist and statistician, born in Kharkov, Ukraine. He emigrated to the United States in 1922, studied at Columbia, and investigated business cycles for the National Bureau of Economic Research from 1927. He was professor of economics at Pennsylvania (1930–54), Johns Hopkins (1954–60), and Harvard (1960–71). His major publication was *National Income and its Composition, 1919-1938* (1941). Kuznets' life work was the collection and organization of the national income accounts of the United States, an accomplishment paralleling that of

Richard Stone in Great Britain. Kuznets' work coincided with the emergence of econometrics and the Keynesian revolution, both of which found in Kuznets' data an important resource for their advancement. He received the Nobel Prize for economics in 1971. Kuznets was also one of the earliest empirical development economists. Among his several discoveries, which sparked important theoretical research, was his discovery of an inverted U-shaped relationship between income inequality and economic growth.

Lewis, Sir W. Arthur (1915–90). British economist, born in St Lucia in the West Indies. He studied and taught at the London School of Economics, before becoming professor of economics at Manchester (1948–58), where he did some of his most important work on development economics. He then became the first president of the University of the West Indies (1959–63). From 1963 until his retirement in 1983, he taught at Princeton, and his lectures on economic development were masterful, but most Ph.D. students in those days preferred to specialize in more technical fields. Sir Arthur advised international organizations and national governments, especially in West Africa and the Caribbean. In 1979 he shared the Nobel Prize for economics for his contributions to development economics. He was president of the American Economic Association in 1983.

Lucas, Robert E., Jr. (1937–). American economist, born in Yakima, Washington. He was a professor of economics at Carnegie Mellon (1970–4) before joining the faculty at the University of Chicago (1974). He helped formulate the theory of rational expectations, according to which monetary and fiscal policy actions only affect output and unemployment for a short time, if at all, because economic agents with rational expectations can see through the government's policy intentions and can thus offset them to their own advantage. Lucas has also made important contributions to the theory of investment, business cycles, and endogenous economic growth. He was awarded a Nobel Prize in 1995.

Malthus, Thomas R. (1766–1834). English economist. He studied at Cambridge, and was ordained in 1797. In 1798 he published anonymously his *Essay on the Principle of Population*, arguing that the number of people has a natural tendency to increase faster than food supply, and that efforts should be made to cut the birth rate, either by self-restraint or birth control—a view which later was widely misrepresented under the name of Malthusianism. In 1805 he became professor of political economy in the East India College at Haileybury, where he wrote his *Principles of Political Economy* (1820) and other works.

Marshall, Alfred (1842–1924). English economist, born in London, fellow and later professor of political economy at Cambridge, the dominant figure in British economics in his time. Although he wrote infrequently, his teaching at Cambridge was a major source of influence on his contemporaries. An able mathematician, he sought to express himself in the simplest language possible, adding the mathematical and quantitative material as appendices and footnotes. Like Irving Fisher, he wanted his works to be read and understood by businessmen as well as by students and colleagues. Marshall's partial equilibrium analysis—the chief element of his method—was designed to be appropriate to a dynamic or biological view of economic life. His welfare economics was of central importance, since his decision to take up economics originated in a moral purpose, and his general conclusion was that a redistribution of income from rich to poor would increase total satisfaction. His main works are his *Principles of Economics* (1890) and *Industry and Trade* (1919).

Marx, Karl (1818–1883). German economist and agitator, born in Trier. He began studying law in Berlin, but turned later to philosophy. In 1842 he became editor of *Rheinische Zeitung*, but the paper was closed down by the authorities because of its revolutionary content. Marx fled to Paris, whence he also had to flee, in 1845. He met Friedrich Engels in 1844 and, with him, published *The Communist Manifesto* in 1848. Marx moved with his family to London in 1849 and laboured, with the financial support of Engels, in the British Museum, where he gathered much research material on the economy of Britain and other countries and made useful contributions to the analysis of the workings of a market economy and property rights. His *magnum opus* is *Das Kapital*, thousands of pages. Marx completed only the first volume in his lifetime (1867). The remaining volumes were published posthumously by Engels and others.

Menem, Carlos S. (1935–). Argentinian politician and president (1989–), born in Anillaco, Argentina. While studying for the legal profession he became politically active in the Peronist movement (the Justice Party), founding the Youth Group in 1955. He was elected president of the Party in La Rioja (1963), and became governor of the province in 1983. In 1989 he won the presidency on a populist platform, but steered the Peronists quickly towards a market-friendly programme aimed at maintaining economic growth, keeping inflation under control, and attracting foreign investment. His policy of privatization and currency reform helped bring inflation down from 3,000 per cent in 1990 to 3 per cent in 1996, but unemployment doubled from 9 per cent of the labour force to 18 per cent. Despite inflammatory speeches during the election campaign, he declared a wish to resume normal diplomatic relations with the United Kingdom regarding the future of the Falkland Islands. His decision to pardon military officers tried, after the military's fall from power in 1983, for the murder of thousands of 'suspects' remains controversial.

Mill, John Stuart (1806–73). Philosopher, economist, and social reformer, born in London. His father, James Mill, took care of his son's education, and in 1823 Mill jun. began a career under his father at the India Office. One of the major intellectual figures of the nineteenth century, he helped form the Utilitarian Society, was a major contributor to the *Westminster Review*, and became a regular participant in the London Debating Society. He published his major work, *A System of Logic*, in 1843. In 1851 he married Harriet Taylor, having waited 20 years for her husband to die; she helped him draft the brilliant essay *On Liberty* (1859), the most popular of all his works. His other main works include *Utilitarianism* (1863) and *Three Essays on Religion* (1874). He was elected to parliament in 1865, campaigning for women's suffrage and liberalism. To economists, he is best known for his *Principles of Political Economy* (1848):

> John Stuart Mill,
> By a mighty effort of will,
> Overcame his natural bonhomie,
> And wrote *Principles of Political Economy*.[2]

Museveni, Yoweri Kaguta (1945–). Soldier, politician, and president of Uganda (1986–). He studied at Dar es Salaam University, then worked for President Milton Obote until his overthrow by Idi Amin (1971). From exile in Tanzania he formed the Front for National Salvation, and helped defeat Amin in 1979. He became minister of defence (1979–80), but was in disagreement with Obote, who returned to the presidency in 1980 with the help of Tanzanian troops. When they withdrew in 1982, a virtual civil war ensued, and reasonable normality did not return to Uganda until 1986, when Museveni became president, pledging to follow a policy of national reconciliation.

Myrdal, Gunnar (1898–1987). Swedish economist, politician, and international civil servant. He was born in Dalarna, and studied at Stockholm University, where he became professor of political economy (1933). He wrote a classic study of race relations in the United States, *An American Dilemma* (1944), then was minister of trade and commerce in Sweden (1945–7), and executive secretary of the United Nations Economic Commission for Europe (1947–57). His later works include *The Challenge of Affluence* (1963). He shared, with Friedrich von Hayek, the 1974 Nobel Prize for economics, principally for his work on the critical application of economic theory to developing countries. 'Science is criticism,' he wrote, 'and social science must be critical of the social order.'

Ne Win, also known as Thakin Shu Maung (1911–). Burmese general and head of state. He studied at University College, Rangoon, and in the Second World War became chief of staff in the collaborationist army after the Japanese invasion of Burma, but joined the Allied forces later in the war. He held senior military and cabinet posts following Burma's independence (1948), before becoming caretaker prime minister (1958–60). In 1962, following a military coup, he declared the Burmese Way to Socialism and ruled the country as chairman of the revolutionary council and became state president in 1974. From 1981, he dominated political affairs as chairman of the ruling Burma Socialist Programme Party, but was forced to step down in 1988. His rule was characterized by economic stagnation and pervasive political corruption.

Newton, Sir Isaac (1642–1727). English physicist and mathematician. He studied at Cambridge. In 1665–6 the fall of an apple is said to have suggested the train of thought that led to the law of gravity. He studied the nature of light, concluding that white light is a mixture of colours, which can be separated by refraction, and devised the first reflecting telescope. He also examined the mechanics of planetary motion and derived the inverse-square law, which states that the intensity of, say, the gravitational pull between the Earth and the Moon varies inversely with the square of the distance between the two. He became professor of mathematics at Cambridge in 1669, where he resumed his work on gravitation, expounded finally in his famous *Philosophiae naturalis principia mathematica* (1687, *Mathematical Principles of Natural Philosophy*). In 1696 he was appointed warden of the Mint, and was master of the Mint from 1699 until his death. He also sat in parliament on two occasions, was elected president of the Royal Society in 1703, and was knighted in 1705. During his life he was involved in many controversies, including the lifelong quarrel with Leibniz over the question of priority in the discovery of calculus.

Nkrumah, Kwame (1909–72). Ghanaian statesman, prime minister (1957–60) and president (1960–6), born in Nkroful, Ghana (formerly, Gold Coast). He studied in both the United States (Lincoln University and the University of Pennsylvania) and the United Kingdom (London School of Economics), returned to the Gold Coast in 1947, and in 1949 formed the nationalist Convention People's Party. In 1950 he was imprisoned, but was elected to parliament while still in gaol. Released in 1951, he became leader of government business in parliament, and then premier. Called the 'Gandhi of Africa', he was a significant leader both of the movement against white domination and of pan-African feeling. He was the moving spirit behind the Charter of African States (1961). Economic reforms led to political opposition and several attempts on his life, interference with the judiciary, and the formation of a one-party State in 1964. An author of several books and a Marxist, he argued that Africa's struggle for independence 'forms part of the world socialist revolution'. His regime was overthrown in a military coup during his absence in Peking (1966), and he sought asylum in Guinea, where he was given the status of co-head of state. He died, from cancer, in Bucharest.

Perón, Juan D. (1895–1974). Argentinian soldier and president (1946–55, 1973–4), born in Lobos, Buenos Aires. He took a leading part in the army coup of 1943, became Secretary of Labour, gained widespread support through his social reforms, and became president in 1946. He was deposed and exiled in 1955, having antagonized the Church, the armed forces, and many of his former Labour supporters. He returned in triumph in 1973, and won an overwhelming electoral victory, but died the following year. His third wife, Isabel, a cabaret singer, took over as president, but the military removed her from office two years later (1976). Under the brutal military dictatorship that followed, over 10,000 'left-wing suspects' disappeared and the Argentinian navy tried unsuccessfully to take the Falkland Islands (population 2,000) by force. The junta lasted until 1983, when Raúl Alfonsín was elected president.

Pol Pot, also called Saloth Sar (1926–98). Cambodian politician and prime minister (1976–9), born in Kompong Thom province, Cambodia. He was active in the anti-French resistance under Ho Chi-Minh, and in 1964 joined the pro-Chinese Communist Party. Following studies in Paris (1949–53), he worked as a teacher (1954–63), and became leader of the Khmer Rouge guerrillas, defeating Lon Nol's military government in 1976. As prime minister, he set up a totalitarian regime, which caused the death of about 1½ million, more than a fifth of the country's population, and imprisonment or exile of many others. Overthrown in 1979, when the Vietnamese invaded Cambodia, Pol Pot withdrew to the mountains to lead the Khmer Rouge forces. He announced his retirement in 1985, but remained an influential figure within the movement. A soft-spoken man, he asked an inquisitive journalist in the last interview he gave, in late 1997: 'Do I look savage?'

Ricardo, David (1772–1823). English economist and politician, born in London. He set up in business as a young man, and by 1814 had made a fortune. In 1817 he published his main work, *Principles of Political Economy and Taxation*. In 1819 he became a member of parliament, and was influential in the free-trade movement. Despite his own considerable practical experience, Ricardo's writings are abstract and frequently difficult. His law of rent was probably his most notable and influential discovery. It was based on the observation that the differing fertility of land yielded unequal profits to the capital and labour applied to it and, hence, differential rent. This principle was also noted at about the same time by Malthus and others. His other great contribution, the law of comparative cost, or comparative advantage, demonstrated the benefits of international specialization as regards the commodity composition of international trade. This was at the root of the free trade argument, which set Britain firmly on the course of exporting manufactures and importing foodstuffs.

Romer, Paul M. (1955–). American economist, educated at the University of Chicago (BS 1977, Ph.D. 1983). He taught at Rochester, Chicago, and Berkeley, before joining the faculty of the Stanford Graduate School of Business in 1996. He has been sr. research fellow at the Hoover Institution at Stanford since 1994. 'More than any other person, Paul Romer is responsible for the revival of interest in economic growth,' says Robert Solow. 'He has produced a succession of ideas that have captured the imagination of economists all over the world.'

Sachs, Jeffrey D. (1954–). American economist, born in Detroit, Michigan, and educated at Harvard (BA 1976, MA 1978, Ph.D. 1980). Since 1980, Sachs has taught at Harvard, where he also directs the Harvard Institute for International Development. He has written extensively on macroeconomic policy, economic transition in post-communist countries, and economic development. In addition to his scholarly books and articles, he is the co-author, with Felipe Larrain, of an undergraduate text, *Macroeconomics for the Global Economy* (1993). He serves as an economic adviser to several governments in Latin America, Eastern Europe, the former Soviet Union, Asia, and Africa. He has also been a consultant to the IMF, the World Bank, the OECD, and the United Nations.

Sala-i-Martin, Xavier (1963–). Catalan economist. Educated at Universitat Autònoma de Barcelona and Harvard, where he got his Ph.D. in 1990. He taught at Yale 1990–6, where the graduate students awarded him with the Distinguished Teacher Award for his flamboyant classes on economic growth, and then moved to Columbia, where he is professor of economics. He is also a research fellow of the National Bureau of Economic Research and of the Centre for Economic Policy Research and a consultant to the IMF.

Samuelson, Paul A. (1915–). American economist, born in Gary, Indiana. By age 26, he had obtained his Ph.D. from Harvard and landed a teaching position at MIT, where he built up one of the best economics departments in the world. At the end of his doctoral defence at Harvard, Schumpeter is said to have turned to Leontief and asked, 'Well, Wassily, have we passed?' Samuelson's distinguished academic career has included path-breaking work on a wide variety of subjects in economics—international trade, public finance, production, capital, growth, and the history of economic thought. His textbook, *Economics* (1948; 16th edn., with William Nordhaus, 1998), is the economic equivalent of Feynman's *Lectures on Physics*: it changed beyond recognition the way economics is taught to beginners. Samuelson was the first American to receive the Nobel Prize for economics, in 1970. Of himself, he has written, 'Although positivistic analysis of what the actual world is like commands and constrains my every move as an economist, there is never far from my consciousness a concern for the ethics of the outcome. Mine is a simple ideology that favours the underdog and (other things equal) abhors inequality.'

Schumpeter, Joseph A. (1883–1950). American economist, born and educated in Austria. Following a quick doctorate at Vienna, he moved from place to place until he rejoined academia in 1909. While teaching at Czernowitz (now in the Ukraine), he wrote his *Theory of Economic Development* (1911), where he outlined his theory of entrepreneurship. Entrepreneurs create technical and financial innovations in the face of competition and falling profits, and these spurts of activity generate economic growth. In 1919, Schumpeter became minister of finance in Austria, presiding over the hyperinflation of the period, and was dismissed later that year. After a brief teaching stint at Graz, he returned in 1921 to the private sector and became the president of a small Viennese bank, which collapsed in 1924. He emigrated to the United States in 1932, and became professor at Harvard. His theory replaced Marx's view of greed-driven capitalism with dynamic, innovative entrepreneurship, clearly differentiating the capitalist from the entrepreneur. He published several books, but *Capitalism, Socialism, and Democracy* (1942) stands out. There he rejects the Marxist diagnosis of the imminent breakdown of capitalism, and at the same time predicts the almost inevitable emergence of socialism due to a betrayal of capitalist values by intellectuals. His last book, *History of Economic Analysis* (posthumously published in 1954), is a brilliant exposition of the history of economic thought.

Shaw, George Bernard (1856–1950). Playwright, essayist, and pamphleteer, born in Dublin. In 1876 he left clerical work in Ireland and moved to London. In 1882 he turned to socialism, joined the committee of the Fabian Society, and became known as a journalist, writing music and drama criticism, and publishing critical essays. He began to write plays in 1885, and among his early successes were *Arms and the Man* (1894), *Candida* (1897), and *The Devil's Disciple* (1897). There followed *Man and Superman* (1905), *Major Barbara* (1905), *The Doctor's Dilemma* (1906), and several others, displaying an increasing range of subject matter. Later plays include *Pygmalion* (1913), adapted as the musical play *My Fair Lady* in 1956 (filmed, 1964). He wrote over 40 plays, most of them permeated by his passion for social reform, and he continued to write them even in his nineties. In 1935 he was awarded the Nobel Prize for literature. Of his native country, he said: 'As long as Ireland produces men with sense enough to leave her, she does not exist in vain.'

Smith, Adam (1723–1790). Economist and philosopher, born in Kirkcaldy, a small fishing village near Edinburgh, Scotland. He studied first at Glasgow (1737–40) and then at Oxford, which, compared with Glasgow, the centre of the 'Scottish Enlightenment', was an educational desert. After six years of self-education at Oxford, Smith returned to Scotland and became professor of logic at Glasgow in 1751, at the age of 27. He took up the chair of moral philosophy the following year and published *The Theory of Moral Sentiments* (1759), where he introduced his idea that men are often 'led by an invisible hand . . . without knowing it, without intending it, [to] advance the interest of the society'. At Glasgow, he lectured for an hour or two every morning to classes of up to 90 students, aged 14 to 16. He was famous: his classes attracted foreign students from Russia and other European nations. In 1776 Smith moved to

London, where he published *The Wealth of Nations* (1776). His appointment as commissioner of customs in 1778 took him back to Edinburgh. He never married.

Solow, Robert M. (1924–). American economist, born in Brooklyn, New York, educated at Harvard (BA 1947, MA 1949, Ph.D. 1951). He is best known for his pathbreaking work on capital and growth. Since 1950, he has taught at MIT; he has never had or wanted any other job. He was president of the American Economic Association in 1979 and was awarded the Nobel Prize for his work on economic growth in 1987. Recently, he wrote: 'Maybe the main function of economics in general is not, as we usually think, the systematic building of theories and models, or their empirical estimation. Maybe we are intellectual sanitation workers. The world is full of nonsense . . . Maybe the higher function of economics is to hold out against nonsense, . . . All those theories and models we invent and teach are just nature's way of making people who know nonsense when they see it.'

Stalin, Joseph (1879–1953). Georgian Marxist revolutionary who became Soviet dictator (1928–53), born Joseph Vissarionovich Dzhugashvili, the son of a cobbler and ex-serf. He studied at Tiflis Orthodox Theological Seminary, from which he was expelled in 1899. He became active in the revolutionary underground, and was twice exiled to Siberia (1902, 1913). As a leading Bolshevik he played an active role in the October Revolution. In 1922 he became general secretary of the Party Central Committee, a post he held until his death, and also occupied other key positions which enabled him to amass enormous personal power in the party and government apparatus. After Lenin's death (1924) he gradually isolated and disgraced his political rivals, notably Trotsky. In 1928 he launched the campaign for the collectivization of agriculture in which millions of peasants perished, and the first 5-year plan for the forced industrialization of the economy. In 1934–8 he inaugurated a massive purge of the party, government, armed forces, and intelligentsia in which millions of so-called 'enemies of the people' were imprisoned, exiled, or shot. In 1938 he signed the Non-Aggression Pact with Hitler, which bought the Soviet Union two years' respite from involvement in the Second World War. After the German invasion (1941), the USSR became a member of the Grand Alliance, and Stalin, as war leader, assumed the title of generalissimo. He took part in the conferences of Tehran, Yalta, and Potsdam, which resulted in Soviet domination of East and Central Europe. From 1945 until his death he resumed his repressive measures at home. He was posthumously denounced by Khrushchev at the Twentieth Party Congress (1956) for crimes against the Party and for building a 'cult of personality'. Under Gorbachev, many of Stalin's victims were rehabilitated, and Stalinism was officially condemned by the Soviet authorities.

Truman, Harry S. (1884–1972). American president 1945–53, born in Lamar, Missouri. A farm boy, he could not afford college. In the 1920s he joined the local Democratic Party. He entered the US Senate in 1935. His personal integrity helped him get re-elected in 1940 despite the exposure of the Missouri Democratic Party machine's corruption. He came to national attention heading the so-called Truman Committee, which investigated government wartime production and saved taxpayers millions. That prominence brought him to office as Franklin D. Roosevelt's new vice-president in 1944, an office he held for only 82 days, during which he met with the president only twice. When Roosevelt died the following year, Truman became president; he went on to win a close election in 1948. He surprised everyone with his boldness in a troubled time: he dropped the first atom bombs on Japan; authorized the Marshall Plan to aid post-war Europe; proposed the 'Truman Doctrine' of communist containment and support for free peoples; organized the Berlin Airlift (1948–9); ordered the desegregation of the armed forces (1948); established NATO (1949); sent American troops to deal with the communist invasion of South Korea in 1950; and dismissed the popular General MacArthur for insubordination in Korea. His visionary, Roosevelt-style social programme, which he called the 'Fair Deal', was largely stymied by a conservative Congress. Truman declined to run in 1952 and settled in Independence, Missouri, for a long retirement of writing and speaking his mind.

Notes

1. Einar Benediktsson, 'Íslandsljóð' ('Poems for Iceland'), in his *Sögur og kvæði (Stories and Poems)*, Reykjavík, 1897. Translation from Icelandic by Kristján Karlsson.
2. By Edmund Clerihew Bentley (1875–1956).

Name and Place Index

Subject Index